Antonio Enríquez Gómez

Twayne's World Authors Series
Spanish Literature

Donald W. Bleznick, Editor
University of Cincinnatti

Janet Pérez, Editor
Texas Tech University

TWAS 803

A Gallis habuit tua Portugallia nomen
Clarum à te, GOMES, Gallia nomen habet.

ANTONIO ENRÍQUEZ GÓMEZ
(1600–1663)

Courtesy of Special Collections,
Van Pelt Library, University of Pennsylvania

Antonio Enríquez Gómez

By Glen F. Dille

Bradley University

Twayne Publishers
A Division of G. K. Hall & Co. • Boston

Antonio Enríquez Gómez
Glen F. Dille

Copyright 1988 by G. K. Hall & Co.
All rights reserved.
Published by Twayne Publishers
A Division of G. K. Hall & Co.
70 Lincoln Street
Boston, Massachusetts 02111

Copyediting supervised by Barbara Sutton.
Book production by Janet Zietowski.
Book design by Barbara Anderson.

Typeset in 11 pt. Garamond
by Williams Press, Inc., Albany, New York.

Printed on permanent/durable acid-free paper
and bound in the United States of America.

Library of Congress Cataloging-in-Publication Data

Dille, Glen F., 1940–
    Antonio Enríquez Gómez / by Glen F. Dille.

    p.   cm.—(Twayne's world authors series ; TWAS 803)
    Bibliography: p. 184
    Includes index.
    ISBN 0-8057-8234-6 (alk. paper)
    1. Enríquez Gómez, Antonio, 1600–1663—Criticism and
interpretation. I. Title. II. Series.
PQ6388.E5Z64   1988
862'.3—dc19   87-35097
                                                                              CIP

To Dean W. McPheeters,
Emeritus of Newcomb College, Tulane University:
teacher, scholar, and good friend.

Contents

About the Author

Glen F. Dille received his B.A. and M.A. from the University of Colorado. After a period of service with the U.S. Air Force he returned to graduate studies at Tulane University where he received his doctorate in 1973. His doctoral dissertation, *A Critical Edition of the "Comedia Serafina" (1521)*, was later published by Southern Illinois University Press. Dille is the author of several articles and papers concerning sixteenth- and seventeenth-century Hispanic literature on topics ranging from Celestinesque literature to Sor Juana Inés de la Cruz. For the past few years his investigations have concentrated on the Golden Age drama and, in particular, on the works of Antonio Enríquez Gómez. Dille has been awarded fellowships to attend two summer seminars sponsored by the National Endowment for the Humanities as well as a Fellowship for Independent Study. He is currently associate professor of Spanish at Bradley University, Peoria, Illinois.

Preface

A study of so prolific a writer as Antonio Enríquez Gómez in so small a volume as this cannot pretend to be more than a general and rapid look at one of the most representative New Christian writers of the seventeenth century, a man whose life seems to be the distillation of all the trials that society reserved for the Jew or, in this case, a person of Jewish descent.

While the following nine chapters are not exhaustive or definitive, they will give an introduction to the breadth and depth of Enríquez Gómez's works through descriptions of the various compositions, consideration of the salient themes, and identification of the continuity of thought that unites his work. It is hoped that this volume will stimulate further investigation in all aspects of the author's life and work, for, although Enríquez Gómez was relatively popular in his day, the nineteenth and early twentieth centuries have not been very kind to his memory. Now, however, his work is fast gaining critical attention. The past few years have seen the appearance of several of his compositions with excellent introductory studies, and there is the promise of more in the near future.

Enríquez Gómez was an exceptionally personal writer who viewed his compositions as vehicles to address his own vital concerns. Because the repressive atmosphere of his day dictated the often obscure manner in which he wrote, the author's feelings are quite difficult to interpret. The opinions expressed in this work concerning the troublesome question of Enríquez Gómez's religious beliefs are, as I see them, the best approximations to the truth that available evidence allows. Others will disagree, and I welcome that as constructive consideration long overdue this author.

Enríquez Gómez's major works are presented in separate chapters in a roughly chronological order by publication data except for several less extensive compositions that are considered together in chapter 8. For the sake of convenience, in spite of its oversimplifications, I have considered Enríquez Gómez's work as divisible into three epochs: the Madrid period, the period of the French exile, and the Seville period. In chapters 3 and 9, dealing with his dramatic compositions, I felt it more valuable to discuss in relative detail representative titles of each period rather than to try to squeeze into the book a very short summary of each of his fifty-odd plays. In these two chapters general comments do supply at least some information on the plays not selected for more detailed discussion.

Except for Professor Oelman's translation of the poem on Lope de Vera used in chapter 8, all translations from primary and secondary sources are my own. My translations concentrate on intention and meaning and certainly neither do justice to Enríquez Gómez's poetic ability nor convey the eloquent nature of his prose. I also recognize that the translations of titles of his works are often especially stilted. They are not artistic renderings, but instead are intended to be as close as possible to the original title. At first I had thought not to include many citations and their translations, but I later decided that since the majority of his works are not readily available, it would be well to let the author speak for himself as much as possible, even if only in translation.

Many people and agencies have aided in this project, more than such a short work would seem to indicate. The National Endowment for the Humanities and the Bradley University Board for Research have been very generous in their support. Above all, I must give credit to my esteemed professor and good friend, D. W. McPheeters, for suggesting the topic and thank him for his continuous support over the years. Additionally, professors B. W. Wardropper, S. A. Armistead, Michael McGaha, and John Wooldridge have all been supportive and most helpful in this project. Technical assistance was vital to this effort, and for that I gratefully acknowledge the skill and patience of the staff of the Bradley University Library—Marina Savoie, Elisabeth von Glasenapp, Laura Corpuz, and especially Barbara Tunks who cheerfully and carefully copied hundreds of pages of microfilm for me. My friends and colleagues Helen D. Goode, Warren Dwyer, and Margaret Carter kindly read the manuscript and tried to correct its worst passages. The infelicities that remain are my own. Finally, the preparation of the numerous revisions of the manuscript was undertaken by my wife, Lee, and by Kathie Strum, to both of whom I owe a very special acknowledgment of thanks.

Glen F. Dille

Bradley University

Chronology

1600   Antonio Enríquez Gómez born in Cuenca.

1618   Marries Isabel Basurto in Zafra. Three children are born of this marriage: Diego Enríquez, Leonor, and Catalina.

1624   Establishes as a merchant in Madrid.

1625   Attempts to recover property confiscated when his father was arrested by the Inquisition.

1633   18 May, *Fernán Méndez Pinto* staged in Madrid; 22 May, *Diego de Camas* staged in Madrid.

1634   12 May, testifies before the Inquisition in the case of Bartolomé Febos. 4 December, *El capitán Chinchilla* staged in Madrid.

1635   5 August, *La soberbia de Nembrot* staged in Madrid; 9 December, *El capitán Chinchilla* staged in Madrid.

1636   His sonnet included in commemorative volume on the death of Lope de Vega.

ca. 1636   Abandons Spain for France.

1637   15–25 February, mentioned in a literary academy celebrated at the Buen Retiro. 1 November, his play *El rayo de Palestina* in possession of a theatrical agent.

1641   *Triunfo lusitano.*

1642   *Academias morales de las musas.*

ca. 1643   Moves to Rouen with his wife, son, and daughter Leonor.

1644   *La culpa del primer peregrino* and *El siglo pitagórico y vida de don Gregorio Guadaña.*

1645   *Luis dado de Dios.*

1647   *La política angélica. Academias morales* reprinted in Valencia.

1649   *La torre de babilonia. Engañar para reinar* (play) published in Lisbon.

ca. 1649   *El rey Salomón (El trono de Salomón)* (play) smuggled into Spain.

ca. 1649   Clandestine return to Spain.

1650   *La hija del aire* (part 2), attributed to Enríquez Gómez.

1652   *Celos no ofenden al sol, Contra el amor no hay engaños,* and *No hay contra el honor poder* (plays).

1656   *Sansón nazareno* (all but the last canto written before 1649).

1658   *Contra el amor no hay engaños.* Writes *La loa de los siete planetas.*

1660   *Academias morales* reprinted in Madrid. *El valiente Campuzano* printed in Spain. April, effigy of Enríquez Gómez burned in an auto-da-fé in Seville. 5 April, autograph MS of *El noble siempre es valiente.* 24–26 April, *El maestro de Alejandro* staged in Madrid; 27–28 April, *El valiente Campuzano* staged in Madrid.

1660   20, 23 May, *A cada paso un peligro* staged in Madrid. 26 July, autograph MS of *La montañesa de Burgos.*

1661   *Entremés del zapatero, Entremés del alcalde de Mayrena,* and the play *El obispo de Crobia.* 10 March, autograph MS of *Las misas de S. Vicente Ferrer.* 21 September, arrested in Seville by the Inquisition.

1663   The plays *Quererse sin declararse, Mudarse por mejorarse* and *Los filósofos de Grecia.* 19 March, Enrique Gómez dies in prison in Seville.

Chapter One

Historical Background: Jews and New Christians in Iberia

Definition of Terms

"La existencia de los conversos, más aún que la de los propios judíos, envenenó la vida española durante siglos y constituye uno de los rasgos más significativos de nuestra historia durante toda la Edad Moderna: exactamente, desde fines del XIV a comienzos del XIX" ("The existence of the *conversos* [converts], even beyond that of the Jews themselves, poisoned Spanish life for centuries and constitutes one of the most significant traits of our history during the whole of the Modern Age: that is from the end of the fourteenth century to the beginning of the ninteenth").[1] With these words the Spanish scholar Antonio Domínguez Ortiz calls attention to a situation that for many centuries characterized all aspects of Spanish society. Thus, before we begin to discuss the life and works of the *converso* Antonio Enríquez Gómez, it is essential to briefly consider the Jewish and New Christian presence in the Iberian Peninsula as well as the role in Spain of the Inquisition.

It is useful to begin with a definition of terms that will be used throughout this book. The Iberian Jews are the Sephardim or Sephardic Jews, as differentiated from the Ashkenazim, or eastern Jews. A *marrano* is a crypto-Jew, a baptised Christian, who secretly observes all or some of the practices and tenets of Judaism. The origin of the word *marrano* is not certain, but it may be derived from an old Spanish word meaning "pig," originally used as an insult. Today the term is frequently used to denote that group of Spanish or Portuguese practicing secret Judaism.[2] Another term used often in this work is *converso*, which in its strictest sense applies to any convert from one religion to another. Its use, however, is almost always restricted to converts from Judaism to Christianity and their descendants. Technically the converted Moors were also *conversos*, but the usual term applied to them was *morisco*. *Conversos* were also commonly referred to as New Christians even though the conversion of the family might have occurred as much as three or four

1

generations earlier. In this study the terms *converso* or New Christian are neutral words used merely to refer to people descended from Jewish ancestors and do not convey any supposition of Jewishness, or Christianity for that matter.[3] Old Christians were those Spaniards who supposed that their ancestry was pure, that is, free from any Jewish or Moorish taint.

The Sephardim

Medieval Spanish Jews claimed that their presence in the Iberian Peninsula antedated the time of Christ. As such they maintained that they had no responsibility for the Crucifixion and were exonerated from the charge of deicide that Christians held against them. However, the date of arrival of Jews in the Iberian Peninsula is a subject of much conjecture. In the past there have been efforts to identify the biblical Tarshish (1 Kings 10:22) with the legendary pre-Roman Tartessus of the Iberian Peninsula, but this identification is extremely tenuous. Nevertheless, a recent work by L. García Iglesias maintains that, given the trading alliance between Phoenicians and Israelites during King Solomon's time, there were Jewish merchant-traders in Iberia as early as 1200 B.C. and that there were permanent Jewish settlements at least by the second or third century B.C.[4]

Despite his supposition of a pre-Christian era Jewish presence in Spain, García Iglesias notes that there is no extant artifact attesting to it earlier than the first century A.D. Ibiza amphora, and no certain inscription until that of the child Salomonuela in Almería in the third century A.D. From the fourth century A.D. there are the remains of an ancient synagogue at Elche and the regulations concerning Christian-Jewish relations that came out of the Synod of Elvira (ca. 306 A.D.). An analysis of the deliberations of that Synod leads García Iglesias to conclude: "De las actas conciliares se puede concluir sin temor a las deducciones exageradas que los judíos peninsulares, y sobre todo, los béticos constituían minorías influyentes y de importancia númerica destacable, cuya vitalidad religiosa y su afán proselitista provocaban las preocupaciones de las autoridades del cristianismo hispánico" ("From the Synod's regulations one can conclude without fear of exaggerated deductions that the peninsular Jews, and especially those in the Southern region, constituted an influential minority of numerical importance whose religious vitality and proselytizing zeal provoked fears on the part of the Christian Hispanic authorities").[5]

But whenever they came, the fortune of the Sephardim (the name deriving from *Sepharad,* presumably the ancient Hebrew name for the Iberian Peninsula)⁶ rose and fell according to the policies of their gentile rulers. It seems that their Roman-era existence was undisturbed until repression began soon after Christianity became the official religion of the empire. With the coming of the Visigoths in the fifth century A.D. the Sephardim fared better because the first Visigothic kings were not Roman Catholic but Arians who believed that Christ was not consubstantial with God the father.⁷ The tolerance of Jews ended with the conversion to Roman Catholicism of King Recarred in 589 A.D. which initiated a long period of discrimination, persecution, and forced conversion of Jews that continued in greater and lesser proportion until the Muslim invasion of 711 A.D. The remarkably speedy conquest of the peninsula resulted in accusations that the Jews aided and abetted the Moorish invasion, a charge that may have some basis in fact. The harsh treatment by the Visigoths indeed disposed the Jewish population favorably toward the Muslims, and they eagerly accepted the new masters under whom, save for brief periods of repression, they fared well during the long period of Islamic presence.⁸ Whether they lived in Muslim or Christian areas of the peninsula, Sephardim generally prospered until the repressions beginning in the late fourteenth century, and there were few cities that did not contain a Jewish ghetto or *aljama.*⁹ The administrators, merchants, and intellectuals of the Sephardic community gained much esteem throughout Europe. In fact, the wealth and culture of peninsular Jewry made it the envy of other communities and led Sephardim to assume an aristocratic role among world Jewry that persisted until this century.¹⁰

The *Conversos*

The end of a long period of relative religious tolerance came in 1391 when anti-Jewish riots broke out in Seville and quickly spread to other cities. The widespread plunder and massacres forced many thousands of Jews to undergo baptism, producing, for the first time since the Visigothic era, a sizeable number of *conversos.* Obviously, these conversions under duress were suspect, and many Jews of this generation either later fled the country or remained Catholic in name only. The problem for them was, however, that even though the conversions were forced, the church regarded the baptisms as valid and any backsliders guilty of heresy.

Throughout the fifteenth century there were more and more forced conversions, and, as a result of the pogroms, a number of voluntary conversions by disspirited Jews who did not wish to flee their homeland. Even though the first generation *conversos* were perhaps rightly suspect of Marranism, there is ample evidence that through a process of assimilation with the Old Christian population, by the third generation a majority of their descendents were authentic Catholics.[11] Nevertheless, though greatly reduced in numbers and importance, Jews were still officially tolerated in Spain to the end of the fifteenth century. Thus the Spanish population offered quite a range—from practicing "public" Jews and secret Jews *(marranos)* to sincere converts, Old Christians, *moriscos,* and probably also a number of New Christians who, in their hearts, were religiously indifferent.

The famous Edict of Expulsion of 1492 was designed not only to rid the country of the last vestige of its Jewry, but also to remove the potential for Marranism, the fear being that many *conversos* were relapsing and in this were being encouraged to return to Judaism by the remaining Jews. It seems that the Old Christians were not the only ones to promote anti-Jewish legislation: recent investigations have shown that in the persecution and expulsion of the Jews some of their worst enemies were their ex-correligionists, the *conversos.* Many *conversos* supported the expulsion of Jews not only out of fear, but also because of their desire to take over the last positions of importance that Jews held. In addition, they badly wanted to be rid of a group that called attention to their own ancestry, a background that many New Christians were trying to live down.[12]

The number of people affected by the Edict of Expulsion has been the subject of intense debate. Domínguez Ortiz discusses the various figures offered by historians and comes up with a compromise number. To begin with, he assumes that, by the end of the fifteenth century, out of a total population of seven million there were no more than 500,000 Jews. Of these he estimates that 180,000 refused to convert and left the country.[13] Thus, almost exactly a century after the massacres and conversions of 1391 another enormous number (320,000) of *conversos* was suddenly added to the church. As far as the Old Christians were concerned these New Christians were little more than Jews in disguise. Even though by the second and third generations the process of assimilation produced authentic Catholics from most of their descendants, they suffered the stigma attached to New Christians and their heirs until the final part of the seventeenth century. This discrimination continued even longer in isolated areas such as Mallorca where the unfortunate *chuetas* (New Christians) were social outcasts well into the nineteenth century.

The separation of society into New and Old Christians was kept alive by the requirement of proof of blood purity *(limpieza de sangre)* that became widespread in the sixteenth century. This certification was necessary for knighthoods, for governmental positions, for entry into some religious orders, for entry into the most distinguished colleges of the universities, and for a host of honors and positions. The cost of the genealogical investigations required for the *limpizea* was exorbitant, but, perhaps worse than financial ruin, was the danger to a person's reputation if denied a certificate because of questionable ancestry. In the investigatory process neighbors, acquaintances, and strangers were interviewed to gather hearsay information about a candidate, a procedure that offered a splendid opportunity for personal revenge or even blackmail.

The *Marranos*

Vigorous activity by the Inquisition and pressure to assimilate reduced the number of identifiable Spanish New Christians throughout the sixteenth and seventeenth centuries. Concomitantly the number of *marranos* decreased greatly during this period as shown by the records of the Inquisition. But even before the Expulsion and the Inquisition the decline of Spanish Judaism was evident. B. Netanyahu, in fact, postulated the almost total disappearance of Judaism by 1478, the year the Inquisition was authorized, and, as a result, concludes that subsequent *marranos* were more Christian than Jewish. Other investigators, however, have rejected Netanyahu's statements as extreme.[14]

Historical events, however, contrived to add to Spanish society a new group of suspect *conversos* who began to arrive from Portugal when that country was annexed to the Spanish crown during the period 1580–1640. As physicians, retailers and wholesalers, bankers, and literary figures they came in increasing numbers to Spain seeking a larger theater of activity than that afforded in Portugal. The more wealthy of the Portuguese *marranos* were encouraged to set up business in Madrid by the Count-Duke of Olivares, the all-powerful minister of Philip IV.[15] It was hoped that their commercial and financial talents would improve the dismal Spanish economy as well as provide competition for the Genoese bankers who effectively owned the country. Exact numbers of Portuguese who came into Spain are not available, but an idea of their presence can be inferred from an estimate of two thousand residing in the important commercial center of Seville in the year 1640.[16] As opposed to their counterparts in Spain, many more Portuguese New Christians had managed to retain varying degrees of crypto-Judaism.[17] The dubiousness of their Catholicism became so well-known that during that period the word "Portuguese" became synonymous with *marrano*. The inquisitional records from the seventeenth century confirm the tendency toward Marranism of the Portuguese immigrants in the overwhelming preponderance of Portuguese prosecuted for heresy.[18]

The numbers of Portuguese New Christians in Spain began to diminish after the restoration of the Kingdom of Portugal in 1640, and especially after the fall from power of Olivares in 1643. As was the case with the Spanish *conversos,* these people were either exterminated, assimilated, or left the country to establish themselves in more hospitable parts.

The Inquisition

The Spanish Inquisition is a fascinating and repugnant institution that has elicited varying interpretations of its purpose, methods, and effect on Spanish society.[19] The following summary is included in order to make more comprehensible the subsequent chapters of this work concerning the life and works of one of its many victims, Antonio Enríquez Gómez.

A papal bull of 1478 authorized the establishment of the Spanish Inquisition which was set up two years later. Cecil Roth provides a statement of the agency's purpose: "The object of the Inquisition was to deal with heretics *within* the Church—that is to say, persons who had been baptised, or who asserted that they were Christians, but departed from the practice and teaching of Roman Catholicism. Normally, then, professing Jews did not come into the scope of its activities, unless they had been guilty of interfering with the faith of some baptised person and thus 'favoring' heresy, or were 'dogmatisers' who preached it."[20]

The Inquisition, or Holy Office, was a uniquely powerful agency in that it was a centralized organization, operating effectively throughout the many kingdoms and colonies that made up the Spanish Empire. Although its organization changed over the centuries, at its peak of power there were fifteen or sixteen peninsular tribunals headquartered in the principal cities. All tribunals reported to the *Suprema,* the Supreme Council, composed of about six members including the inquisitor general.

Over the years the bureaucracy grew to include theologians, prosecutors, clerks, notaries, secretaries, jailers, chaplains, spies, and, in general, all the various offices associated with a law enforcement agency. At the bottom of the organizational pyramid were the *familiares,* agents of the Inquisition, who functioned rather like an auxiliary police force. The title of *familiar* was eagerly sought and eventually had to be limited in number; its desirability was that it publicly affirmed an individual's Old Christian status.

Among the Inquisition's practices that contributed greatly to its fearsome reputation was the habit of shrouding its activities in absolute secrecy. Fortunately the agency was also meticulous in its record keeping, every step of a case being fully documented in files that can run on to hundreds of pages. While many records have disappeared over the centuries, thousands more remain for study and interpretation and, until a good deal more archival work is done, it can be truly said that knowledge of the Inquisition and its operations is even now superficial.

Persons suspected of heresy or denounced to the Inquisition were placed under surveillance until enough evidence was accumulated for an arrest warrant to be issued. In theory, the evidence was supposed to have been examined by a panel of theologians before an arrest order was issued. The Inquisition had a long memory and many agents at home and abroad who contributed information to the files of suspected heretics that might build up for many years before action was taken. Once detained, the accused were brought to the "secret" prisons of the Inquisition. These were not secret in the same sense that their locations were unknown but because, contrary to the civil prisons, the detainees of the Holy Office were allowed no contact with the outside world and were kept strictly separated from other prisoners. Also, upon arrest the accused's goods were confiscated, a practice that often left their families completely destitute.

Inquisitional proceedings also differed from secular courts in that their prisoners were not allowed to know the names of their accusers or the specific charges brought against them. A person was considered guilty until he proved otherwise and, under these circumstances, any defense was difficult if not impossible. The only recourse permitted to the accused was to submit lists of all persons they felt might have spitefully and falsely denounced them. If the names listed coincided with the accusers the inquisitors might conclude that the accusations were motivated by personal malice.

The Inquisition functioned as judge, jury, and prosecutor and was relentless in its pursuit of the details of a case. All prisoners were not considered repentant until every detail of the presumed heretical act had been admitted and the accused had denounced every person he knew or even suspected had acted suspiciously. As with cases in secular courts, a part of the process might involve torture, although investigation has shown that the Holy Office was remarkably forbearing in its application, employing it in perhaps as little as ten percent of the cases.[21]

The sentence handed down ranged from acquittal or suspension, to prison terms, public whipping, or being sent to row in the king's galleys. Almost always the prisoners had to appear in a public ceremony, an auto-da-fé (act of faith) where they acknowledged their heresy, received their punishment, and ·were reconciled to the church. The more unfortunate whose crimes were considered grave might be confined to prison for life or condemned to death. In the inquisitorial terminology the condemned were "relaxed" or handed over to civil authorities to be burned at the stake. Even in death there was no escaping the Inquisition. For those who died before they could be prosecuted, their corpses would be dug up to be publicly burned. Others who had fled to other countries were symbolically executed by burning a dummy or effigy painted to look like the fugitive.

Even if the sentence were not too severe, the act of appearing in an auto-da-fé was designed to be a humiliating affair. In addition to the confiscation of assets, the subject and his family were declared ineligible for any future public offices or honors. The sacklike garment called the *sanbenito* worn during the ceremony would be hung up in the parish church so that the disgrace would be shared by the entire family for years to come.[22] The disastrous economic and social consequences for a family are obvious, and it is little wonder that names were changed, genealogies fabricated, and people moved to escape the opprobrium of being identified with a relative denounced by the Inquisition.

The prosecution of the Portuguese *marranos* during the seventeenth century marks the last period of vigorous inquisitional activity, so that by the eighteenth century there is a marked decrease in the number of cases. But, although all but dead in the last half of its existence, the Holy Office managed to survive officially until its final abolition in 1834.

Chapter Two
The Life of Enríquez Gómez

Introduction

Like many seventeenth-century Spanish writers, Antonio Enríquez Gómez has left a corpus of material as notable for its volume as for its variety. Enríquez Gómez himself, proudly conscious of his accomplishments, enumerates and classifies his production as follows: "Si entro en la *Torre de Babilonia* es para sacar documentos de confusión. Si deseas verme filósofo moral lee mis *Academias;* si político, la *Política angélica;* si teólogo, mi *peregrino;* si estadista, *Luis dado de Dios;* si poeta, este poema; si cómico, mis comedias: y si burlas y veras, el *Siglo pitagórico*" ("If I enter the *Tower of Babylon* it is to testify to the confusion of this world. If you wish to see me as a moral philosopher read my *Academies;* if as a theologian, my *Pilgrim;* if as a diplomatic writer, *Louis The God-given;* as a poet, this poem *[Samson the Nazarene];* as a dramatist, my plays; and if you enjoy social satire, the *Pythagorean Century*").[1] But these works represent only a part of his total output. This statement was probably written in 1649, after which Enríquez Gómez had approximately another decade of production encompassing some thirty more plays.

Yet, apart from the voluminousness, variety, and intrinsic merit of his compositions, there is another valuable aspect in that through and in Enríquez Gómez, the man, we have the expression of an important segment of seventeenth-century Spanish society. The drama of Enríquez Gómez life and works is that of the New Christian struggling to find a place for himself in a nation preoccupied with religious purity. The Spanish obsession with Jewishness is a specter that haunts its literature, reflecting a collective phobia that has produced long-lasting political, economic, and psychological effects. The Spanish response to heterodoxy, the Inquisition, contributed much to the creation of the Black Legend, that stereotype of cruelty, backwardness, fanaticism, and intolerance that has dogged Spain's footsteps to the present and has been transmitted intact to the Hispanic countries of the New World.

Within this setting we see that the works of New Christian writers such as Enríquez Gómez offer another dimension to the period, especially as they present an alternate view, one from without the establishment. In them we have the expression of an important but despised class that was not easily allowed to forget its Jewish origins, no matter what service is rendered, no matter how faithfully it observed Catholicism. Among the various *converso* writers active in the seventeenth century, Antonio Enríquez Gómez is one of the most representative because of the circumstances of his life and the volume and nature of his writings.[2] In his work we find constant expressions of the *converso's* aspirations and anxieties. Particularly intriguing are the indications of his personal religious struggle and another dilemma—that of loving his native country while, at the same time, being repelled by its policies of discrimination.

Background and Early Years

For many years very little was known of the life of Antonio Enríquez Gómez.[3] He was thought to be Portuguese or born of Portuguese parents and to have pursued a military career leading to the rank of captain under the alias Enrique Enríquez de Paz. Later it was thought that he fled the country, finishing his days in Amsterdam among the members of the Spanish Jewish colony there. Rare is the early biography that does not repeat as gospel the witicism attributed to him—"Allá me las den todas"—supposedly his reply to a man that announced that he had seen the burning of Enríquez Gómez's effigy in the Sevillian auto-da-fé of 14 April 1660.[4] However, in 1962 the late professor I. S. Révah published a biography of Enríquez Gómez that completely revised the details of the author's life and demonstrated that, once the misinformation is discarded, the truth is indeed stranger than the fiction, for what emerges is a pathetic but fascinating drama.[5]

The first important correction is that Antonio Enríquez Gómez was not Portuguese but Spanish. He was born in Cuenca in 1660, the son of Diego Enríquez Villanueva (or Diego Enríquez de Mora) and Isabel Gómez. On his father's side Enríquez Gómez was descended from some of the few Spanish *marranos* that managed to survive into the seventeenth century. Their survival was not without cost: C. H. Rose reports finding at least fifty inquisitorial cases against members of the family.[6] Antonio Enríquez Gómez's paternal grandfather, Diego de Mora, died in the inquisitional prison toward the end of the sixteenth century, and some years later (ca. 1624) Antonio Enríquez Gómez's father was likewise arrested by the Holy Office. Diego Enríquez Villanueva was more fortunate than his father and managed to secure release. Obviously, the charges against him were not very serious but, nevertheless, his assets were confiscated according to the standard practice of the Inquisition. Some years later Antonio Enríquez Gómez went to court to recover that portion of the assets that he claimed belonged to his mother and, therefore, should not have been seized. His suit was not successful.

Antonio Enríquez Gómez's mother, Isabel Gómez, was an Old Christian. After her death his father left Spain for Bordeaux where, it seems, he formed an active part of the *marrano* community. One indication of his crypto-Judaism is that Diego Enríquez Villanueva married again, this time to a Portuguese lady he had brought from the large Jewish community at Amsterdam. The second marriage produced three much younger half-brothers for Antonio Enríquez Gómez— Miguel Enríquez, Esteban Enríquez and Diego Enríquez.

Antonio Enríquez Gómez entered into the family's merchant tradition at an early age. We know that for a time he was apprenticed to his paternal uncle, Antonio Enríquez de Mora, who was established in Seville and who, like his brother, Enríquez Gómez's father, found it expedient to escape the Inquisition by fleeing to Bordeaux. Regardless of the examples of his grandfather, father, and uncle, Antonio Enríquez Gómez remained in Spain and by 1624 had established himself in Madrid as a dealer in imported French goods. Apparently he was the commercial correspondent in Spain for both his father (by that time at Nantes) and his uncle in Bordeaux.

The endurance that enabled generation after generation of *conversos* to remain in Spain in spite of continual humiliation, arrest, confiscation, and even death is astonishing. Julio Caro Baroja, who has devoted much research to the *converso,* concludes that their persistence cannot be totally due to the general prosperity they often enjoyed but must also be explained in sentimental terms—they simply felt more "at home" in the Iberian environment which was, as we have noted, their native land since perhaps before the Roman colonization.[7] Certainly this sentimental attachment to Spain was intense in Enríquez Gómez as we shall see when we consider his works.

The fact that Enríquez Gómez remained behind in Spain would seem to indicate that he felt he had little to fear from the Inquisition. Either he had not engaged in any *marrano* practices that would cause him problems or he had been very discreet about them. Enríquez Gómez was, after all, only half *converso,* and in 1618 he had married Isabel

Basurto, an Old Christian like his mother. Isabel Basurto's brother was a priest and commissioner of the Inquisition. No doubt Enríquez Gómez hoped this connection would be to his advantage. One cannot help but wonder how his wife's family felt about the marriage.

The thorny question of Enríquez Gómez's religious preference throughout his lifetime will be discussed in more detail in relation to his individual works. But, in general, both Judaism and Catholicism exerted powerful attractions on him, and there are periods in his life during which one seems to predominate over the other. In his early years he seems to have been as much inclined to his mother's Catholicism as to his father's Marranism. For while it is never possible to speak with certainty about Enríquez Gómez's Christianity, there are many passages in the *Política angélica* (Angelic politics), published years later, that return over and over to the theme of innocence. In this work he is particularly concerned with the sufferings of innocent, presumably Christian, children of heretics at the hands of the Inquisition. He writes: "Los libelos infamatorios no los solicita la fe; antes los condena como perjudiciales a la Iglesia, no digo sólo en los hijos inocentes que no pecaron, pero en los mismos padres que cometieron el crimen" ("The degrading broadsides published by the church do not serve to bring them into the Faith; rather they condemn them as enemies of the church. I say this not only with regard to those innocent children who have not sinned, but also for the very parents who committed the crime").[8] In another passage dealing with the opprobrium attached to the descendants of Jews and Judaizers he speaks of "sus hijos y descendientes, cuya inocencia y cristiano celo ha sido vituperada y afrentada de las gentes, contra toda razón y justicia" ("their children and descendants whose innocence and Christian zeal has been vituperated and affronted contrary to all reason and justice").[9] As he penned these statements it is difficult to imagine that Enríquez Gómez did not have in mind his own unfortunate experiences and the tribulations of his father's family.

The Years in Madrid

In addition to the mercantile affairs that, of necessity, occupied his entire life. Enríquez Gómez also devoted considerable time to literary studies and to writing. By his own admission his formal education had been minimal, but in his youth Enríquez Gómez recognized this lack of polish and set about to instruct himself, as he explains in the prologue to *Sansón nazareno* (Samson the Nazarene): "Si Sansón no estuviere adornado de tanta ciencia como debe llevar un poema, paciencia y volver a nacer, que si mis padres en los primeros años me negaron el estudio no trabajé poco en mi juventud sobre las noticias más importantes de las ciencias" ("If *Samson* is not adorned with as much knowledge as a poem ought to contain, patience and try again; for if my parents denied me education in my early years, in my youth I worked a good deal on the most important elements of learning"). The prologue to *La culpa del primer peregrino* (The first pilgrim's guilt) echoes the same lament: "pues mis estudios más son sobrados alientos de mi natural, que centíficos aciertos de la ciencia" ("since my studies are more due to natural audacious inspiration than to solid learned accomplishments").

The first epoch of his literary career was dedicated primarily to poetry and especially to the theater. Enríquez Gómez certainly took part in the numerous but ephemeral literary academies that flourished in the period—perhaps in the Apollo which he mentions in his prologue to *Samson the Nazarene*. In these literary salons, often elaborately organized, the poets met to read their works and participate in competitions that frequently led to acrimonious disputes. In his *Vida de don Gregorio Guadaña* (Life of Don Gregorio Guadaña) he describes a session in which the "poets" compete in the exaggerated obscurity of the style of the immensely popular Luis de Góngora. Even though from the pompous ridiculousness of the verse this scene is satirical, from what we know of these sessions Enríquez Gómez's description may be more fact than fiction.[10] This is also a period in which the theater enjoyed tremendous popularity and therefore required the production of a large number of plays to satisfy the constant public demand for something new. Fortunately for the investigator, Enríquez Gómez was never shy about promoting his work; we know from the prologue to *Samson the Nazarene* that during this time he wrote twenty-two plays. Some of these, he says, were printed in Seville and presumably the remainder in Madrid. Enríquez Gómez's nostalgic reminiscences of his halcyon days as a young dramatist in Madrid include a thumbnail sketch of Spanish drama of the early seventeenth century:

En mi tiempo (dejado aparte al Adán de la comedia que fue Lope) hubo lucidísimos poetas. Don Antonio de Mendoza, Secretario de Apolo, se llevó el Palacio; el doctor Juan Pérez de Montalbán, entre muchas comedias que escribió, puso en las tablas la de un castigo dos venganzas con que se vengó de sus émulos (notable ingenio fue éste). Don Pedro Calderón, por las trazas se llevó el teatro; Villayzán por lo conceptuoso, los ingenios; el doctor Godínez por las sentencias, los doctos; Luis Vélez por lo heroico fue eminente; no olvido don Francisco de Rojas, ni a don Pedro Rosete, Gaspar de Avila, don Antonio de Solís, don Antonio Cuello, y otros muchos que con acierto grande escribieron comedias.

In my time [leaving aside Lope who was the Adam of drama] there were very outstanding poets: Don Antonio de Mendoza, the secretary of the Apollo, was popular at the Palace; Doctor Juan Pérez de Montalbán, who among the plays that he wrote staged one that called for two vengeances with one chastisement and with which he chastised his detractors—a notable idea was this; don Pedro Calderón was popular because of his ingenuity; Villayzán popular among the wits for his conceits; Doctor Godínez popular among the erudite for his maxims; Luis Vélez eminent for his heroic qualities. I should not forget Don Francisco de Rojas, nor Don Pedro Rosette, Gaspar de Avila, Don Antonio de Solís, Don Antonio Cuello, and many others who with much success wrote plays.

In spite of the fact there are records and testimony indicting that at least eight of his plays had been written and produced in Spain by 1635, the dramatist's name does not appear in any of the several contemporary listings of playwrights of the period. In fact, the first printed acknowledgment of his existence as a literary figure is the inclusion of his sonnet in the commemorative collection, *Fama póstuma,* published in 1636 by Juan Pérez de Montalbán on the occasion of the death of Lope de Vega.

Self-Exile to France

Just when it seemed that Enríquez Gómez was beginning to enjoy some artistic success, the first epoch of Enríquez Gómez's career ends in 1636 or 1637 when he judged it expedient to abandon Spain for France. Although his exact reasons for leaving Spain are not known, most likely he feared that being called to testify before the Inquisition in the case of Portuguese financier Bartolomé Febos was an indication of future problems with the Holy Office.

The proceedings against Febos apparently had their origins in commercial rivalries among the thriving *converso* merchant population of Rouen.[11] Febo's father, Rodrigues Lamego, was the head of a group of crypto-Jewish merchants that was opposed by another group of authentic converts. Each band had agents in Madrid. The Christians, wishing to ruin their competitors, evidently contacted the Inquisition, which in turn began investigating the links between *marrano* merchants and their Spanish correspondents. While Enríquez Gómez was not listed as one of these suspect agents, his inquisitional dossier by this time would have included the record of his paternal Judaizers and also records of his business trips to France where his *marrano* father, uncle, and other relatives were living. Additionally, the fact that Enríquez Gómez was called to testify about Febos indicates that the Inquisition had reason to believe that the two were acquainted, if not because of business perhaps artistically; the wealthy Febos was famous for his patronage of the arts and liked to surround himself with the literati of the day. It seems likely that one of the poets to enjoy Febos's hospitality was his fellow New Christian, Enríquez Gómez.[12]

Enríquez Gómez's appearance before the tribunal to testify in the downfall of Febos must have brought to his mind the examples of his grandfather, father, and uncle. As a result in or about the year 1636 he abandoned Spain to set himself up in France with his wife, son Diego, and daughter Leonor. Another daughter, Catalina, remained in Madrid. She, like her father and grandfather, had married an Old Christian and agent of the Inquisition, Constantino Ortiz de Urbina. It is interesting to note that Enríquez Gómez's departure did not disrupt relations with his son-in-law who became Enríquez Gómez's commercial correspondent during his self-exile in France. In fact, Enríquez Gómez's sudden flight from Spain to France during a period of war between the two countries may have also had economic motives as he left unpaid certain rather large debts.

Writing in France

The second epoch of Enríquez Gómez's literary production encompasses the years in France where the author lived principally in Bordeaux and Rouen. As in Spain Enríquez Gómez engaged in commercial activities, but now his dedication to writing intensifies in proportion to his need to communicate his feelings of injustice and disillusionment. Although some of the twenty-two plays he listed in *Samson the Nazarene* may have been written while in exile, his major works of this period are in nondramatic genres more sited to the expression of his unhappy circumstances. The sheer volume of his literary activities during these years becomes a source of pride as if the more he wrote the greater the chances of influencing reform: "Los libros que he sacado a luz . . .

hacen nueve volúmenes en prosa y verso, todos escritos desde el año de cuarenta al de cuarenta y nueve, a libro por año, a año por libro" ("The books that I have brought out . . . constitute nine volumes in prose and verse, and all written between 1640 and 1649, one book per year, one year per book").[13] And, as if this were not enough, several prologues to these works promise even more compositions that apparently were not written.

Understandably, the circumstances of this move to France impart a note of bitterness to his writings. The introduction to the *Academias morales* (Moral academies), his first important work done in exile, contains the following notice to the reader:

Extrañarás (y con razón) haber dado a la imprenta este libro en extranjera patria. Respóndate la elegía que escribí sobre mi peregrinación: si no voluntaria, forzosa, y si no forzosa, ocasionada por algunos, que, infeccionando la república, recíprocamente falsos, venden por antídoto el veneno a los que militan debajo del solio.

You will wonder, and rightly so, at my having printed this book in a foreign land. The elegy that I wrote on my wanderings will give you the answer. These involuntary and enforced wanderings were occasioned by some doubly false persons, who, after infecting the republic, sell poison as if it were an antidote to those close to the throne.

The topic of the informer or false friend in the preceding citation appears with such obsessive frequency in his exile compositions that Enríquez Gómez must have known or at least suspected that his problems with the Inquisition were due to information that implicated him in crypto-Jewish activities. The informer, *malsín,* was the terror of the New Christians and especially of the crypto-Jews. According to the definition of a *converso* of the period, "Malsines son los que descubren el secreto de sus amigos para hacer que los maten y que los roben, y algunas veces con levantamiento de falso testimonio" ("Malsines are those who ferret out their friends' secrets so that they can be bilked or killed; sometimes they do it with false testimony").[14]

Although Enríquez Gómez's sojourn in France would have allowed him an opportunity to practice Judaism with little risk, it is not clear at this time to what extent he considered himself Jewish. Certainly during his stay in the various New Christian communities of seventeenth-century France Enríquez Gómez lived and worked with *marrano* relatives and acquaintances who, in the relatively tolerant country, were allowed to observe privately the Law of Moses if they publicly appeared to be Christians. Révah has no hesitation in classifying Enríquez Gómez as a crypto-Jew, but it is never totally clear from Gómez's writings just how strongly attached he was to the religion of his paternal ancestors. While Enríquez Gómez often questioned the practices of Christianity in his satires, it is also clear that his printed French period writings contain no criticism whatsoever of Catholicism. In fact, quite the opposite is true—the church is defended and praised. In general, Enríquez Gómez's criticisms are directed toward the hypocrisy of those Christians whose activities are contrary to Christian tenets, and chief among his targets is, quite naturally, the Inquisition.

On the other hand, it would be naive to expect from Enríquez Gómez an attack on Catholicism. Tolerance in France had its limits, and the French government was also subject to diplomatic pressure from Spain, as Enríquez Gómez was to find out. While he did defend and praise the church in some compositions, this is the same period in which he supposedly wrote two works that most openly express sympathy and admiration for Judaism—*Samson the Nazarene* and possibly "Romance al divín mártir, Judá creyente" (The ballad to the divine martyr, Judah the Believer). These two compositions have traditionally been taken as the sincerest expressions of his religious beliefs.

The truth about Enríquez Gómez's religious beliefs is most likely neither black nor white. In such complicated and contradictory circumstances he doubtless found himself for much of his life in a middle ground between the two religions—alternatively repelled and attracted to each by powerful and conflicting reasons. Indeed, there is evidence in his writing to conclude that he experienced periods of religious indecision. His comments in *The Angelic Politics* on the state of mind of the victim caught up in the Kafka-like inquisitional proceedings are poignantly revealing: "Como al reo se le niega el nombre del testigo, el que padece inocente, como no le conoce y se halla en el tormento, confiesa que es hereje, siendo cristiano; y muchas veces, con la desesperación, ni queda uno ni otro" ("Because the names of the witnesses are denied to the accused, the innocent victim, as he knows not his accusers and finds himself subjected to torture, confesses to being a heretic even though he is Christian, *and many times because of his desperation winds up not being either*").[15]

During the exile period Enríquez Gómez continued to function on the mercantile scene and maintain an intense literary activity. In addition, because of his interest in political science and through the activities of his friend, Fernándes de Villareal, he became interested in the Portuguese restoration of 1640 that separated that country from the Spanish Empire in which it had been incorporated for sixty years.[16] In an effort to marshal international support for his restored kingdom, King John IV of Portugal sent a delegation to France. An important member of the Portuguese diplomatic team was the *converso* Fernándes de Villareal who, already residing in France, offered his services to the new government and worked tirelessly to propagandize the Portuguese cause. Fernándes de Villareal relied heavily on the writing skills of his friend Enríquez Gómez in a number of projects. One of Enríquez Gómez's first tasks was to chronicle the arrival in France of the Portuguese ambassador in 1641. The result was *Triunfo lusitano* (Lusitanian triumph) published in both Paris and Lisbon. Later, notwithstanding his services, Enríquez Gómez called down upon himself the wrath of the Portuguese ambassador with the publication of the second part of his anti-inquisitional pamphlet, the *The Angelic Politics*.

Clandestine Return to Spain

Enríquez Gómez's decision to return to Spain was made about the year 1649. Just why he chose to leave the relative safety of France to return to a land in which he had every reason to fear detention remains to be determined. Certainly he must have realized that his inquisitional dossier would include reports on his association with Judaizers in France as well as a copy of *The Angelic Politics* that Enríquez Gómez himself had sent to one of the tribunals of the Inquisition.

Professor Amiel suggests that Enríquez Gómez's return was primarily motivated by the failure of his business in Rouen and his need to retrieve certain sums owing to him by his son-in-law in Madrid.[17] C. H. Rose and Timothy Oelman feel that the troubles caused by Enríquez Gómez's publication of the second part of *The Angelic Politics* may have caused the French government to pressure him to leave.[18] But along with economic and political motives, sentimental and artistic factors must have also come into play. The *converso* attachment to the Iberian ambience, the exile's nostalgia and longing for repatriation is strongly and frequently expressed in Enríquez Gómez's writings. One suspects that for a writer as dedicated to his art as was Enríquez Gómez, there was a compelling need to work and produce in a Spanish milieu; after all, his compositions could not hope to achieve wide diffusion or appreciation in a French language and cultural environment. From his commercial dealings in France, his visits there and eventual residence, he must have had at least an elementary knowledge of French; however, there is no evidence to indicate that he ever wrote in any other than his native Spanish.

According to Amiel's investigations, Enríquez Gómez returned to Spain with the idea of turning himself into the Inquisition for rehabilitation.[19] Obviously, if he entertained this notion, Enríquez Gómez must have felt that his lapses against Catholicism were not very grave. He must also have been prepared to tell everything he knew of *marrano* activities of friends and relatives in France, an indispensable element of the process. But before he could do this, his brother-in-law, Pedro Alonso Basurto, an official of the Inquisition, convinced him that the charges were indeed serious and the risk too great.

For at least the last years of his life Enríquez Gómez established himself clandestinely in Seville in spite of the danger incurred because he had lived there, had published there, and his uncle had fled that city under a cloud. Even after twenty-five year's absence the risk of being recognized was greater there than in any Spanish city except Madrid. But Seville was the entrepôt for trade with the New World, an important city for people with commercial interests in America, and we know from Révah's investigations that Enríquez Gómez had relatives in the colonies with whom he had business dealings. And so under the alias Fernando de Zárate y Castronovo he passed eleven years in Spain until his arrest in Seville by the Inquisition on 21 September 1661. We can only imagine the constant apprehension he must have suffered during this time. When, for example, the Inquisition began to suspect that Zárate and Enríquez Gómez were one, it was discovered that, although a well-known figure in Seville, his private life was so discretely managed that no one knew where he lived.[20] Any hope he may have entertained of the Inquisition forgetting about him was dispelled when, in the year prior to his arrest, on 14 April 1660, Enríquez Gómez had the dubious pleasure of seeing his own effigy burned along with other victims in a large auto-da-fé in Seville. This notoriety must have alarmed him, for at the time of his arrest he was making plans to leave for Naples as soon as he could collect funds arriving with the annual fleet from America.

Antonio Enríquez Gómez died in prison in Seville on 19 March 1663, reportedly of natural causes, after having been reconciled to the church and having received the sacraments. Despite the fate of his effigy three years earlier, it seems that the inquisitors did not in fact deal very harshly with Enríquez Gómez.

As ever he continued to write after his return to Spain. However, the political and philosophical treatises of his French exile were no longer suitable nor possible in his new circumstances. In this last epoch we see a return to his first love—the theater, a return that may have been economically motivated as successful dramatists were rather well compensated according to the standards of the time. The thirty-odd plays Enríquez Gómez wrote under the Zárate alias were praised by nineteenth-century critics for their Catholic zeal and *castizo* nature (for their "Spanishness").[21] These critics believed that Zárate was a separate and distinct person from the New Christian Enríquez Gómez whose works, they felt, reeked of Marranism. Of course, the orthodox nature of the Zárate plays is not surprising; considering the author's masquerade as an Old Christian gentleman, he could hardly have written otherwise. Nevertheless, unless the Catholic spirit is a complete pose, the religious zeal of the plays indicates that at least during the final decade of his life Enríquez Gómez was resolving his religious dilemma in favor of Catholicism. The problem of the apparent Catholic sincerity of the Zárate plays has generally been overlooked by commentators: both Amiel and Révah flatly affirm that Enríquez Gómez remained faithful to his Jewish faith until the end, and even J. A. Cid is inclined to go along.[22] However, the surprising leniency of the Inquisition, Enríquez Gómez's death as a Catholic, and his internment in consecrated ground seem to indicate otherwise. The fact that the Inquisitors were inclined to accept the sincerity of the author's Catholicism should carry a good deal of weight—they were, after all, experts in sniffing out heresy.

Chapter Three

The Twenty-two Plays
of the First Epoch

Prologue to *Samson the Nazarene*

The prologue to *Samson the Nazarene* contains, in addition to his reminiscences on the state of dramatic art in the first half of the seventeenth century, a list by title of all Enríquez Gómez's plays to the year 1649, the approximate year of his clandestine return to Spain. All in all, the prologue reveals a writer dedicated to his work and, as a result, preoccupied with the fate of his compositions. Because he was so keenly aware of the precariousness of his existence, Enríquez Gómez sought a remedy through the written word that would be a testimonial to his life: "Poeta soy, pero si no me puedo excusar de ser mortal, justo será que busque una pequeña luz de la inmortalidad" ("I am a poet, but if I cannot remedy the fact that I am also mortal, it is only just that I seek a small portion of the light of immortality"). In many respects this prologue appears to be a conscious commemoration of the end of one phase of his life and the beginning of another, as he knew he would be returning to Spain or else had, in fact, already returned. One of his vital concerns is to establish the paternity of his intellectual offspring. For once back in Spain living under an alias, the plays he authored as Antonio Enríquez Gómez would be on their own. Even for dramatists who were not in hiding an active concern for one's own compositions was a necessity given the unscrupulous practices of the printers of the period, as Enríquez Gómez notes: "Las mías [comedias] fueron veinte y dos, cuyos títulos pondré aquí para que se conozcan por mías, pues todas ellas o las más que se imprimen en Sevilla les dan los impresores el título que quieren y el dueño que se les antoja" ("My plays came to twenty-two, whose titles I will list here so that they can be known as mine, since all or the majority of those that are printed in Seville are given whatever titles the printers dream up and are attributed to whatever author strikes the printers' fancy"). The singling out of the Sevillian printers is interesting. Surely they were no different than printers in other cities with regard to these practices. This may indicate that he wrote the statement after returning there and being particularly offended by the intentional or unintentional inaccuracies of Sevillian printers.

This list of plays is reproduced in the primary bibliography of this work in the order established by Enríquez Gómez, an order that is neither alphabetical nor apparently chronological, according to the little information there is on the date of composition of any of his plays. Of all his plays of this period only a few relate to any date or indicate their order of composition. The last lines of *To Deceive in Order to Reign* proclaim this play as the author's first work, but there is no indication as to when it was composed. For some other plays performance and publishing information establishes termini ad quem: *Fernán Méndez Pinto* 1633; *The Valiant Diego de Camas* 1633; *Captain Chinchilla*, 1634; *The Overweening Pride of Nimrod*, 1635; *The Lightning Bolt of Palestine*, 1637; *The Great Spanish Cardinal*, prior to 1642; *The Prudent Abigail*, *What Honor Obliges*, *Love is Proof Against Deceit*, and *Love Pure and Sane*, all 1642; and *The Throne of Solomon*, 1649.[1]

Of the twenty-two plays in Enríquez Gómez's list only fourteen are extant in manuscripts, individual printed copies *(sueltas)*, and in the various seventeenth-century collections of plays (the *partes*). Investigation has not uncovered the whereabouts of copies of *The Lightning Bolt of Palestine*, *What Goes on in the Middle of the Night*, *The Rights of an Heir*, *The House of Austria in Spain*, or the two parts of *The Throne of Solomon*. Two other titles on his list that do still exist, *The Chevalier of Grace* and *The Sun Stopped in its Tracks*, seem not to be the plays Enríquez Gómez wrote but works with the same titles by Tirso de Molina and Lope de Vega respectively. As in the case with the works of most of the dramatists of the period, there are problems of attribution; thus, also included in the primary bibliography are the titles of several plays that have been credited to Enríquez Gómez but which he did not set down in his 1649 list.

Categorizing the Plays

In spite of the obvious generalizations in dividing Enríquez Gómez's extant plays into discrete categories, such a division is convenient in attempting a brief discussion of the plays he wrote under his true name. Of the fourteen plays only two are cape and sword plays: *Love is Proof Against Deceit* and *The Valiant Diego de Camas*.[2] The rest fall into a category that can be generally characterized as plays of palace intrigue, all of which involve a subversive threat to a legitimate monarchy. This type of play can be subdivided into two groups: those based on historical and biblical personages—the two parts of *The Great Cardinal, Don Gil de Albornoz,* the two parts of *Fernán Méndez Pinto, The Overweening Pride of Nimrod, The Prudent Abigail, Love Pure and Sane* (dealing with Emperor Marcus Aurelius), and, to some extent, *What Honor Obliges* (concerning King Peter I, the Cruel); and those plays involving fictional situations—*To Deceive in Order to Reign, Jealousies Cannot Obscure the Sun,* and *What Jealousies Oblige.* Of course, as with the vast majority of seventeenth-century drama, the plays of palace intrigue also incorporate most of the romantic mix-ups that fuel the traditional cape and sword plays, and they include the comic relief that the servant (*gracioso*) traditionally provides.

The play of palace intrigue, often associated with that type of play concerning the rise and fall of kings' ministers or favorites (*comedias de privanza*), is by no means an invention of Enríquez Gómez, the careers of great men and the deeds of princes being among the oldest topics in literature. However, the theme of the king's favorite (his *privado* or *valido*) was especially prominent during the first third of the seventeenth century due to the weakness of Philip III and his son Philip IV, both of whom allowed court favorites to run the government in sharp contrast to previous monarchs. During the reign of Philip IV the gradual assumption of all powers by the Count-Duke of Olivares naturally brought about the minister's increasing unpopularity and subjected him to constant literary attacks.[3] The disastrous economic and political conditions of Spain as well as its gradual decline on the international scene gave added impetus to writers concerned with correct governance, a topic that already had a long tradition in peninsular literature. Enríquez Gómez's interest in right-government was heightened by his *converso* status, which made him more directly affected than others by official policies of tolerance or persecution.

Because the characteristics of the Spanish *comedia* have been amply treated in other works concerning Golden Age dramatists,[4] the remainder of this chapter is devoted to first, a general discussion of Enríquez Gómez's drama, drawing upon all the available plays; and second, to a more detailed consideration of three specific plays—*What Honor Obliges, Love is Proof Against Deceit,* and *The Prudent Abigail.* These three plays have been chosen because they represent Enríquez Gómez at his best, because they are undoubtedly authentic, and because they represent three different types of his *comedia*—tragedy, comedy, and historical drama. Notes to this chapter include references to the few studies to date of the individual plays and will show that the dramatic works of this author are largely unexplored.

Spirit of Forgiveness

One notable characteristic of Enríquez Gómez dramaturgy is his aversion to punish his villains with the full rigor that their treachery would normally demand in seventeenth-century drama, or even in real life. Or, to put it more positively, with the notable exception of *What Honor Obliges,* Enríquez Gómez's tendency is always toward forgiveness of transgressions. While in the Spanish *comedia* the restoration of societal harmony is very often accomplished by the elimination of the opposing disruptive forces, for Enríquez Gómez a reintegration of contending factions into a harmonious society is most often brought about by reason and persuasion to effect admission of error and forgiveness.

This feature of his drama is, of course, most evident in the treatment of evildoers for whom the death penalty would seem justified but who instead are shown remarkable tolerance and mercy. The most notable illustrations occur in the cases in which the crime is the most grave, as, for example, that of Ludovico of *To Deceive in Order to Reign,* who is guilty of attempted fratricide, regicide, sedition, and rape, among other crimes.[5] Nevertheless, his brother, the rightful king, on regaining his kingdom pardons Ludovico and, as if that were not enough, weds him to a princess with a dowry of half the kingdom. Another example is that of *Jealousies Cannot Obscure the Sun,* in which Federico not only plans the king's murder but also imprisons the king's favorite advisor and personally murders the king's cousin. Although well deserving of execution, Federico's punishment for these horrendous crimes is only to be exiled. Exile is likewise the only punishment for the two villains of *What Jealousy Obliges;* they, among other nefarious plots, attempt to murder the prospective wife of their king.

In all the extant Enríquez Gómez plays only four include cases of unnatural death of a principal figure, and of these only three characters are real villains. The fates of these three are interesting: divine justice causes Nimrod and Caidem of *The Overweening Pride of Nimrod* to fall to their deaths in an abyss, and Pinol, one of the traitors of *Fernán Méndez Pinto,* is killed by a lion as he attempts to assassinate the sleeping hero. In each of these three cases we note that death is not brought about by human hands but by a higher power. The fourth case, that of the untimely death of the heroine Elvira in *What Honor Obliges,* is unique in Enríquez Gómez's dramaturgy and is discussed in more detail later in this chapter.

Perhaps a passage in *The Prudent Abigail* best sums up the generally benign philosophy of Enríquez Gómez with regard to punishment: Abigail responds in the following manner to her avaricious and evil tempered husband, Narval, who wishes to punish one of his shepherds: "No pidáis estrecha cuenta / al inocente pastor. . . . Todos somos peregrinos, / y hermanos. Es menester / hacer bien, y no perder / de la virtud los caminos" ("Do not demand such strict accounting from the innocent shepherd. . . . We are all wanderers on this earth and brothers. It is necessary to do good and not to stray from the path of virtue."[6]

Flawed Heroes or Human Beings?

If Enríquez Gómez's tolerance of treachery seems not true to life according to the norms of the *comedia* or of society, the combination of virtues and defects of his characters makes them very lifelike. In fact, Amador de los Ríos found Enríquez Gómez's gentlemen altogether too human for his liking: "Los caballeros pintados por Enríquez Gómez no siempre son igualmente discretos o pundonorosos; no en todas ocasiones guardan con el mismo empeño, con la misma constancia los fueros de la hidalguía y se postran rendidos ante las aras del amor y de la belleza" ("The gentlemen . . . painted by Enríquez Gómez are not always equally discrete and honorable; they do not in all occasions conserve with the same zeal and constancy the obligations of the well-born, and they prostrate themselves submissively before the altars of love and beauty").[7] It is true that Enríquez Gómez's gentlemen, nobles, and even royals do not hesitate to lie or commit acts that, although common in human experience, in the idealistic *comedia* is conduct more often associated with servants and villains. Their foibles add interesting dimensions to many of his characters as the following examples suggest.

By far Enríquez Gómez's least attractive monarch (but most interesting) is the king-protagonist, Iberio, of *To Deceive in Order To Reign.* Iberio, pursued by palace intrigue and unhappy over an impending arranged marriage with the princess Isbela, instead of combating his enemies and being honest with Isbela, runs off to the forest to live as a shepherd, at the side of his true love, Elena. Iberio shrugs off his royal responsibilities with these remarks:

> . . . Yo hallo
> por mejor, dejar el reino
> a que le goce un bastardo
> como Ludovico, que es
> como tú sabes, mi hermano,
> y vivir en estos montes.[8]

I deem it better to leave the kingdom to be enjoyed by a bastard like Ludovico, who is, as you know, my brother, and to live in these hills.

In no hurry to regain his rightful place, while all presume him dead, Iberio passes three years with Elena in the pastoral setting. All this time his fiancée, the princess Isbela, remains true to his memory and rejects valiantly the advances of the usurping Ludovico. When Iberio finally moves to retake the throne he deceives Isbela with a promise of marriage in exchange for vital help. Isbela naturally imagines herself queen on Iberio's restoration, but on attempting to take her place on the throne Elena stops her with the humiliating words, "Está, señora, occupado"[9] ("It is already occupied, my lady"). As if this were not shabby enough reward for her constancy, Iberio proceeds to marry Isbela to the very traitor whose threats she has heroically rejected for the past three years. The title of the play is ennunciated by the king in a speech justifying his poor conduct vis-à-vis Isbela—"Si puede llamarse engaño / Engañar para Reinar"[10] ("If one can call it deceit to deceive in order to reign"). Iberio's self-indulgence and deceit makes for one of the most extraordinary presentations of the king in the whole of the *comedia*. Clearly, in spite of the play's setting in a fictitious Polish-Hungarian empire, the monarch's name indicates that the dramatist had the Spanish political situation in mind.

Another royal person with an equally curious sense of honor is the King of Tartary in the first part of *Fernán Méndez Pinto*. This youth, because of a grievance, ignobly murders the old Emperor of China while the latter is alone and is asleep on his throne. The king-assassin then flees the scene and lets the blame fall on the innocent Méndez Pinto. One can scarcely imagine a series of deeds less worthy of a monarch but, in spite of it all, the King of Tartary later marries the Emperor's feisty daughter in the second part of the play and wars on the side of right.

Even that valiant knight, Méndez Pinto, has moments in which he displays unworthy attitudes. After having suffered many misfortunes in his wanderings, Méndez Pinto is naturally interested in finding stability. This desire at times leads him to adopt opportunistic stances. In part 1 of the play he does not hesitate to respond quite cynically to the amorous advances of the Princess Pantalisa and, at the same time, to those of her lady in waiting Tituliana. In the second part of the play Méndez Pinto attains the high post of tutor to the king's nephew, a position that promises potential stability and favors. But when the nephew, for whom Méndez Pinto professes much affection, falls gravely wounded, the only thing that occurs to him to say is the rather callous observation "Aquí dió fin mi privanza" ("There is the end of my royal favor"), a phrase that he repeats twice.[11] For a moment then, human nature shines through the veneer of the gentleman.

As a final observation on the subject, while one would have to agree with Amador de los Ríos concerning the lack of discretion and even honor of many an Enríquez Gómez hero, the worst cases do not "prostrate themselves submissively before the altars of love and beauty," but before the altar of self-interest, a situation that seems much less pardonable, but more true to life.

Aggressive Heroines

Whereas Enríquez Gómez's male roles are customarily valiant when the occasion calls for physical response, in their relationships with women they are, more often than not, reduced to jelly before a woman's wrath or completely befuddled by their actions. Few dramatists of the time consistently created ladies of such strength of character, constancy, and aggression. As they pursue their objectives with an extraordinary single-mindedness of purpose, they inspire admiration and quite often a certain amount of fear on the part of the males. Generally their objective is to wed their man and, as such, there are no "coy women" (the *mujer esquiva*) that McKendrick found to be the most popular type of the seventeenth-century drama.[12] To the contrary, Enríquez Gómez ladies love and pursue their men with a persistence not to be denied.

In several plays the Enríquez Gómez heroine is the Amazon type, strongly imbued with a sense of her own worth. For example, Pantalisa of *Fernán Méndez Pinto* and Calmaná and Delbora of *The Overweening*

Pride of Nimrod proclaim themselves the equals of any male. Pantalisa
describes herself as "Rayo / fatal del orbe . . . venerada por diosa de
elementos, si no por ser cometa, / por hija heroica del mayor planeta"[13]
("Deadly lightning bolt of the world. . . . Venerated as goddess of
the elements, and, if not as a comet, as the heroic daughter of the
sun"). Not too different from the Amazons are Elena of *To Deceive
in Order to Reign* and Laura of *What Jealousies Oblige,* the beautiful
huntress types, more at home in the skins of wild animals and with
their bows and arrows. If others are rulers of nations, these women
hold sway over the forests. Elena proclaims:

> El alma soy de estas fieras,
> el corazón de estos montes,
> la corona de estas selvas,
> la reina de estas montañas
> blanca aurora de estas breñas.[14]

I am the soul of these wild beasts, the heart of these woods, the crown of
these thickets, the queen of these mountains, and the pure dawn of these
crags.

Others of his heroines are less obviously Amazonian, but nevertheless
are undeniably formidable. The cases of Juana and Leonor of *Love is
Proof Against Deceit* and the character of La Padilla of *What Honor
Obliges* are discussed in the individual sections on these *comedias* at the
end of this chapter, but Anarda of *What Jealousies Oblige* will illustrate
a common Enríquez Gómez heroine. Anarda is so fiercely jealous that
she proclaims to her fiancé that she herself is perfectly capable of doing
away with him and the woman she suspects is his lover: "Mujer soy
tan celosa y atrevida, / que a Flor de Lis y a vos en un instante /
a mi proprio aliento quitaré la vida"[15] ("I am a woman so jealous and
daring that, with my own hand and without hesitation, I will take
your life and that of Flor de Lis"). Naturally it never comes to this,
but Anarda does not hesitate to cruelly beat and scratch her fiancé's
servant to try to get him to talk. Another equally fearsome woman is
the queen in *Jealousies Cannot Obscure the Sun;* she manages to intimidate
everyone including the king.

Amador de los Ríos noted a similarity with Tirso de Molina with
regard to the forceful and willful nature of Enríquez Gómez's ladies:
"presentando a sus damas dotadas de afectos poco nobles. . . . Tal

vez pinta demasiado fáciles y celosas a estas mismas damas que atropellan las leyes del decoro, para lograr sus amorosos intentos" ("presenting his ladies graced with less than noble inclinations. . . . Perhaps he paints these ladies as too easy and too jealous as they run roughshod over the rules of decorum to obtain their amorous intents").[16] Naturally, indecorousness and forcefulness are most obvious in the works containing female antagonists who exhibit various degrees of culpability. As we shall see later in this chapter, María de Padilla of *What Honor Obliges* undermines Elvira's conjugal fidelity and causes her downfall. Another aggressive type is the formidable queen of *Jealousies Cannot Obscure the Sun* who causes considerable mischief that has to be pardoned her, since her jealousies are fomented by the king's enemies. Also in this category is the empress of *Love Pure and Sane* whose maternal devotion blinds her to the mental instability of her son, an instability that threatens the peace of realm. In these examples the female roles are involuntary accessories to the principal male villains, but there is one interesting comedy in which the main antagonist is a woman, Leonor of *Love is Proof Against Deceit.* (This work is discussed in more detail later in this chapter.) Nevertheless, it should be noted that not everyone of Enríquez Gómez's ladies are so aggressively forward—one immediately thinks of the prudent Abigail whose strength and virtue lie in her calm determination to do right. Moreover, the ladies' lack of attention to decorum is most often a response to circumstances beyond their control— machinations of an enemy, or undesired amorous interest from a rival suitor. Finally, we might note that trampling on decorum or the appearance of it is the norm in the *comedia;* if all the ladies and gentlemen acted with propriety there would be no conflict and thus no play.

General Observations

The plays of Enríquez Gómez are often quite baroque in their plot intricacies. To modern eyes they are frequently overburdened with too many characters and too much action. As with other playwrights of the epoch, Enríquez Gómez made no pretense of following the dramatic unities of time, place, or action; thus the multiplicity of competing actions often fragments his plays, giving the impression of several works artificially compressed into one. *The Valiant Diego de Camas,* for example, unsuccessfully tries to incorporate the unrelated adventures of two ladies in distress plus the various adventures of the hero within one work.

The second part of *The Great Spanish Cardinal* is another in which the author fails to unite what supposedly is the main action, the recital of the Cardinal's heroic deeds, with a competing story line of the amorous difficulties of his younger brother.

By far the least interesting of Enríquez Gómez's plays are those that show the greatest tendency toward the spectacular; the large number of roles leads to more complications and consequently a dilution of any central theme. Perhaps the most representative of this problem is the play *The Overweening Pride of Nimrod* which is fragmented to the point of incomprehensibility by its overabundance of incidents, motifs, characters, and scenic changes. In general, the plays of Enríquez Gómez's first period demonstrate his penchant for special effects, the exotic, and the dramatic moment, elements that are even more developed in the plays of his Zárate period.

A number of interrelated themes may be adduced from the collective works of Enríquez Gómez's first period. Because they are also present and developed to an even greater degree in the nondramatic literature of his exile years it would seem that they represent an increasing consciousness of concerns arising out of the author's New Christian status. There are, in summary, five distinct themes: (1) The persecution of the hero or heroine and especially that which results in exile—two of the best examples are the cases of Fernán Méndez Pinto and that of David of *The Prudent Abigail*. (2) Treachery, especially of those who pretend to be friends all the better to betray the protagonist: almost every play has an example of this type, one of the most representative being Leonor of *Love is Proof Against Deceit*. No doubt this preoccupation is an outgrowth of the *converso*'s bogey-man, the stool pigeon (*malsín*), whom we have already noted as a prime concern of the author. (3) Tolerance and forgiveness, as previously discussed. (4) The true worth of a person is shown by his deeds and not the nobility of lineage. (5) The well-ordered state directed by an enlightened prince: all the plays of political intrigue express this expectation, but the foremost example of this ideal is the Emperor Marcus Aurelius of *Love Pure and Sane*. As the creation of a merchant-writer, this monarch is concerned with even such bourgeois matters as the protection and encouragement of commerce.

At his best Enríquez Gómez shows a dramatic flair that is generally well-formed and well-employed, and a comic spirit that finds its principal expression in sarcasm and satire. The several confrontation scenes between rival women are highly entertaining and magnificent pieces for the actresses to demonstrate their skill in portraying suppressed rage, injured dignity, and cattiness. At the other end of the dramatic spectrum the pathetic crises of the husband and wife of *What Honor Obliges* can be said to equal anything that Calderón de la Barca can offer. Unfortunately, what we do not often find in Enríquez Gómez is a memorable poetic talent to complement his gift for the dramatic. The best moments of his verse are those that come closest to reproducing normal conversation, but his lyric passages frequently lapse into a prosaic verse revealing a general poverty of rhyme.[17] Also unfortunate is that Enríquez Gómez felt obligated by the conventions of the time to include long artificial and bombastic passages that are never integrated harmoniously into the drama and tend to tedious repetition of image and metaphor.

The Popularity of Enríquez Gómez's Plays

It is difficult to judge the popularity of Enríquez Gómez's drama in his day. His friend, Fernándes de Villareal, in his apology to the *Moral Academies* wrote that Enríquez Gómez "por muchas veces se llevó los aplauso a pesar de sus émulos" ("was frequently applauded in spite of his rivals") and, further, his plays "eran envidiadas, pero también eran aplaudidas" ("were envied, but also applauded"). Given the circumstances, Villareal's comments could be expected to exaggerate his friend's fame and must be taken with a grain of salt, there being no evidence to show that Villareal ever saw one of them performed in Spain. However, the equal attention to Enríquez Gómez's detractors in Villareal's statements and the absolute silence concerning his existence as a playwright would indicate that the budding dramatist Enríquez Gómez had not made much of a mark before his exile to France.

After his exile and, in particular, after his death, the numerous *sueltas* that remain and the various documents relating to theatrical activity indicate that several of his first period plays became very popular indeed. *The Prudent Abigail*, for example, appears with astonishing frequency in collections of Spanish theater, and others that are conserved with relative abundance are *What Jealousies Oblige, To Deceive in Order to Reign, Jealousies Cannot Obscure the Sun, Love Pure and Sane, What Honor Obliges, Love is Proof Against Deceit*, and *Fernán Méndez Pinto*. The popularity of some of these is perhaps due to the fact that four were included in Enríquez Gómez's *The Moral Academies of the Muses* which enjoyed considerable success, seeing six editions betwen 1642 and 1734.

For all the popular success of his plays during the eighteenth century, critics beginning with L. Fernández de Moratín have been less than enchanted with the Enríquez Gómez works. Moratín detested them because of their baroque excesses, and nineteenth-century Spanish critics added an element of anti-Semitism to the complaints.[18] Mesonero Romanos found nothing at all commendable about the plays, for "aunque no se declaren absolutamente las creencias religiosas del autor, se nota cierta predilección a ocuparse de la antigua historia hebraica . . . y no hay una sola cuyo asunto sea tomado del nuevo testamento, de los misterios de la religión cristiana ni de la vida de los santos" ("even though the author's religious beliefs are not absolutely declared, one notes a certain predilection to occupy himself with ancient Hebrew history . . . not one play's plot is taken from the New Testament, from the Christian mysteries, nor from the lives of the saints").[19] The very influential Marcelino Menéndez y Pelayo was somewhat more charitable, although his characterization of the author is clearly denigrating: "tenía este judaizante muy despierto y lucido ingenio, aunque de segundo orden e incapaz de la perfección en nada, y contagiado hasta los tuétanos de los vicios de la época y de otros propios y peculiares suyos" ("this Judaizer had a lively and clear genius, although of the second rank and incapable of perfection in anything, and infected to the very marrow by the vices of the epoch as well as by others of his own particular type").[20] On the other hand, it is not surprising that Jewish literary historians are more enthusiastic, Graetz referring to him as the Jewish Calderón.[21] It is only very recently that Enríquez Gómez's dramatic works have begun to receive any sort of balanced attention.

Because the scope of this work does not allow for comments on all his plays, the remainder of this chapter concentrates on three representative plays of Enríquez Gómez: *What Honor Obliges, Love is Proof Against Deceit,* and *The Prudent Abigail.*

What Honor Obliges

Enríquez Gómez consistently rejects the fatal solution to punish the woman who has dishonored her family. This tendency is evidenced by *Fernán Méndez Pinto, Love is Proof Against Deceit,* and *The Valiant Diego de Camas,* and again later in his semipicaresque story, *Don Gregorio Guadaña.* So it is surprising that of all his existing plays *What Honor*

Obliges is the only one that presents a tragic interpretation of the love-honor conflict between a married couple.[22]

We will give first a synopsis of the plot. With the very best intentions King Alfonso decides to reward the long and faithful services of Don Enrique by arranging his marriage to the beautiful and much younger Elvira de Liarte. Neither is pleased by the prospective match: Enrique, the old soldier, considers love and courting as frivolous pursuits, and Elvira is already in love with Prince Pedro, the future King Peter "The Cruel." In spite of their personal desires, neither wishes to offend the king, and the first act ends with their engagement ceremony amid indications of an ill-starred union.

The marriage has taken place as the second act opens. Although obviously not a love match, the pair make the most of the situation and treat each other with the courtesy and respect that the sacred union demands. However, Elvira continues to frequent the palace where she suffers at the sight of Prince Pedro and from the ironies of María de Padilla, Elvira's rival for the prince's affection. Encouraged by Elvira's presence, the prince determines to visit her one night. Unfortunately, Enrique returns unexpectedly and, in a tense scene, discovers the prince in hiding. Without letting Elvira know, Enrique shows the prince out of the house and takes his place in the dark alcove in order to judge the culpability of Elvira. Elvira, believing at first that she is addressing the prince, defends herself vigorously, convincing her husband that she had no part in his clandestine visit. The act closes with Enrique's expressions of confidence and respect and, in fact, he is so impressed by her spirited defense of his honor that his previous indifference to her changes to care.

In the third act, by a combination of fatal circumstances, it becomes obvious to Enrique that neither can Prince Pedro desist in his intended seduction nor does Elvira have enough strength to resist indefinitely the temptation. Moreover, the danger grows that the attraction will become public knowledge. Enrique appeals to the king for remedy, but before the latter can act the prince's pursuit of Elvira determines her fate. During a hunt at his country villa, Enrique forces Elvira to accompany him to a precipice from which she falls to her death.

Without doubt *What Honor Obliges* is the dramatist's finest work. Of all his dramatic roles none are developed with as much depth as those of this play. The first act establishes Enrique as the unsentimental, mature man making the best of a situation that was forced upon him by loyalty to his king. The crisis that shakes him in the second act sets off a progression of emotions that changes polite indifference to suspicion, to admiration, to fear, and finally to sorrow. For Enrique the situation is impossibly complex; because of the potential of personal dishonor, the temptation to react immediately and drastically is strong but, even disregarding his own fate, he has to consider the royal status of his opponent and his love for the king. He suppresses his impetuous tendencies and calls on his deep-seated sense of justice, which requires that Elvira be given an opportunity to defend herself. Her self-exoneration is a tremendous relief for Enrique and one that initiates a completely new view of this woman who heretofore scarcely existed for him.

This final act reverses Enrique's newfound confidence in Elvira. Notable is his desire to give her every opportunity to prove her innocence, and notable are his attempts to avoid the catastrophe that he foresees. His extreme reluctance to take Elvira's life is reflected even in the equivocal manner of her death—she seems not to be pushed but rather led to a position from which her fall is inevitable. In this way her death is a perfect mirror of the circumstances that led to it, that of having placed herself in a dangerous position vis-à-vis the prince and her husband.

Elvira's dilemma receives as much of the play's attention as that of her husband. From the beginning we see that there are two impediments to any future happiness with the prince, one being the difference in rank between them and the other being competition from María de Padilla. In the first act Elvira's initial joy in what promises to be the culmination of her amorous expectations and her triumph over her rival turns suddenly to ashes at the king's announcement of his intention to honor Enrique with her hand. The farewell scene between Elvira and the prince that ends act 1 is tender and moving. With sad resignation Elvira renounces her past and states her determination to fulfill her obligations as Enrique's wife.

Elvira's fatal flaw seems not so much a result of any deep love she maintains for the prince but rather from her not wanting to lose him to her archrival María. Although in act 1, with all good intention, she had nobly released him from any obligation and even suggested he find solace in María's arms, her generous resolve crumbles when it seems that such a match might actually happen. Elvira's struggle to maintain her honor as Enrique's wife is set against her consuming jealousy of María and produces a state of indecision that keeps alive the prince's attention. As a sorrowful Enrique observes, Elvira's downfall is brought about by her jealousy, not her love.

The plot of this play naturally leads one to a comparison with the famous Calderonian tragedies. For its unaccustomed violence against the wife it seems likely that Enríquez Gómez was inspired particularly by Calderón's *El médico de su honra* (The doctor of his honor) and *A secreto agravio, secreta venganza* (For secret slight, secret vengeance).[23] Because there is no evidence at present as to which dramatist first wrote a play about uxorcide, we can only assume that Enríquez Gómez's followed Calderón's. While there is no doubt that Enríquez Gómez was familiar with Calderón's dramaturgy (Enríquez Gómez mentions him with admiration several times in the prologues to his exile works), it cannnot be said that *What Honor Obliges* is merely an imitation of Calderón. There are, however, some points of contact. The most intriguing similarity with *El médico de su honra* is that Calderón also has the wife tempted to an illicit affair with a prince, this time don Enrique, the son of King Pedro. Otherwise the plays are dissimilar: when Calderón's husband finds out he tells his wife to prepare for death, and he then orders a barber to open her vein so that she will bleed to death. The king not only pardons but condones the murder and orders the husband to wed a lady whom he had dishonored some time before. *For Secret Slight, Secret Vengeance* is set in Portugal. Here the chief similarity is that a young wife is married to an older man. In Calderón's play she then learns that her first love, whom she thought dead, is very much alive. The play's resolution has the husband murdering the lover while the two are fording a river and then murdering the wife by setting fire to his villa.

In spite of some superficial resemblances, the plot of Enríquez Gómez's play is more complex than either of the Calderón plays. Enríquez Gómez joins together two people completely indifferent to each other and from here the characters develop, especially the husband, who comes to admire and then love his wife, the first time in his life that he has experienced love. The subsequent process of Enrique's disillusionment is likewise presented artfully with all the nuances of his interior conflict. In the same way we see played out the psychological process of Elvira's struggle to conform and accept her responsibility and her inability to do so caused, in large measure, by the presence of her rival, María.

Another point that deserves note is Enríquez Gómez's flair for the dramatic moment, especially evident in the intense scene of the second act in Enrique's confrontation with the prince and his testing of Elvira's loyalty. A complement to this dramatic sense is his excellent talent for dialogue. Enríquez Gómez may lack Calderón's sustained poetic genius,

but he is not less talented in the creation of exchanges that sparkle
with a natural conversational freshness, as evidenced by the scenes
between Elvira and María with their serious and comic moments, and
between the prince and Enrique when he discovers the prince hiding
in his house. Another noteworthy scene is the emotion-charged moment
in the third act in which Enrique reveals his fears to the king and
pleads for aid. Even Menéndez y Pelayo, perhaps Enríquez Gómez's
severest critic, praised the passages in which Enrique pours out his
desperation:

> El rey quiso darme honor;
> pero no advirtió que cuando
> su amor me fue levantando,
> mi honor, sin hacer estruendo,
> iba al abismo muriendo.
> ¡Oh, mal haya la balanza
> que levantó mi privanza
> cuando mi honor fue cayendo!
> Cielos, quitadme la vida
> o remediad mi dolor;
> que quien vive sin honor,
> siempre la tuvo perdida.
> . . . .
> Quitóme el honor el rey
> Y entendió que me la daba.[24]

The king thought to honor me, but he did not realize that while his loving
favor was lifting me up, my honor was silently sinking into the abyss. Oh,
a curse on the balance beam that on one end raised up my royal favor while
on the other lowered my honor! Merciful heavens, either end my life or
remedy my pain, for he who lives without honor can never have been said
to have any. . . . Thinking to honor me the king has done just the opposite.

A detailed analysis of *What Honor Obliges,* one that would also relate
the play to wife-murder dramas of other playwrights of the period, has
yet to be undertaken, and is much to be desired.

Love is Proof Against Deceit

We have seen that *What Honor Obliges* delves into the dark side of
love and jealousy, but Enríquez Gómez was probably even more talented

in the comic-satiric vein. Along this line *Love is Proof Against Deceit* is one of his very best comedies.

This cape and sword comedy begins with a tempestuous lovers' quarrel between Juan and Juana. Juan complains that another man was seen at her window the night before and is certain that it is Count Carlos. The count is Juana's father's candidate for her hand, the relationship of Juan and Juana having been kept a secret. Juan's suspicions of Juana's double-dealings increase as the count arrives to speak to her father concerning the proposed marriage. While all this is going on we learn that the cause of all the confusion is Leonor, Juana's poor cousin. Leonor, wishing Juan for herself, has instigated the count's hopes by impersonating Juana at the dark window. Her purpose is to fan jealousy to the point that Juana marries the count and leaves Juan for her. The remainder of the play is a constant series of confusions created by Leonor to keep the lovers apart. At one point Leonor finds one of Juana's love letters to Juan and redirects it to the count who in turn innocently shows it to his friend Juan. But Leonor's *pièce de résistance* is to convince Juana that Juan has another girlfriend, and, to substantiate that fiction, Leonor hires a girl to come to Juana's house looking for him. With all this there are various night scenes in which both pretenders visit the house at the same time with much scurrying back and forth from darkened room to darkened room— obligatory scenes in almost all seventeenth-century plays. Finally, Juana discovers the machinations of Leonor, and things are put to right by the usual matrimonies, in this case Juan's with Juana and Leonor's with the count.

In this play the author's considerable dramatic skill is brought to bear to move the plot forward at a rapid and humorous level of confusion. Enríquez Gómez accomplishes this by situation comedy and by dialogue that is vivacious and sparkles with witticisms. It is not surprising, given Enríquez Gómez's healthy respect for women, that the female roles come to dominate the comedy completely. The plot pits two clever women against each other in a contest between the devious schemes of Leonor to break up the lovers and Juana's ability to soothe Juan's ruffled feathers.

Of the two contending women, the antagonist Leonor is by far the more interesting of the piece. Her motivation seems not so much that she is in love with her cousin's boy friend, but rather stems from her unhappy role as the poor relative obliged to live on the generosity of others. In revenge for the subservient position circumstances have forced

upon her she takes delight in breaking up Juana's romance and a
notable pleasure in manipulating others and authoring the most outrageous confusion. Her pleasure is all the more exquisite because of the
secrecy with which she operates. Enríquez Gómez's fascination with his
own female creation is apparent in the manner in which Leonor is
"punished" after the inevitable discovery that she is the culprit behind
all the mix-ups. She is, of course, made to admit her guilt but, for
all that, Leonor winds up with the count. Far from punishment, this
advantageous marriage with the thoroughly decent, rich, and noble
Carlos is, if anything, a reward for her ingenuity.

For her part, Juana is an example of the customary Enríquez Gómez
heroine. Above all, his women possess a degree of determination that
surpasses that of their men, and so it is Juana who always keeps the
relationship alive in spite of Leonor's schemes. It is Juana who risks
everything with her reiterated opposition to the arranged marriage, and
it is Juana who undertakes to find solutions to their problems while
Juan complains and wrings his hands. It is also the forthright Juana
who in every act tells the count plainly that she has no intention of
marrying him while Juan says nothing for fear of upsetting his friend.
While the title of the play proposes that Leonor's deceits are bound
to fail because of love's power, in truth they are thwarted because
Juana's pride will not permit the loss of a lover in whom she has
invested two years of her life.

The play is clearly intended first and foremost to entertain. Its message
is the not very original one of opposition to arranged marriages, a topic
that is evident in many of his plays and the staple of the romantic
comedies of the day. Rather different from the usual submissive daughter
who is afraid to inform her father of her wishes is Juana's spirited
defense of her right to choose her own destiny, strongly expressed in
several statements. In act 2, for example, she tries to discourage the
attentions of the amorous count in this manner:

> En fin vos me pretendéis
> como decís, por esposa;
> mi padre lo da por hecho;
> y como si fuera cosa
> el matrimonio que apenas
> se dice cuando por obra
> se ejecuta, así venís
> a capitular ahora

conciertos . . .

. . . .

Y no os espantéis, señor,
que de esta suerte os responda;
que si todas las mujeres
hablaran en esta forma,
ni se perdieran las vidas,
ni se acabaran las honras,
que verdades no admitidas,
muy brevemente se lloran.[25]

In sum, you are my self-proclaimed suitor for marriage; my father assumes that it will be thus; and, as if the wedding were little more than said and done, here you come to negotiate the contract. . . . Do not be shocked, sir, if I respond to you in this manner; for if every woman would speak so plainly lives would not be lost nor honors sullied, for truths that are not owned up to will soon be cause for tears.

For its cleverness of plot, agility of dialogue, and fascinating female roles, Enríquez Gómez's *Love Is Proof Against Deceit* can well stand comparison with the best comedies of other more well-known dramatists.

The Prudent Abigail

Of the twenty-two titles in the 1649 list of his plays, six appear to have been based on the Old Testament topics that for Mesonero Romanos insinuate the dramatist's Marranism: *The Prudent Abigail, The Lightning Bolt of Palestine* (perhaps a *valiente* play with Samson as its hero), *The Overweening Pride of Nimrod, The Sun Stopped in its Tracks* (a dramatization of Joshua's siege of Gibeon?), and the two parts of *The Throne of Solomon.* Of these only those concerning Abigail and Nimrod survive to give us an idea of Enríquez Gómez's biblical plays. The fact that Enríquez Gómez chose *The Prudent Abigail* for inclusion in his *Moral Academies* may indicate that he regarded it as one of his best.

As the play opens David has made a daring visit to King Saul's camp hoping for a cessation of his persecution by the king. David, instead of taking the opportunity to avenge his mistreatment, forces the king to listen to a review of the injustices that have sent him into armed exile; and he so convincingly maintains his loyalty that Saul agrees to readmit him to royal favor. Nevertheless, David is not entirely convinced of Saul's sincerity and withdraws his troops to Mt. Carmel

near the estate of the wealthy Narval and his wife Abigail. To feed
his starving soldiers David dispatches his trusted lieutenant, Reuben, to
request assistance from Narval. The avaricious Narval not only refuses
aid but also gravely insults Reuben and sends him packing. Narval's
rash behavior worries Abigail, and to protect her husband from certain
reprisals, she secretly makes ready provisions for David's army.

In act 2 David receives Reuben's report and in a towering rage
prepares to erase Narval, his household, and possessions from the face
of the earth. While he makes ready his attack the scene returns to
Narval's house as he receives a visit from Saul. The emotionally disturbed
monarch has resumed his march against David. As David and his troops
approach, Abigail rides out to meet them with the necessary supplies.
Her beauty and concern for her unworthy husband captivates David
and he abandons his plans for vengeance.

Act 3 begins with a repeat of the opening of act 1 as David steals
again into Saul's camp and again passes up an opportunity to kill his
sleeping persecutor. This time, in more detail, he confronts the king
with a résumé of his services and the king's ingratitude. Once more
David's sincere protestation of loyalty softens the king's hostility and
peace is made between them. From this reconciliation the scene shifts
to a harvest festival at Narval's estate. When the miser learns of Abigail's
generosity in provisioning David's army he suffers a fatal stroke. The
final scene announces the eventual marriage of David and Abigail.

Enríquez Gómez turned often to the Old Testament for examples
of life's tribulations and for lessons in dealing with them. As reworked
by Enríquez Gómez, the story of David and Saul becomes an extended
metaphor on prudence, understood as the all-embracing virtue that
regulates good life, or correct existence. Not only does prudence supply
a set of values that dictate one's actions toward others, but it also
offers a mechanism to deal with the evils that beset us. Abigail and
David symbolize the ideal of prudence according to their traditional sex
roles—Abigail by her steadfast loyalty, support, and honor of even such
an unworthy husband as Narval, and David by his unswerving faithfulness to an annointed king who is bent on David's destruction. Rather
like Job, both Abigail and David are on trial. The reward for their
"right doing" is Abigail's winning a worthy husband with the promise
of the future children that her union with Narval has failed to produce,
and David's truimph over the enemies who have poisoned the king's
mind against him.

As in the two previously discussed plays, the author again takes up the cudgel against forced or arranged marriages. These loveless matches that, in the extreme case, can cause tragedy, as in *What Honor Obliges,* or occasion family conflict, as in *Love is Proof Against Deceit,* are given a different treatment in *The Prudent Abigail.* After Elvira's incorrect handling of her loveless marriage it almost seems as though Enríquez Gómez created Abigail to exemplify the right course of action in such cases—that of patience and forbearance.

A more important theme is that of persecution and exile, perhaps indicating that this play was written after the author's own exile to France around 1636. David's laments on his unjust treatment by Saul and the application to David of the epithet *peregrino* ("pilgrim, wanderer") echoes elements very frequent in Enríquez Gómez's exile works. The following are excerpts from David's first confrontation with his king:

> Si el brazo de Dios te incita,
> persígueme. Mas si locos
> aduladores se atreven
> a infamar mi pecho heroico,
> acaben en su delito,
> mueran en su mismo oprobio,
>
> . . . .
> ¿Cómo, señor, te sujetas
> a corazones tan propios
> hijos de la vanidad?
> ¿Por qué me persigues? ¿Cómo
> me vas siguiendo en los campos,
> en los valles, y en los sotos?[26]

If God's will incites you, then persecute me. But if mad sycophants dare to defame my heroic breast, may they perish in their own crime and die in their own opprobrium. Sire, how can you listen to people whose hearts are so full of vanity? Why do you pursue me? How is it that you chase me through fields, valleys, and woods?

At the heart of David's problems with King Saul is that envious tongues have undermined the king's confidence in him. This brings to mind the "doubly false ones" of Enríquez Gómez's prologue to the *Moral Academies,* the ones who treacherously advise the crown and who had to do with the dramatist's exile. David's attitude of patiently enduring his experience with the knowledge of his self-worth and confidence in the future may reflect at this period of the author's life optimism for his future vindication.

There are two story lines in this play that on first reading appear to be in competition but which, upon examination, are seen to be complementary. The action of heroic nature is David's dramatic struggle with Saul and is undiluted by a *gracioso*'s tomfoolery as befits its solemn nature. The obligatory action of comic character is assigned to the peasants who support Abigail's virtuous efforts to reform the stingy Narval. The scenes alternate between those two story lines and should not be viewed as competing, but rather as two circles revolving about the same theme, that of prudence. As such they present the moral lesson in two modalities—the heroic and the comic. The circles become more and more congruent as two centers, David and Abigail, come closer and closer together until they are unified by the promised marriage of two.

The misogyny, noticeable in earlier plays and so frequent in Enríquez Gómez's exile poetry and prose, is absent in any form in this play. In contrast to other heroines, the presentation of Abigail is so idealized as to be an effort on the author's part to fashion his concept of the perfect woman—an ideal of feminine conduct, one might point out, that seems to offer a contrast to the Virgin, the Christian symbol of feminine perfection. Abigail's presentation is almost exclusively concentrated on her role as a wife. Her perfection is put to the test under the difficult circumstances of marriage to the ill-tempered Narval, whose personality could lead any woman to infidelity. As the ideal wife, however, Abigail not only puts up with Narval but honors him and defends him against the criticism of the peasants and the potential physical punishment of David. Her gentle efforts to correct her husband's miserliness are truly disinterested and made with the intention of saving him from self-humiliation. But her gentleness and passivity aside, there is still a trace of the general forcefulness of previous Enríquez Gómez women in Abigail's decisive action to avoid the wrath of David.

Narval is an interesting character. He is a complete caricature of the avaricious Jew who meanly laments the expenditure of each penny. His total absorption with his possessions blinds him to the feelings of others and even to his own danger. It is his miserly character that provides the comic element through the tricks played on him by his peasants and through the total lack of dignity and magnanimity that a master ought to display. Even his death is comical, for if he rages at the loss of a few chickens and at the expenditure of wine for his workers, it is not any surprise that the news of his wife's generous gift of food for David's soldiers brings on a fatal stroke. Narval is practically a unique creation in the whole of Enríquez Gómez's literary production, which naturally avoided the presentation of Jews in unflattering roles and never presented Judaism in an unfavorable light.[27]

Narval entertains with his comic greed, Abigail edifies by her noble comportment and David inspires by his loyalty. But equally interesting is the exposition of the tormented existence of King Saul, torn between his fears that David will usurp his throne and exterminate his dynasty, and the realization of the debt he owes to David for his past services. Saul's dilemma is futher compounded by the voice of his conscience in the person of his son, Jonathan, whose undying friendship for David aggravates Saul's fears and is a constant thorn in his side. As in other Enríquez Gómez plays, the king for all his divinely annointed majesty is also a flesh and blood man liable to the same errors as any other.

Chapter Four

The Moral Academies of the Muses

General Considerations

During the exile years in France Enríquez Gómez wrote constantly, producing at least one major work per year. This extraordinarily fecund period began with the appearance in 1641 of *The Lusitanian Triumph* (see chapter 8). The following year saw the publication of *The Moral Academies of the Muses* in Bordeaux. In spite of the author's troubles with the Inquisition, this poetic collection was reprinted in no less than six Spanish editions during approximately the next hundred years. (See the bibliography of the author's works for these editions.) The *Academies,* in fact, became second in popularity only to his *Life of Don Gregorio Guadaña.* The reprintings of the *Academies* until 1734, the date of the last edition, illustrates how long the baroque style enjoyed the favor of the reading public, and is an indication of the popularity of Enríquez Gómez's considerable poetic talents.

The rather curious title refers to that popular seventeenth-century institution, the literary academy, that abounded in Spanish cities and in which Enríquez Gómez no doubt took part.[1] Modeled along the lines of Italian literary associations, these academies were salons under the patronage of a notable in which the habitués met to read and discuss their works, engage in poetic contests on given topics, and argue the latest of the many polemics in that era of combative personalities. Of course, the agglomeration of poetic egos virtually guaranteed the ephemeral nature of these societies. The "moral" portion of Enríquez Gómez's title refers to the author's intention to center the major poems on moral philosophy, that is, ethics.

The Moral Academies of the Muses is a poetic collection including the broadest range of lyric and narrative verse plus four plays. All of this is contained within a pastoral envelope that supposes a congress of characters in a *locus amoenus* based on the idealized geography of Enríquez Gómez's native Cuenca. In this setting the various figures present their compositions during festivities lasting four days, hence the four Academies. Each section or Academy consists of a lengthy introduction, the Academy itself, and a play that brings the Academy to a close. The result is not, as might be expected, a hodgepodge of poems but a rather well thought out, well-constructed composition that is unified around certain themes, all of which spring from the circumstances of the author's life. The intimate relationship between the Academies and the author's life has become more evident since Révah definitively reconstructed the poet's biography.

The Academies are introduced by a number of laudatory poems in Latin, French, and Spanish contributed by the author's acquaintances in France, as well as by the author's dedicatory verses to the Spanish Anne of Austria (1601–66), queen of France and Navarre and mother of Louis XIV. More interesting than the poems or the dedication is the prose apology written by the ill-fated Portuguese *converso* and friend of Enríquez Gómez, Manuel Fernándes de Villareal. Enríquez Gómez and Fernándes de Villareal were associated in France in propagandizing the restoration of the Portuguese monarchy in 1640.[2] Both the apology and author's prologue underscore the perceived uniqueness of the work— that of poeticizing moral philosophy and presenting it in combination with less weighty verse so as to both instruct and entertain. Fernándes de Villareal gives a naturally favorable review to his friend's artistic merits and literary versatility, subjects that were always particular sources of pride for Enríquez Gómez. Among his comments Fernándes de Villareal touches on Enríquez Gómez's skill as a playwright and the applause his works merited in Madrid. At the same time, however, he notes that the plays had their detractors. Fernándes de Villareal also lauds his friend's prose works and his talent for epic poetry as evidenced in his *Poema de Tubal* (The poem of Tubalcain), a work that has evidently not survived and that curiously was not mentioned some years later when Enríquez Gómez enumerated his compositions during the decade.

The author's prologue proclaims his sincerity and personal involvement in the work, and digresses briefly to return the compliment of Fernándes de Villareal by extolling his literary accomplishments. Enríquez Gómez then acknowledges previous works of the same type, mentioning specifically two by Lope de Vega, *Arcadia* (1599) and *Los pastores de Belém* (The shepherds of Bethlehem, 1612). He also cites Pérez de Montalbán's *Para todos* (For everyone, 1633), Tirso de Molina's *Enseñar deleitando* (To delight while instructing, 1630), and Matías de los

Reyes's *Para algunos* (For a few, 1640). It is clear, however, that Enríquez Gómez feels that his effort is both a continuation of this popular literary form as well as an improvement upon it. The fact that *The Moral Academies* is totally in verse is noted as one element distinguishing it from previous miscellanies. And, although he affects modesty concerning his works, there is an unmistakable element of pride in his talents and enough mention of jealousy and envy to indicate that he felt his artistic merit was not duly recognized in Spain. The prologue is likewise suffused with a tone of bitterness of being forced into exile, the reason for which he "explains" in a well-known passage already cited in chapter 2.

Excluding the four plays, the index of the *Moral Academies* lists a total of ninety-seven individual poetic compositions (There are some additional poems not included in the index.) The transition passages between the poems are accomplished with a verse form known as a *silva,* a flexible combination of seven and eleven syllable lines that may or may not have consonantal rhyme (Enríquez Gómez's almost always do rhyme). By far the most frequently employed verse form is the sonnet, of which there are fifty-four listed in the index. The number of sonnets decrease in each succeeding Academy (23, 16, 10, 5) in favor of longer works that are obviously intended to be the major compositions of the collection. In his prologue Enríquez Gómez calls attention to several of these, specifically "The Voyager" (Academy 1), "The Pilgrim" (Academy 3), "The Epistles of Job" (Academy 2), and the "Elegies of Heraclitus and Democritus" (Academy 4).

The following comments on *The Moral Academies* attempt to give a general view of each in turn. Since each of the ninety-odd poems could not be mentioned, the remarks are confined to those compositions that seem the most important in terms of topic or expression.

The First Academy

The introduction to the First Academy introduces the fiction that provides an excuse for the individual poems. As in other works of this type a framework situation is created, a stage to provide a background for the characters who declaim the verses. To begin, four pairs of lovers drift onto a pastoral setting reciting verses, both serious and comic, concerning love and jealousy. The sonnets and ballads are elegant creations replete with conceits typical of the era. Then Albano arrives on the scene to recount a lengthy adventure in ballad meter concerning Duke

Antilo who, lost while hunting in the forest, slays a dragon and frees a beautiful damsel whom he decides to wed. The marriage provides the excuse for the next day's Academy that the Duke orders held in celebration. This is the characteristic plan of the entire work. The introductions with their amorous verses and adventure ballads are intended to capture the readers' attention and to provide a pleasant prelude to the really serious subjects to be addressed in the Academies themselves.

The lengthy poem in *silvas* that inaugurates the First Academy is "El pasajero" (The voyager) declaimed by Albano. Among the eleven participants in the dramatis personae, the characters Danteo and Albano are the main voices through which the author speaks and, of the two, Albano seems to be the author's principal spokesman.[3] "The Voyager," with its pessimistic and disspirited recital of Albano's tribulations, disturbs the tranquil tone established by the introduction. The abrupt transition from the idyllic Cuencan setting to the image of a storm-tossed boat vainly navigating toward a safe port underscores the fragility of existence and recounts poetically the author's perception of his life—"naufragué cuarenta años" ("forty years of shipwreck" [18]).[4] The symbolism of the poem is explained by the poet himself: the central image of the sea represents the chaotic state that is this life; onto this vast and uncertain body the voyager (the soul) embarks on a flimsy craft (the body) in search of a refuge from life's problems.

The general spirit of "The Voyager" is disillusionment, warning of the false nature of the world and all its pleasures, wealth, and honors. Albano's unhappy wanderings inspire many intensely lyric passages but, unfortunately, after a promising beginning the poem settles into a monotonous series of warnings to the unwary. The advice is noteworthy only as it clearly is the result of firsthand knowledge of the precarious life of the *converso* merchant—"no fíes de ninguno tu secreto. . . . Ni al hijo ni al hermano / des en vida tu hacienda. . . . Sepan pocos tu nombre en las ciudades. . . . Haz muy pocas firmas si pudieres. . . . No hagas fianza por el más amigo" ("Do not trust anyone with your secret. . . . While you live, do not trust your assets to son or to brother. . . . Let few persons in the cities know your name. . . . Sign as few documents as you are able. . . . Do not be guarantor for even your best friend"). Other causes for lament are the inequality imposed by the caste system and the failure of the government to exercise its proper role in unifying and directing a nation. But, of all the misfortunes cataloged in the "Voyager," the most painful is the forced separation

from the native land: "Y si te quieres ver libre de penas / no trueques
por tu patria las ajenas" ("If you wish to live free of pain to not
exchange your native land for foreign shores" [23]).

A characteristic rhythm is generated in the First Academy with the
major pieces swinging back and forth between passages of agitation and
despair and those of a calmer, more contemplative nature. The topics
throughout the Academies are naturally those associated with exile:
memories of happy and unhappy moments, alienation, hopelessness over
the future, the desire to return home, confusion, and anger at unjust
treatment that alternates with a sense of guilt at past mistakes.

The loss of peace of mind that exile imposes is compensated in some
measure by a turning inward toward memory. The construction of an
idyllic setting based on the landscape of his birthplace reflects a desire
to escape through memories of the past. Thus, the lovely *silvas* beginning
"Humilde albergue mío, / líquidos arroyuelos" ("Humble lodging of
mine, bubbling brooks" [39]) celebrate in the time-honored *beatus ille*
fashion the peaceful countryside that offers an asylum from the madness
of the court which in this and other works is symbolized by Babel or
Babilonia.

But memory can also be treacherous because it stores the good with
the bad. The ten-verse stanzas *(décimas)* on "Mudanzas siempre temidas,
pero nunca remediadas" ("Misfortunes always feared, but never re-
medied" [43–44]) remind us that the past can never be reconstructed
or undone: "Volver a ser lo que he sido / no es posible, que un error
/ es abismo del valor / y sepulcro de un perdido" ("To become again
what I was is impossible, for an error is the abyss of valor, the sepulcher
of the lost soul" [43]). His reference to past error is intriguing and
offers an ambiguity characteristic of much of Enríquez Gómez's writings.
The obvious interpretation of this "error" of his past would be that
of a flirtation with heterodoxy, some involvement with the Marranism
of his father's family. On the other hand, another lengthy composition
in this Academy, "El robo de Dina" ("The rape of Dinah" [45–58])
presents the story of Dinah (Gen. 34:1–31) whose curiosity causes her
dishonor by the gentile Sichem.[5] Here, the most obvious interpretation
is as a warning against erring from Judaism, but one might also
understand the message in the opposite sense, that is a warning against
straying from Catholicism.

The anguish of memory leads to one of the finest expressions of
exile poetry in the Spanish language. Beginning with a well-known line
that served a number of Spanish sonneteers and ultimately traces back

to Petrarch—"Cuando contemplo mi pasada gloria" ("When I contemplate my past glory" 59)—Enríquez Gómez develops an extensive poem in tercets that reflects on happier days:[6]

> Perdí mi libertad, perdí mi nido,
> perdí mi alma el centro más dichoso,
> y a mí mismo también pues me he perdido.
> ¿Cómo puedo aguardar ningún reposo
> si el reloj de mi vida se ha quebrado,
> parándose el volante perezoso?

I lost my liberty, I lost my nest, my soul lost its most happy center, and I myself also have I lost. What repose can I expect if my life-clock has been broken, stopping the already slow moving hand?

(60)

And perhaps the greatest loss for a man so attuned to communication as Enríquez Gómez is the loss of the native language, the relief of his escape soon paling as he finds himself in the Babel of a foreign land. Albano pines for the sound of Spanish: "Hablaba el idioma siempre grave / adornado de nobles oradores / siendo su acento para mí suave" ("I spoke the ever dignified language, adorned by noble orators, its accents for me so sweet" [61]). The one hope that sustains him is to return to his homeland, preferably with honor restored but, if not that, to face whatever the consequences. The last lines of this composition address other would-be exiles and invite them to be warned by the poet's experience: "Que no hay segura vida / cuando la libertad está perdida" ("For there is no secure life when freedom is lost" [66]).

Several sonnets on human ambition, vanity, and ingratitude follow before the melancholia abates somewhat in a sonnet on the triumph of humility. The topic of humility leads into Albano's "Canción a la felicidad de la vida amando la soledad" ("Song to the happiness of life, enjoying solitude" [70–73]) which, as evening approaches, brings to a close the First Academy. As the title indicates, after the anguish of the elegy on his past glory, the poet finds a measure of comfort through the contemplation of nature as created in the pastoral landscape.

In general, the First Academy focuses on topics related to exile and is suffused by a tone of world weariness and regret. Any sort of consolation is mainly to be found in memories of happier childhood days in Cuenca or in escapist fantasies of retreat to a tranquil place of refuge. The lack of statements indicating a hope for compensation for suffering in another life is notable, and, indeed, there are no elements apparent in any line that would place the First Academy in an obviously Christian context. On the other hand, there is nothing that is obviously non-Christian either. The general pessimistic air is continued in the play that closes the section *What Honor Obliges* (see the comments in chapter 3).[7]

The Second Academy

The mainstay of the four introductions to the Academies is conceit-ridden, amorous verse following the usual topics—love's power, unrequited love, jealousy, the beloved's disdain, and other related lover's complaints. As a counterbalance to so much grandiloquence, the contributions of Pacor and Elisa in this and other introductions often add humerous touches in their parodies of the recherché style. To introduce the Academy itself, one of the characters charges onto the scene to relate a heroic adventure ballad in celebration of which Duke Antilo orders the next day's Academy. Notwithstanding their poetic form, the adventure ballads, with their fantastic tales of ladies in distress and brave heroes operating in incredible settings, add a novelesque element to the overall work.

While the First Academy tends to concentrate on the sentiments that are the consequences of exile, the major compositions of the second deal more generally with man's lot in this confused and troubled world. As if to provide historical perspective, the first important selection turns back to the beginning of time with Albano's "Panegírico a la creación del universo" ("Panegyric on the Creation of the World" [135–48]). In forty octaves the sonorous baroque verses detail the six days of Creation ending with the creation of man. The sublime beauty and perfection sprung from God's perfect knowledge are brought together in His greatest achievement which is man. But the achievement also brings with it the seeds of future disappointment, for the final lines of stanza 39 take note of the ruin that man is to suffer through the beautiful and fatal Eve: "Aquella, de la luz divina copia . . . flor de Edén altiva y propia . . . incendio de mayor centella. . . . Aquella, ruina del gustoso Imperio, / Origen del pesado cautiverio" ("That copy of the divine light . . . the proud and very flower of Eden . . . the flame of a larger fire . . . that ruin of the delightful Empire, that origin of the gloomy captivity" [147]). The misogynous references that creep into the penultimate stanza are fairly frequent in all the Academies but even become more developed in later exile works of a more satiric nature.

The implied ruin of Eden establishes the linkage with the next composition of thirteen-verse stanzas in rhymed *silvas* "Canción a la ruina de un imperio" (Song on the ruin of an empire [148–52]). From the Divine Creation Enríquez Gómez passes to human creation and, employing the *ubi sunt* topic, contemplates the remains of Babylon, once so mighty, then brought low by the pride and cruelty of its people. The rise, corruption, and fall of Babylon is seen as the paradigm of man's history, and its ruin the consequences of his error: "Así acaba, y recibe / justo premio quien muere como vive" ("Thus it ends, and he receives just punishment who dies as he lives" [150]). Given the poet's own experiences, there is little doubt but that he had clearly in mind a warning to the greatest empire of the day—that of Spain. The rather vague references to military conquest and overseas expansionism foreshadow more specific criticisms of imperialism he was to make later in *The Tower of Babylon* and in the play *The Conquest of Mexico*.

After several intervening sonnets the poet passes from the Fall of Adam and that of the first empire to the individual in the tercets of the three "Epistles of Job" (158–74). In these there is no doubt but that the poet's own life is presented in cypher. Quite different from the glorious "birth" of Adam with its promise, the "First Epistle of Job" begins with his lament on having been born into a world of woe. It is obvious that what on the surface is an exposition of the doctrine of Original Sin has another and very real manifestation for the *converso* poet to whom the stigma of being New Christian was attached by accident of birth. Again, later works develop this theme in almost obsessive detail, particularly *The Angelic Politics* and *The Tower of Babylon*.

While the "First Epistle" concentrates on present affliction and on his aimless wandering, the second calls for sympathy and understanding for one born under an unlucky star. Forsaken by friends and family, the protagonist wanders an outcast, stripped of honor and wealth. He looks back to a previous happy state, realizing how vain were his worldly aspirations. Nevertheless, there is always time for change: "Antes que larga cuenta ajuste y goze; / debe la enmienda ser constante y firme; / pues lo vivido, errores reconoce" ("Before the long standing bill is settled the reform must be constant and true since every lifetime must acknowledge errors" [168]).

In the "Third Epistle" the fiction separating author and narrator becomes more transparent. The persecuting agent that in the "First Epistle" was referred to as "hidra cruel" ("cruel hydra" [158]) and "aguda espada" ("sharp sword" [162]), and in the "Second Epistle" as "poder incircunscripto" ("all encompassing power" [165]), is now identified as the "tribunal sagrado" ("the sacred tribunal") (168), clearly the Holy Office of the Inquisition. In this, one of the most hopeful compositions of the entire work, a plan of future action is outlined:

> Del tribunal sagrado pienso asirme,
> pidiendo mi justicia y mi derecho,
> a quien orden me dio para partirme.
> Sacaré los testigos de mi pecho.
>
> . . . .
> Desde luego pretendo presentarme,
> diciendo "la serpiente me ha engañado."[8]

I intend to throw myself upon the mercy of the sacred tribunal calling for justice and appealing to my rights to those who gave the order for my departure. . . . I will be my own witness. . . . I will present myself saying "the serpent tricked me."

(168)

Although he does not totally deny the blame that brought about his sufferings, he alleges that his guilt is simply ignorant imprudence that let him be misled by those who nurtured him (a suggestive statement that would seem to throw blame on the author's *marrano* relatives). Veiled references to his "errors" were also noted in the First Academy. But no matter that he finds himself brought so low, in spite of everything he retains his faith in God's mercy for an ignorant sinner. Thus the epistle ends on an optimistic note that, for the first time in the composition, indicates the consolation of an after life.

> Yo aguardo en la divina omnipotencia
> mercedes soberanas sin medida,
> fiado en los perdones de su esencia.
>
> . . . .
> Y diré lleno de virtud y ciencia,
> accordóse el Señor de mi paciencia.
> Que aquél que en los trabajos la ha tenido,
> siempre llevó su premio merecido.

I await in the divine omnipotence sovereign rewards without measure, trusting in the pardon that his essence promises. . . . And I will proclaim, filled with virtue and knowledge, God remembered my patience. For he who in his tribulations maintains patience always wins his well-merited reward.

(174)

The "Three Epistles of Job" are outstanding compositions in terms of their verses and original treatment of a popular topic. Moreover, the three poems have the distinction of being perhaps the only verses of the Academies to have received detailed critical attention. They have been the subject of an analysis by Judith Rauchwarger, whose informative article also well illustrates the difficulty of interpreting Enríquez Gómez's statements.[9] Although Rauchwarger assumes, as do most recent critics, that the author was a *marrano,* she concludes that "The doctrines Job articulates in the 'Epístolas' are not at variance with those espoused by Catholic exegetes (though they do omit essential dogmas), nor do they contradict rabbinical hermeneutics, but they do not definitively adhere to one or the other."[10] Rauchwarger points out that Enríquez Gómez's "Epistles of Job" mainly lack a Christian interpretation in the absence of references to Job as a "prefiguration of the Savior, or in the Hagiographa, an anticipation of the events of the New Testament."[11] This same lack of any Christian references is notable in Enríquez Gómez's early plays and in practically all his exile works and gives a decidedly marranistic cast to his writing. The lack of Christian references becomes much more obvious when the early plays and exile compositions are compared with Enríquez Gómez's last plays written under the Zárate alias.

The closing composition of the Second Academy is the satirical poem "El hombre honrado" (The honorable man), a humorous dialogue in ballad meter between Albano and Pacor, the rustic. Albano's idealistic definition of honor based on virtue is ridiculed as old-fashioned by Pacor because, as he says, modern honor depends entirely on money. This introduces a tirade on the dishonorable characters of contemporary society that Albano has to interrupt with the warning that they are getting out of the pastoral mode. Like many of Enríquez Gómez's compositions, the poem winds up with a lengthy list of advice and warnings for those who would be honorable.

A sonnet by Pacor ends the Academy and calls for the reader's patience if the work so far has not been to his liking because "Cúrense con amor las opiniones, / que cuando son los males accidentes, / no

hay salud como amar oposiciones" ("Let differences of opinion be settled
with love for, when the faults are accidental, nothing is as salutary as
the promotion of love between opposites" [180]). There is no doubt
but that this closing sonnet is also intended to be an appeal to tolerance
and to conciliation for those, like he, who have erred. The lesson is
repeated in the play *La prudente Abigail* (The prudent Abigail) which
closes the Second Academy. For David's fortitude in the face of unjust
persecution by King Saul and for Abigail's steadfastness in honoring
an unworthy husband both eventually find their reward for patience.
In its portrayal of a period of testing and trial the play complements
nicely the "Epistles of Job." The appeal of the story for Enríquez
Gómez is obvious.

The Third Academy

As in the previous Academies the introduction to the third provides
the playful respite from the seriousness of the overall work. In addition
to, or perhaps as a consequence of, the usual stilted love verse of the
introductions, the baroque style itself is the subject of Pacor's three
satirical poems, carrying to the ultimate nonsensical extreme the poetic
extravagancies of the day. As ever, the introduction is terminated with
a wild adventure story of the beautiful maiden's rescue from the clutches
of a horrible giant, a story that seems at least suggested by the famous
poem, *Polyphemus and Galatea,* of Luis de Góngora.[12]

The Third Academy continues a downward progression of material
(the first has fifty-nine pages, the second forty-seven, and the third has
thirty-two). The diminution in length accords with the somewhat lighter
spirit of this Academy, no doubt an attempt to balance the gloom of
the preceding section.

The comic figure, Pacor, opens the third day's offerings with a poem
on a figure very dear to Enríquez Gómez—"El peregrino" (The Wanderer
[243–57]). The lengthy poem in *silvas* is divided into four *vistas* or
"views" and anticipates Enríquez Gómez's later satires in its targets
and in its framework, that of an ingenuous man drawn to the teeming
bustle of the corrupting court. But, all in all, this satire is less bitter,
less drawn out, and much more lighthearted than the subsequent works
in which the passing years of exile obviously caused the wounds to
fester. Once again the first verses of "The Wanderer" establish a quasi-
autobiographical sketch of Enríquez Gómez's own progress from the
provinces to the capital as the protagonist leaves Cuenca bound for the

hypocrisy, vanity, greed, and conspicuous consumption of the court as illustrated by commonplace targets—coaches, palaces, luxurious clothing, and lineage. A theme developed in the poem's "Second View" is that the lust for money rules the day. All virtues are turned upside down by the self-interest that reigns supreme, as, for example, when the wanderer witnesses a competition for an academic chair and sees a venerable sage forced from the lectern by a mocking crowd of ignorant spectators who reserve their applause for the absurdities of their friends. Everything, as the wanderer's guide explains, can be reduced to one fact, that the world has two lineages only—the haves and the have-nots.

The most entertaining "view" is the third section involving a visit to an insane asylum where the guide, a poet, is one of the inmates. The poet explains to the bewildered wanderer that, in spite of appearances, the really mad people are the ones on the outside, those who knowingly do wrong for money or power's sake. Among the long list of examples that the poet-inmate gives to illustrate his thesis are false friends, false women, and, once again, the *converso*'s nightmare, stool pigeons *(malsines)*.

The topic of deception that pervades the three parts of "The Wanderer" in the Third Academy (the fourth part is continued in the Fourth Academy) is also contained in Albano's subsequent verses "Al engaño de la naturaleza" (On nature's deception [258–65]), which is ideologically and artistically one of the very best compositions of the *Moral Academies*. "On Nature's Deception," arranged in thirteen-line stanzas of rhymed *silvas,* renews the concept of the birth trauma introduced in the "Epistles to Job." Albano ponders his suffering. He has been born into a world in which the reason for the struggle to exist is a mystery that defies solution: "Naturaleza, averiguar pretendo / ¿quién soy? porque me dice mi pecado / que estoy de vanidad alimentado" ("Nature, I seek to find who I am, for my sins tell me that I am by vanity fed" [258]). All that one strives for—wealth, friends, knowledge, honors—is hard won and, in the end, not worth having as these worldly items are stolen or else stray from our grasp. Albano's verses examine the puzzlement of life and death and their meaning in a composition of great nobility:

> A la memoria traigo lo que he sido.
> Lo que soy ya lo ves, y voy buscando

lo que seré, y el alma está ignorando
adónde le darán otra posada.

I call to mind what I have been. What I am now is what you see, and on
I go searching for what I will be. My soul is ignorant of where it will be
given other shelter.

(265)

In the face of such doubts about the meaning of this life and the
nature of the next, the only possible solution that offers him any promise
of relief is retirement from the world, and thus the Third Academy is
brought to a close with the poem "A la quietud y vida de la aldea
y cabaña" (On the peacefulness of village life), a work that, although
artistically successful, offers little different to the *beatus ille* motif present
in any number of compositions from the First Academy on.

Love is Proof Against Deceits is the play selected to conclude the
Third Academy. Because the Third Academy in general adopts a less
tragic perspective concerning society's foibles, Pacor's introductory sonnet
to the play announces that love mixed with comedy is an appropriate
end to the section, and that the play "desengaños articula" ("articulates
'disillusionment' " [274]). "Love is Proof Against Deceits" is one of
Enríquez Gómez's finest comic works, worthy of comparison with the
best of plays by better known writers. In brief, this comedy of lovers'
intrigues deals with the efforts of a poor relative, Leonor, to sabotage
her cousin's love affair and gain the gentleman for herself. The cunning
Leonor's motivation combines her desire to obtain a suitable husband
in spite of her second class status in the household plus the fact that
she enjoys formulating elaborate stratagems to confound others for the
pure fun of it. The artful Leonor who relishes pulling the strings from
behind the scenes is one of Enríquez Gómez's most memorable female
characters. (For more on this play see chapter 3.)

The Fourth Academy

The downward progression of length is reversed in the fourth and
longest of the Academies. This final section contains the fewest sonnets,
preferring more extensive compositions. No doubt, Enríquez Gómez
reserved what he must have considered his most important poems to
close the *Moral Academies*.

In the fourth introduction, along with the usual amatory verse, Pacor sustains a comic exchange with his Elisa that produces more lines ridiculing the unintelligibility of some contemporary poetry. But in the midst of Pacor's humorous poem is buried a punning line—"Soy culto cuando me oculto" ("I occult myself in cultured verse" [329])—that is typical of the personal aspect of Enríquez Gómez's compositions. In this and in many other compositions he leaves a clue to let the reader know that there are both overt and covert messages in his works, the problem being that the covert message is generally maddeningly ambiguous.

The Fourth Introduction is unusual as it includes not one but two adventure ballads. The first, related by Danteo, tells the story of a doughty heroine who stabs to death the servant of her would-be rapist, flees to the mountains and is rescued by a passing gentleman who helps her restore her honor. This aggressive and decisive action on her part is, as we have seen in many plays, characteristic of Enríquez Gómez's female characters. The second narrative ballad, also dealing with the tribulations of two lovers, is built upon the sleeping beauty motif that is a favorite of Enríquez Gómez.[13]

The Fourth Academy proper opens with the fourth and final part of the satire, "The Wanderer" (346–51), that began in the previous Academy. The fourth view, which is separated from the other three, seems inserted into the Fourth Academy with little forethought. There are no *silvas* to connect it to the following poems or to introduce it as is usual in the other Academies. As the entire poem proceeds more or less chronologically according to a life span, the final installment finds the wanderer at the magnificent palace of an acutely ill man. This sets the stage for a satire directed against those age-old targets, the doctors, whose remedies are more likely to hasten death than arrest it, and against the lawyers who then pick clean the deceased's estate.

However, the key sections of the Fourth Academy are the debates between the two most important figures of the work, Danteo and Albano, characters representing the author's confused feelings with regard to his situation. Whereas previous Academies were primarily concerned with the protagonist's (that is to say, the author's) perceived suffering and the historical precedent for it, the final portion debates the appropriate attitude to cope with life. Hence we have the cycle of four elegies in tercets, two on "La risa de Demócrito" (The laughter of Democritus [352–68]) and two on "El llanto de Heráclito" (The tears of Heraclitus [369–401]) that Danteo and Albano exchange. The Democritus-Her-

aclitus opposition was attractive to Enríquez Gómez, who often employed
it to symbolize the opposing stances that one could take with regard
to the difficulties of this world.[14]

In essence, Danteo advocating Democritan laughter feels that, as the
problems of the world are so insurmountable and evil so deeply
entrenched, the only possible solution is that of living one's life as
virtuously and sanely as possible and accepting with indulgent laughter
the follies of the rest: "Bueno será que yo me está muriendo / de ver
mal gobernado el siglo, cuando / él de mi necedad se está riendo"
("A lot of good it does me to kill myself over the evil governance of
the world when it is laughing at my foolishness" [352]). It is therefore
a waste of time and effort to grieve over the world's difficulties since
nothing can be changed. Danteo's attitude is pragmatic: "De bonísima
gana yo llorara, / si pudiera mi llanto dar remedio / a la malicia
deste siglo cara" ("Very gladly would I cry if my tears would remedy
the costly malice of this world" [354]. The fact that the world is in
such disarray leads Danteo to adopt a state of detachment "Como entré
he de salir; no hay más razones / y en todos cuantos libros he leído
/ no hay más verdades que en estos dos renglones" ("I will leave the
world as I entered; that is all there is to it. In all the books I have
read, there are no more truths than in these lines" [362–63]). The
seeming agnosticism of these lines is tempered by other statements
indicating a general belief in an afterlife in which good will be rewarded
and evil punished.

Albano's response is in opposition to Danteo's indulgent attitude
concerning human nature. Albano supposes that the situation is not
lost even though he concedes the possibility for change is not good:

> El mundo, mi señor, no está perdido;
> el que puede enmendarse, plaza tiene
> para volver a ser el que había sido.
> De estar mal gobernado el daño viene.

The world, sir, is not lost. He who can mend his ways has time enough to
be again what he was. The harm comes from the world being poorly governed.

(370)

But while there is hope, he notes that error and sin are becoming
consecrated as virtues, and what were virtues are now laughingstocks.
Under these circumstances Albano finds little that is funny and much

to lament. As we pile sin upon Original Sin, sorrow ought rather to be the appropriate emotion of the virtuous man.

Albano's "Second Elegy" becomes more and more agitated and is very obscure in parts. His thoughts flood the pages in a rather disorganized fashion, one topic bringing to mind another. One of particular importance for the author, who had been caught between two religions, is the difficulty of knowing what is truth. If there are so many paths that the wanderer can follow but only one that is correct, then how can that one be determined with any certainty? As he puts it: "Si con los ojos interiores veo / opiniones que son damas del sabio, / quién sabe si en la falsa me recreo?" ("If with my intellectual eyes I see various opinions that are the fair ladies of wise men, who knows if with the false one I take my pleasure?" [378]). The image of life is that of an endless stream of doubts, a series of pitfalls man must try to avoid. His meditations on Original Sin lead into a long and especially acerbic tirade against women—"polilla del hombre más discreto" ("The worm that consumes even the most intelligent man" [379]). He traces female desire for control and the inclination to make mischief all the way back to Eve and the apple and asks "¿Ha de durar eterna esta manzana?" ("How long do we have to suffer for that apple?" [379]).

The exchange of elegies between Danteo and Albano is followed by a number of selections that expand on the previous topics. The "Canción a la vanidad del mundo" (Song of wordly vanities) is a rather disorganized satire of a variety of types and evils. Of more interest, however, is the "Ballad to the Torments of Life" (402–6) in which the poet laments the disillusionments he has suffered—false friends and relatives, false witnesses, the Inquisition, the embargo of his goods, and, of course, forced exile. Again the laments are clearly identified as autobiographical—"yo pinto mi vida" ("I paint my life" [402])—but, in keeping with his habitual cautiousness are concealed, this time not by the recherché but by humor—"los disfrazo con la risa / porque nadie los entienda" ("I disguise them behind a laugh so that no one will understand them" [403]). The "Canción al conocimiento de si mismo" (Song to self-knowledge [406–12]) that follows is one of the best poetic compositions of the collection. In rhymed *silvas* he presents a moving *cri de coeur* through a series of nature images in a meditation on the meaning of his life and troubles.

To close the *Moral Academies* Enríquez Gómez once again pairs Danteo and Albano in an exchange of letters in tercets concerning the latter's exile. Albano's exile status reinforces the supposition that Enríquez

Gómez especially identifies this character with his own circumstances. Returning to make use of the nautical imagery that opened the First Academy, Danteo sends a dismal report on what has become of their homeland (obviously Spain) since Albano's departure. The voyaging imagery cloaks his message: "Después de tu partida venturosa / el mar se alborotó de tal manera / que aún dura su borrasca lastimosa" ("After your timely departure the sea became so agitated that the doleful tempest still endures" [416]). For those who remain, the persecution continues, everyone is on guard, there is no more trust or friendship, all has become malice and suspicion. Thus Danteo has resolved to follow Albano into exile.

Surprisingly, Albano's reply is not encouraging. On the basis of six years of exile he advises his friend to remain where he is.[15] For the homesick wanderer the bittersweet memories of his homeland and the feeling of rootlessness is a worse torment than whatever he escaped. For better or worse, one's homeland is infinitely preferable to a foreign land where one is doomed to live forgotten. Exile has also taught Albano that there is no place free from care: "Esta máquina grande y poderosa, / se adorna de mudanza si se mira / pieza por pieza su campaña hermosa" ("This great and powerful machine that is the world is adorned with vagueries if one examines piece by piece its beautiful landscape" [420]).

Finally, it should be noted that the Fourth Academy includes a *décima* (413–14) on the death of the poet's father, Diego Enríquez Villanueva. As the poem does not figure in the index to the work it appears to be a last minute insertion, perhaps indicating the father's unexpected demise. It is, however, a disappointing composition in spite of the fact that this is the only one of the entire work in which the author completely drops his mask by not speaking through one of the characters. Notable only for its artificiality, the poem consists of verses constructed entirely on well-worn conceits involving tears, crying, eyes, hearts, and the like. The New Christian tradition of well-founded reluctance to speak with any openness with regard to family matters shows through clearly in this stilted academic composition that hides whatever were his father's accomplishments and merits and gives no inkling as to the author's feelings for his *marrano* father.[16] Previously noted statements in *The Academies* that seem to blame his relatives for his problems tend to indicate an estrangement between father and son. Perhaps the poet did not involve himself in crypto-Judaism as much as his paternal relatives would have liked.

Enríquez Gómez as Poet

In the past Enríquez Gómez's contribution to seventeenth-century lyric poetry has been either despised or ignored. More modern critics have passed over him with mere acknowledgment of his potential. Juan Luis Alborg characterizes him as "a notably lyric poet who wrote profoundly sincere verses and at the same time was a brilliant creator of Gongoristic metaphor."[17] Díaz-Plaja places him "as one of the foremost representatives of baroque poetry."[18] And even Menéndez y Pelayo admits his "high and generous moral thoughts,"[19] even if he finds the style not to his liking. But to date there has yet to be a comprehensive investigation of the artistic merits of any of Enríquez Gómez's works. This is, no doubt, due in large measure to the lack of modern editions, but an additional problem is that a good deal of his prose and verse can be counted as perhaps the most personal and obscure of all Spanish literature. The sibylline quality of many of his passages inevitably draws the investigator to the decipherment of the message rather than to a consideration of its artistic representation.

The Moral Academies of the Muses is an enormous composition contained in about five hundred pages of the original text. Its daunting length plus the repetition of topics tend to obscure the excellence of many of the compositions that are better appeciated read as individual poems. If one reads the work straight through, it is soon obvious that Enríquez Gómez was not a poetic genius of the first rank. Certainly the quality of the verse is very uneven. At his worst there is a strong tendency to the prosaic and didactic that can become exceptionally ponderous in the lengthy satirical poems. The pastoral poems that fill the various Academies are, with the exception of occasional striking metaphors, rather tedious repetitions of the Petrarchan love dialectic already so overworked by seventeenth-century writers. On the other hand, Enríquez Gómez at his best can be very moving, as the samples throughout this chapter will testify. Time and space has not permitted mention of the many sonnets that are included in the Academies in which the verses are quite finely crafted according to the elegant artistic precepts of the day. Considering only the First Academy, one could point to the three excellent sonnets in praise of Adam, Enoch, and Noah (33–35) and to the three "A la perdida libertad de la patria" (On the loss of the homeland [37–38]) which beautifully distill the essence of the exile's anguish. Additionally, Enríquez Gómez was quite successful with the ballad form he uses in the introductions to the

Academies and especially with the many passages of *silvas* that he employed to knit together the major compositions. All in all, the lyric is often excellent, combining original thought, metaphor, and rhythmic language with a touching sincerity. But perhaps the most impressive quality of the *Moral Academies of the Muses* is that the poet conceived its many individual compositions with their variations of meter and subject matter as integrated elements of a total work. As such, in this first large collection of his compositions, Enríquez Gómez created a corpus of interrelated topics that mirror his spiritual and physical trials as a *converso* and exile.

The point of departure of all his topics is that of birth, which, because of his stigmatized status, appears over and over in this and other compositions. The fatal birth portion and the doctrine of Original Sin go hand in hand. Though it was perhaps an abstraction for most Old Christians, for Enríquez Gómez the idea of sin inherited even before birth was made a real and deadly part of his life by the prejudice and persecution he and generations of his paternal ancestors experienced. For Enríquez Gómez, birth stigma and Original Sin lead inevitably back to the subject of the Creation and especially to Adam and Eve. In this as in later works Adam-like figures such as the Voyager, the Pilgrim, the Wanderer, and the Exile are frequent and meaningful manifestations of the poet's own feelings. References to Eve and Eve-like women likewise abound as temptresses and beguilers of innocent men. Earthly existence is viewed as chaotic, often, as we have seen in the *Moral Academies,* represented as the storm-tossed sea upon which the confused and terrified soul is set adrift. But other representations are common, especially in later works. The Tower of Babel, Babylon, the Babylonian Empire, and related subjects provide imagery that associates the poet's own exile captivity with that of Old Testament Jews as well as symbolizing a vortex of confusion and vice that entices and traps the unwary. In this first large-scale composition of his career we find the germ of many themes and topics that reappear in greater degrees of elaboration in succeeding works, as subsequent chapters will note.

Chapter Five
The Pythagorean Century

El siglo pitagórico y vida de don Gregorio Guadaña (The Pythagorean century and life of Don Gregorio Guadaña) first appeared in 1644 at Rouen, France, from the press of Laurent Maurry. The success of the work is attested by five subsequent printings of the entire composition in France, Spain, and Brussels to as late as the year 1788, and seven more editions of just the *Life of Don Gregorio Guadaña* between 1847 and 1951.[1] The *Life of Don Gregorio Guadaña* is, in fact, the single Enríquez Gómez work to have gained lasting popularity.

Both the dedication and foreword to *The Pythagorean Century* are disappointing compared with those of *The Moral Academies* and *Samson the Nazarene*, which contain valuable information concerning the author's life and thoughts. Given Enríquez Gómez's admiration for the policies of Cardinal Richelieu it is perhaps curious that he should dedicate the work to François de Bassompierre (1579–1646), since his opposition to Richelieu earned him long years in the Bastille, from which he was liberated only upon the cardinal's death in 1643. Possibly Enríquez Gómez sought to curry favor with Bassompierre, hoping that he would again come to a position of power, but more likely the author, acutely sensitive to persecution and injustice, saw in the marshal a fellow sufferer whose years in prison were not unlike his own years of enforced exile.[2] The first line of the dedication alludes to this empathy: "A quien también conoce el siglo como Vuestra Excelencia, justo es que se le dedique el *Siglo pitagórico*" ("To a person such as your excellency who also knows this century, it is just that the *Pythagorean Century* be dedicated" [2]). In Bassompierre's release from prison and the cardinal's death Enríquez Gómez no doubt saw mirrored his own eventual release from exile, especially as the career of the Count-Duke of Olivares, Richelieu's Spanish counterpart and adversary, was also coming to a close. In almost all the dedications to French magnates, in addition to the poet's empathy for their difficult situations, there was a Spanish connection with the honoree. In this case Enríquez Gómez recognized Bassompierre's knowledge of the peninsula through his diplomatic missions, referring to him as "quien tanto honra, quiere y estima el idioma

español" ("he who so honors, loves and esteems the Spanish language"
[3]).

A brief foreword announces the didactic intent of the work which
"sale a luz reprobando errores y aprobando virtudes" ("comes to light
reproving errors and approving virtues" [4]) but, at the same time,
indicates the poet's pessimistic view of the times, which seem to him
to encourage vice rather than virtue. The foreword also explains the
conceit behind the work's curious title. The Pythagorean doctrine of
the transmigration of the soul is declared to be false but useful: "Mi
intento ha sido moralizar el asunto, sacando de una opinión falsa una
doctrina verdadera" ("My intent has been to moralize the topic, ab-
stracting a true doctrine from a false belief" [4]). The foreword also
places the work within the tradition of "dream" literature, a type of
composition that has its roots in classical literature and was popular
among seventeenth-century authors. The celebrated *Sueños* (Dreams) of
Francisco de Quevedo, for example, had already gained international
fame. The "dream" framework is one that we will see used five years
later in Enríquez Gómez's *Torre de Babilonia* (The tower of Babylon).

The introductory material concludes with the customary laudatory
poems in Latin, French, and Spanish from well wishers including his
son, Diego Enríquez Basurto, who contributed a sonnet.

Structure

In a few introductory verses the poet sets the stage for the fiction
whereby the narrator's soul is to migrate from body to body in search
of virtue:

> Dormía a sueño suelto mi cuidado,
> cuando el señor Espíritu, enojado
> de tanta muerte, me salió al encuentro,
> y estas razones me publica dentro:
> "¡Alto a nacer segunda vez!"

My cares were enjoying a good snooze when Sir Spirit came looking for me
and read me the riot act: "Get ready to be born a second time!"

(13)

After a false start—"y en un instante, sin segundo padre, / me zabullí en el vientre de mi madre" ("and instantly, without benefit of a second father, I scooted back into my mother's womb" [14])—from which he is quickly dislodged, the narrating soul proceeds through fourteen chapters or "Transmigrations" that recount the vices of various traditional satiric targets.

Transmigrations 1–4 concern the ambitious man, the stool pigeon or informer *(malsín),* the courtesan, and the king's favorite *(valido)* respectively; 5 is the interpolated tale of Gregorio Guadaña; 6–12 are transmigrations into the hypocrite, the skinflint, the doctor, the too proud parvenu *(soberbio),* the thief, the schemer *(arbitrista),* and the gentleman *(hidalgo).*[3] Transmigration 13 marks a change in the soul's trajectory. Weary and disillusioned by the corrupt bodies it has passed through, the soul is here besieged by a host of potential bodies clamoring to be born. Again a number of conventional types are satirized: a tax farmer, a corrupt judge, a sheriff, a homosexual, an epicurean, a merchant, a poet, and a tailor, among others. In its desperation to avoid these vice-ridden bodies the narrating soul appeals to Pythagoras, who orders it to "Recuerda de tu sueño / y busca la virtud" ("Awake from your dream and search for virtue" [298]) which the narrator is instructed to find in himself—"Vive en ti mismo, búscala si quieres") ("It lives in yourself, look for it if you wish" [298]). Thus, making use of his free will, the final transmigration 14 is into the virtuous man, the ideal man. The remainder of the work is the virtuous man's advice, a summation of all the moral qualities that man must strive to attain. Unfortunately, such perfection is to "soñar el estado / verdadero del hombre" ("to dream the true state of man" [306]), that is to say, another dream.

Except for passages here and there in Enríquez Gómez's earlier plays and some sections of *The Moral Academies, The Pythagorean Century* and the *Life of Don Gregorio Guadaña* is the author's first complete work in the satiric mode, a mode that is later continued in *The Tower of Babylon.* Although *The Pythagorean Century* and the *Life of Don Gregorio Guadaña* have in common their satiric treatment of material, they show different approaches to seventeenth-century Spanish society. The scope of the verse and prose of the entire composition makes it impossible to comment on each incident and character and so, to approach the work in a systematic way, the following remarks concentrate on the main themes uniting the various episodes of *The Pythagorean Century* alone; *Don Gregorio Guadaña* is then considered separately.

Hypocrisy

Hypocrisy is the single most pervasive sin in the world that Enríquez
Gómez creates. As such, expositions of hypocrisy are to be found on
almost every page, although there are certain transmigrations that deal
particularly with the topic—"Into a Hypocrite" (6), "Into a *Malsín*"
(2), and "Into a Thief" (10).

Hypocrisy connected with religion can have no excuse for the *converso*
author and, of all the religious hypocrites, the *malsín* who works for
the Inquisition is especially odious. Julio Caro Baroja relies on the
definition of the celebrated seventeenth-century *converso* physician Vil-
lalobos for *malsín:* "*Malsines* are those who discover their friend's secrets
in order to have them killed or robbed; often they do this by recourse
to perjury.' " Caro Baroja goes on to comment, "The *malsín* operates
within his own circle and is the terror of those who live secret lives.
The plague of *malsines* has constantly harmed the crypto-Jewish society."[4]
The obsessive frequency with which the author excoriates the informer
in this and other works shows Enríquez Gómez's sad experience with
the type, as Amiel has indicated concerning the internecine feuds in the
converso community at Rouen (155). His firsthand knowledge comes
through strongly in transmigration 10 in the description of the future
informer's birth—"y vi que una comadre aceleraba / el paso a cierta
historia, / por mi mal concebida en la memoria" ("and I saw that a
midwife was accelerating the passage of a certain history, conceived for
my woe in my memory" [23]). Since the informer's delight is to
denounce innocent people, even parents and associates, always while
proclaiming ignorance of his treachery, the passages containing the soul's
rebukes reveal the depths of the poet's antipathy—"Tú eres el más
mal hombre de la tierra. / La [sic] hambre, peste y guerra / de la
especie mortal" ("You are the worst of men on earth, the starvation,
plague, and war of the human species" [29]). Enríquez Gómez has his
vengeance on this vermin, at least in print, by having the informer
stabbed fourteen times one night as he goes off to practice his trade.

A more lighthearted tale of hypocrisy concerns the pious fraud of a
friar, the subject of transmigration 6. Amiel has noted that the central
incident of this chapter is probably based on a scandal that occurred
in Seville at a time when Enríquez Gómez was perhaps also there
(333–34). In Enríquez Gómez's version the friar, a Rasputin type, has
built up a following mainly among society ladies by clever shows of

mystic mumbo jumbo. He leads a life of secret self-indulgence while feigning the strictest austerity. Unfortunately, buoyed by the adulation of the crowds, the friar begins to believe his own propaganda concerning his saintliness. In one of the work's most entertaining passages the charlatan predicts his own death, a prognostication that embarrassingly fails to come true when the soul stubbornly refuses to depart. The quick-witted holy man, however, manages to salvage his credibility by announcing, "Dios quiere, por salvar a los estraños, / que trabaje en su viña algunos años" ("God wishes me to work a few more years in the vineyards to save the strangers for him" [198]), a clever double entendre considering the friar's weakness for the grape. The narrating soul's chief complaint is that by passing himself off on a credulous public as a holy man, the friar becomes a false god. The fate of this hypocrite, like that of the informer, is harsh. Enríquez Gómez, in a nice show of irony, eventually has him fall to the mercy of the Inquisition, which decrees two hundred lashes and a year rowing in the galleys. In the inevitable public ceremony he is made to suffer his punishment plus the disdain of those who were formerly his devoted followers: "y cuantos le besaron, le escupían, / y de corridos muchos se escondían" ("and those who before kissed him, spat on him, and from shame many hid themselves" [210]).

The tenth transmigration into the thief is rather curious as he is the only character in the series of transmigrations who is by definition a criminal. The thief elicits at least partial sympathy in that the exposition of hypocrisy is more concerned with that of the society that creates him and then condemns him to death precisely for actions that so-called honorable men are everywhere engaged in. The thief notes: "Ladrones somos todos, pero por varios y diversos modes" ("Thieves are we all but by various and diverse modes" [263]). The overcharges, bribes, and extortions practiced by "decent" professional people and tolerated by society are contrasted with the straightforwardness of the thief, who admits what he is and bravely accepts the consequences. At his execution, "Pidió perdón a todos, / exhortó de mil modos / a muchos compañeros, que le oían / que enmendasen la vida que traían" ("He begged pardon from all and exhorted the many comrades that heard him to enmend the lives they led" [266–67]). His noble bearing in the face of death and his recognition of error contrasts strongly with the less than dignified ends of most of the other bodies.

False Pride

Hypocrisy is directly linked to the theme of false pride or overweening pride *(soberbio)* that runs through this and other works and which Enríquez Gómez often symbolized by the biblical figure of Nimrod. Transmigration 9, "Into a *soberbio*," details the follies of the new rich whose fortunes are based on the hard work and often the dubious business dealings of humble parents. In this case the body is the son of a tavernkeeper, an occupation that, like the tailor's, was synonymous with thievery. The parvenu's efforts to push himself into society is carefully detailed. First, the patent of nobility is purchased, then an official position is obtained with his wealth. Any trace of common sense or humility is quickly erased by the horde of flatterers attracted to the smell of his money. The record of the parents and grandparents in dishonorable trade is erased and replaced with a lineage tracing back to the Goths. With his newfound nobility any notion of labor such as that originating the fortune is now dismissed as undignified. Thus productivity, even though in this case marginal, leads to wealth, then to unproductive idleness and conspicuous consumption, "por mostrar al mundo / que no admito segundo" ("to show the world I am second to none" [247]).

Transmigration 12 develops the theme of false pride on an even more bitter pitch in the satire on the *hidalgo* (gentleman). It would seem that the parvenu of 9 has learned his lessons in arrogance, idleness, and ignorance from the *hidalgo* he strives to emulate. Clearly for Enríquez Gómez the figure was the quintessential Old Christian, as threadbare and proud as his pedigree was long. In the *hidalgo*'s case the soul's comments are particularly strident: "Los sesos podían entrar todos en una cáscara de avellana y sobrar plaza" ("all his brains could be placed in a nut shell and still have room to spare" [277]). Both the parvenu and the gentleman confuse nobility with haughtiness, the latter declaring "que la nobleza y la soberbia . . . eran parientas [*sic*], y que, siendo la soberbia señora y la humildad esclava, tenía por mejor desposarse con una mujer altiva, que no con una que fuese humilde" ("that nobility and haughtiness were related and that, haughtiness being a lady and humility a slave, he thought it better to marry a snooty lady than one that was humble" [279]). If the new rich believe that money can buy nobility, the *hidalgo* believes that merely being born into the privileged class automatically confers nobility. The lesson for each is that true nobility comes from exercise of virtue and not money or birthright. In both cases poetic justice is applied. The parvenu dies in a duel defending the honor he so recently purchased and the *hidalgo* drowns ignobly while viciously attempting to strike down an old peasant who has dared to point out the error of his ways.

Immorality and the State

The Pythagorean Century makes clear in its vignettes that the immorality of individuals, classes, and professions ultimately undermines the state. The national application is best illustrated in transmigrations 4, "Into a *Valido*," and 11, "Into an *Arbitrista*," both frequent targets of seventeenth-century satire. Enríquez Gómez's business interests made him especially sensitive to the dismal Spanish economic situation, which was inextricably linked to political and social concerns. For him and others it was traceable in large measure to the shady activities of what today we would call economic planners (*arbitristas*). As Spain's economic problems multiplied during Philip IV's reign many people came forth with plans to reform or at least shore up the empire's finances.[5] Many of the *arbitrista*'s plans offered comprehensive and beneficial reforms but invariably failed to be implemented because they threatened the vested interest of powerful groups or individuals. As it became apparent that even practical reforms of the system met with storms of opposition, the government began to rely on stop-gap measures to stave off crises, measures that generally involved the raising of existing taxes or imposing new ones. Thus Enríquez Gómez satirizes "El primer arbitro que le dio fue estancar el sol; asegundó con otro y puso un nuevo derecho sobre la luna" ("The first scheme he came up with was to embargo the sun; he followed this with another one putting a tax on the moon" [267]). For Enríquez Gómez the effect of these schemes is the ruination of the nation—"Asaba los pueblos, quemaba las villas, freía las ciudades y destruía poco a poco el género humano" ("He roasted the towns, burned the villages, fried the cities and slowly destroyed the human race" [267]). Worse in the poet's regard is that the *arbitrista*'s chief motivation is self-enrichment, viewing the state as a sheep that requires periodic shearing. What all seems to be comic hyperbole is, in fact, a rather accurate description of the conditions of the time as described by Elliott: "Over the winter months of 1642–3 a pall of despair seems to have descended over the cities of Castile. Life was made intolerable by the lack of coins for ordinary taxation, and poverty was acute."[6]

The career of the king's favorite is examined not only with regard to corrupt internal governance, but also with regard to his handling of foreign relations.[7] For Enríquez Gómez, interested in government since his first play, *To Deceive In Order to Reign*, and doubly so after his exile, the politician's failing is that his government is not based on moral principles; it is not led by example and reason. Instead the *valido* follows the teaching of Machiavelli and bases his rule on force and a theology corrupted to suit his purpose. Along with the expected comments on the inevitable enrichment of the *valido* and his cronies, the soul complains of the endless and futile warfare that impoverishes the country with very little to show for so much bloodshed. The horrors and absurdities of war are eloquently addressed by Enríquez Gómez:

> . . . ¿Por dos piedras indecentes
> acabaste con tantos inocentes?
> ¡O terrible delirio!
> ¡Por un palmo de tierra tal martirio!

For two indecent rocks you terminated so many innocent lives? Oh terrible delirium! For a hand's breadth of land so much martyrdom!

(57)

Regardless of the *valido*'s errors, his response to the soul's criticism shows that Enríquez Gómez is not totally naive about the problems the office entails. The *valido*'s defense is based on two points: first, he cannot please everyone, and second, the adoption of Christian principles by the politician would be disastrous to him and to the nation since the humility, passivity, and peace-loving nature of true Christianity is better suited to the governance of convents than countries. The *valido*'s description of the necessary qualities that a statesman must possess would not be out of place today. The successful minister must show:

> Pocas palabras, religión muy poca,
> más firme que una roca,
> más duro que un Moncayo,
> más activo que un rayo,
>
> . . . .
> y aunque vea los ejes desquiciarse,
> y esta máquina abajo desplomarse,
> ha de decir: "No es nada; todo es risa."

Few words and less religion, more firm than a rock, more resistant than a mountain, more active than a lightning bolt . . . and even if he sees the world come off its axes and plummet into the void, he must say: "It is nothing; all is well."

(61–62)

For Enríquez Gómez, as for others hopeful of reform, it was an article of faith that "El rey es padre de la monarquía" ("The king is the father of the monarchy" [60]). Thus, one perceived solution to the economic and political chaos was the vain one that the indolent Philip IV would emulate his grandfather Philip II and take a direct and active role in the governance of his country—"Dejemos gobernar al propio dueño, / que esto de la privanza es como sueño: / que, cuando recordamos, / con pena y sin dineros nos hallamos" ("Let the proper owner govern, for this business of favoritism is a bad dream from which, when we awake, we will find ourselves pained and penniless" [60]).

Pessimism

All the transmigrations are imbued with the strongest sense of pessimism associated with every level of society and only superficially and rather perfunctorily tempered by the final transmigration, "Into the Virtuous Man." The virtuous man—"jeroglífico ha sido de mi sueño" ("The hieroglyph of my dream" [307])—is really only the impossible dream of another dream, a figure so unimaginably upright and so entirely contrary to every other character of the work that it fails utterly to supply any real hope of remedy for the ills of the world. The general bleak message of *The Pythagorean Century* is witness to Enríquez Gómez's deep-seated disillusionment. In spite of the relative safety that France offered him and his family, his restlessness and confusion is manifest in this work by the soul's frantic and aimless movement from one body to another—much as the poet himself wandered from city to city, country to country. The motif of birth and rebirth, suggested in many of Enríquez Gómez's works, finds its most elaborated expression in *The Pythagorean Century*.[8] By means of this artistic metempsychosis the author can indulge his desires to escape his lot. This literary wish fulfillment, however, is no more successful on paper than in life because, as Transmigration 13, "Into Various Bodies," indicates, the eternal wandering state is everyman's lot imposed by God for the disobedience of the first man and woman—life is "ese cruel calabozo adonde vamos a pagar la culpa del primer hombre, horrible casa es de nuestra noble naturaleza" ("that cruel dungeon where we go to expiate the first parents' guilt, the horrible home of our noble nature" [286]).

Disillusionment, of course, is common to seventeenth-century Spanish literature (the example of Quevedo comes immediately to mind). Enríquez Gómez's pessimism, however, has additional roots in the New Christian experience. If we examine the transmigrations for professions or types that produce the most violent reactions, we may suppose that these are the targets for which the author felt the most antipathy. In this respect the three most bitingly critical portraits are those of the informer (2), the parvenu (9), and the gentleman (13). The obsession with the informer and the condemnation of the Old Christian *hidalgo* are to be expected. (One should note that the ignoble death the latter suffers is not the only revenge the author takes on this intolerant figure; he is subsequently referred to as a *cansado caballero* [literally a "tired gentleman"], which Joseph Silverman has identified as a code phrase indicating impure lineage.⁹) In the portrait of the haughty parvenu the criticism is directed at the ridiculous pretensions to nobility and honors the parvenu assumes after he inherits his wealth. The honorability that he has purchased is not only belied by his conduct, but also by the antihonorability of his ancestry. Like so many New Christians he lives a state of constant tension, on guard for slighting references to his forebearers whom he prefers to forget:

> y quien pusiere mancha en mis abuelos,
> la pondrá como vil en cuantos cielos
> descubrió la arrogante astrología;
> tan limpio soy como la luz del día.

And he who thinks to besmirch my grandparents will search in vain all the heavens that arrogant astrology has discovered. As pure am I as the light of day.

(246)

The new Christian angst becomes more concentrated towards the end of the composition. The thirteenth transmigration into various bodies contains two lengthy passages in tercets (289–92, 292–95) very much in the vein of *The Moral Academies* in which so often the author poeticized his own life. Concerning his birth he recounts:

> nací llorando la terrible audiencia
> que el siglo, entre favores indecentes,
> guardaba a mi larguísima inocencia.
> Torpes gemidos, rudos accidentes,
> nocivos lloros, ásperas prisiones
> fueron mis deudos, cuando no parientes.

I was born lamenting the terrible tribunal that the world, among indecent favors, prepared for my most lengthy innocence. Torpid moans, unpleasant incidents, noxious weepings, harsh prisons were my companions if not my relatives.

                                                                                        (289)

The passage, oblique as usual, appears to call attention to the inquisitional persecution (*terrible audiencia*) he suffered in spite of his proclaimed innocence.

Structure and Style of *The Pythagorean Century*

Leaving aside the interpolated *Life of Don Gregorio Guadaña,* the structure of *The Pythagorean Century* is quite regular and very linear. The transmigrations almost always proceed in the same manner: there is the introduction of the wandering soul into a body, a description of the body's vices, the soul's sermon of admonition, and then the body's rejection of the advice in a passage of self-justification. Immediately after the body's rejection of the right path, some sort of demise is recounted, generally in line with the principles of poetic justice. The episode concludes with a sonnet or a *décima* containing an epitaph warning the reader to take heed.

The majority of the transmigrations are recounted in verse in which the *silva* form predominates, the verses rhyming in couplets. There are, in addition, two sections in the thirteenth transmigration in tercets, as noted above. Transmigrations 5, 11–12, and the first part of 13 are related in prose. The change to prose in the fifth transmigration is obviously to provide a bridge to facilitate the inclusion of the novelette, *The Life of Don Gregorio Guadaña.* The choice of prose in whole or in part for 11–13 is less clear. Combinations of prose and verse are not uncommon in seventeenth-century Spanish works (Enríquez Gómez's *Tower of Babylon,* for example), but the grouping of these prose passages toward the end of the *Pythagorean Century* suggests two possibilities:

that they, like the *Life of Don Gregorio Guadaña*, were parts of an unfinished independent work or works that were inserted to round out a work about to go to press; or, the prose passages were background sketches for sections that Enríquez Gómez had neither the time nor the inclination to turn into verse. The fact that *The Pythagorean Century* does not have the usual lengthy and informative prologue of his other major compositions, plus the truncated ending of *Don Gregorio Guadaña*, would seem to indicate a rush to press.

Within the work's rather rigid plan there is a surprising variety of moods and attitudes expressed. Some of the transmigrations are more developed than others, offering interesting mini-biographies of the various occupations of the time—the career route of the *arbitrista*, for example, or that of the *valido*. The rather detailed machinations of the fake religious of 6 is entertaining reading and, digressing from the biographical form of the majority of the transmigrations, presents an anecdote in verse—that of self-predicted demise. Some vignettes are a good deal more lighthearted than others. For example, 3, detailing the courtesan's wiles, is well within Enríquez Gómez's presentation of the scheming and acquisitive temptress whose danger is obvious but irresistible. The sketch of the type is then fleshed out in *Don Gregorio Guadaña* in several examples, principally in that of the courtesan of Carmona.

Very often the verse has a prosaic quality to it, as perhaps is to be expected in narrative satire, and at times the rhyme is forced and repetitive, especially throughout the didactic passages. Fortunately, the didactic sections are, for the most part, confined to the soul's sermon and the body's reply, passages that are delivered with a good deal of puns and double entendres and all spiced with a fair amount of scatology and eroticism.[10] In terms of lyric excellence, the best testimony to the poet's talents are to be found in 13, "Various Transmigrations." In the prose introduction to the chapter the pace of the narrating soul is first made to falter in despair at "ese teatro de homicidas, vida que no has de gozar, descanso que no has de tener y justicia que no has de hallar" ("That theater of homicides, life that you are not to enjoy, rest you are not to have, and justice you are not to find" [285]). The lyric tercets that follow have a rhythm, flow, and beauty that compare favorably with those of other baroque poets. Here, for example, is his description of the dawn:

> Al tiempo cuando el luminoso día
> recordaba en los brazos de la aurora,

> sacudiendo la sombra helada y fría,
> cuando empezaba a enriquecerse Flora
> de aquella soberana providencia
> que en globos de zafir asiste y mora. . . .

At the moment when luminous day awoke in the arms of the dawn shaking off cold darkness, when Flora began to bedeck herself in that sovereign providence that in sapphire crystals waits and lives . . .

(289)

Subsequent lines splendidly set forth the anguish of man's vain striving to make sense out of his existence, and, at the same time, his attempts to battle the temptation to error that life constantly offers—"Con voz de amante, te llamó su amigo / el siglo, en cuyos mares alterados / te atormentó, cual bárbaro enemigo" ("With the lover's voice your friend, this earthly existence, hailed you; this century in whose turbulent seas, like some barbarous enemy, he tormented you" [293]). The expression of suffering and conflict gradually builds into a heartfelt indication of bewilderment at the gross injustices of the world leading to the inevitable and unanswerable question: "¡Oh altísimo Señor! ¡Oh mar profundo! / ¡Oh ciencia sacra! ¡Oh poderosa idea! / ¿Hasta cuándo tendrá su imperio el mundo?" ("Oh, most high Lord! Oh, profound sea! Oh, sacred knowledge! Oh, puissant idea! How long will this world maintain it rule?" [295]).

The Life of Don Gregorio Guadaña

Summary of the Plot. Transmigration 5 introduces the interpolated short novel, the *Life of Don Gregorio Guadaña,* which is itself divided into twelve chapters that recounts in a quasi-picaresque fashion the amusing adventures of a young man on a journey from Seville to Madrid. The initial chapter sets forth the dubious genealogy of Don Gregorio which Amiel characterizes as "une imposante généalogie du déshonneur—de l'antihonneur" (81). Don Gregorio's father is a doctor and his mother a midwife, his paternal uncle a pharmacist and his maternal uncle a surgeon. Among other members of the larcenous family described in humorous detail, there are a dentist who dabbles in ointments and cosmetics, an alchemist, and a go-between, all experts in the nefarious tricks of their trades. Chapter 2 recounts in almost clinical detail Don Gregorio's birth and then skips ahead to twenty-two years of age and his departure for Madrid en route to law studies at Salamanca. Chapters 3–6 relate the adventures of Gregorio as he travels to the court in the company of a judge, a notary, a bailiff, a priest, a soldier, a scholar, and, most important from Gregorio's point of view, an alluring young lady, Doña Beatriz, who is chaperoned by her *dueña*.

Chapters 3–5 take place during their stopover in Carmona. The central incident concerns the judge's fruitless attempt to arrest a young man who is being entertained in the house of a beautiful and clever courtesan. The young man's escape and the discomfiture of the judge at the hands of the resourceful woman provide one of the most humorous episodes of the work.

Chapter 6 returns Don Gregorio's traveling party to the road where they are robbed and stripped by bandits in the Sierra Morena. Finally, the group arrives in Madrid where Gregorio's roguish activities occupy chapters 7–12.

In the capital Gregorio takes up the idle life of the wealthy playboy. He is taken in tow by a fopish, wastrel cousin and becomes enamoured of a conniving courtesan, Doña Angela Serafín de Bracamonte. In Madrid, Gregorio's life is about evenly divided between womanizing and carousing with his friends. He plays a brutal trick on an offending policeman, has an adulterous affair with the wife of the bailiff resulting in her serious injury, is pursued by the enraged bailiff, and spends some time in jail. The story ends abruptly as Don Gregorio is at the point of going off to jail for the second time on a trumped up breach of promise suit engineered by Doña Angela to force him into matrimony.

The Autonomy of *The Life of Don Gregorio Guadaña*. The separate nature of the novelette has been recognized at least since 1847 when Ochoa first excised the work from *The Pythagorean Century* for inclusion in his *Treasury of the Best Spanish Authors*.[11] In spite of an attempt on Enríquez Gómez's part to provide transitional passages and smooth over the insertion of *Don Gregorio Guadaña* into *The Pythagorean Century*, it is obvious that the two were wedded merely by convenience. The table of contents of *The Pythagorean Century* attests to the autonomy of *Don Gregorio* by the fact that it is the only chapter of the fourteen not to be called a transmigration. Also, the text gives testimony to the separateness of the two works in transmigration 7 where, in a passage in which the soul enumerates its past masters, the list does not include Don Gregorio. Finally, the independence of the work is demonstrable from the obvious differences of style, structure, and purpose.

Perhaps Enríquez Gómez felt that *Don Gregorio Guadaña* was too short to be printed separately and its inclusion in *The Pythagorean Century* was a last minute decision to find a home for the tale. But, for whatever reason, as an independent composition it has become a standard item in anthologies of picaresque works and the best known of all the many Enríquez Gómez works.

Don Gregorio Guadaña and the Picaresque. Over the years *The Life of Don Gregorio Guadaña* has sparked the same sort of ambivalent reaction as have others of the author's works, and perhaps to an even greater degree because it has been more accessible than most of the other compositions. However, attention has been focused on it in a rather external manner; that is to say, it has aroused more interest because of its position in the history of the picaresque genre than because of its merits. For the majority of older critics, purists grounded in picaresque characteristics as established by *Lazarillo de Tormes* and transmitted and developed by Alemán and Quevedo, *The Life of Don Gregorio Guadaña* is cited as an example of how a genre degenerates.[12] More recently, critics have been divided on the worth of the work and whether it really should be called picaresque. R. O. Jones, while he grants it picaresque status, nonetheless dismisses it as a work that "has some entertaining moments, but in its totality is a boring farrago."[13] J. L. Alborg classifies it as an adventure novel with picaresque elements and calls attention to its erotic nature, a Frenchified type of picaresque he presumes.[14] Alborg likewise notes the debt to Quevedo, although he finds it falling far short of the *Buscón*'s intensity. P. N. Dunn has been the most impressed: "The densely woven verbal wit and the comic ingenuity are unmatched by any writer except Quevedo. . . . For brilliant irreverent critical intelligence one can only compare Enríquez Gómez with Valle-Inclán."[15] In general, it appears that the process of reevaluation of *The Life of Don Gregorio Guadaña* is paralleling that of other Enríquez Gómez compositions—as more and more work on his life and works is published his literary worth is seen in more favorable light.

Enríquez Gómez's specific references to the Buscón, the Pícara Justina, and Guzmán de Alfarache in his brief introduction to *The Life of Don Gregorio Guadaña* (68) make it clear that he thought of Gregorio Guadaña in terms of the picaresque tradition. But, as ever, whereas he often sought inspiration in the works of others, the result was always his own original composition. The classic picaresque elements that *The Life of Don Gregorio Guadaña* incorporates are as follows: the autobiographical framework of movement from place to place involving a series of adventures, most of which concern associations with marginal elements of society; the detailing of the antihonorable genealogy of the protagonist; social satire; some moralizing passages; and an open-ended structure.

A nonpicaresque element of the narrative is the apparent contradiction between the protagonist's character and his heritage. The detailed account of his genealogy places the family roots squarely in medicine and related occupations, traditional *converso* professions. But although the antihonorability of the family businesses is exaggerated for satiric and comic effect and perhaps dictated by picaresque convention, the honorability of Don Gregorio himself is not called into question by the other characters or by the author. From the moment he sets out for the court, he is presented as a gallant, courteous, and brave young man who in all his activities abides by the gentleman's code of conduct. We recall, for instance, his facilitating the escape of a man whom he regards as a fellow gentleman during the patrol in Carmona, his gallant attention to Doña Beatriz during the journey to Madrid, and his willingness on several instances to cross swords with adversaries. In fact, in the final lines of the work Don Gregorio affirms his honorability in his refusal to marry the deceitful Doña Angela: "En fin, yo dije que fuésemos a la cárcel norabuena, que más quería acabar con honra en ella que vivir con deshonra toda mi vida en aquella casa" ("Finally, I said that we should depart for jail right away, for I would rather finish my days honorably in it than live all my life with dishonor in that house" [191–92]). Another indication that Don Gregorio's honorability is genuine is shown by his speech to the judge (chapter 11) on the ticklish question of what to do with the judge's sister who gives birth to an illegitimate child, the result of an affair with a lackey. The judge contemplates murder to cover up the dreadful scandal. But Don Gregorio's advice, based on forgiveness, mercy, and understanding, runs counter to the bloody vengeance mandated in the seventeenth-century code of honor. In the end Enríquez Gómez cannot resist adding a sly dig at old Christian honor by having Don Gregorio comment: "Si el agresor del delito natural es indigno de la nobleza de vuestra casa, advertid que no será ése el primer golpe que ha recibido el cuerpo de la nobleza" ("If the perpetrator of this natural crime is unworthy of the nobility of your house, bear in mind that this will not be the first blow that the corps of nobility has received" [173]).

There is no doubt that Don Gregorio's gentility, belying his equivocal genealogy, reflects the experience of class struggle and the aspirations of an author whose *converso* parentage seemed an insurmountable difficulty. The idea that true nobility is that which comes as a result of individual character and not lineage is a constant in Enríquez Gómez's compositions and certainly is exemplified in Don Gregorio. The career of Don Gregorio, who finds acceptance and applause everywhere on the basis of his own worth and personality, contrasts sharply with the *pícaros* Pablo and Guzmán, who are rejected and vilified constantly in their efforts to find higher places for themselves in society.[16] One cannot help but notice the parallel with the parvenu of transmigration 9, who also comes from antihonorable parentage. Don Gregorio Guadaña is a parvenu who listened to the soul's advice, the positive example contrasted with the negative.

Because Don Gregorio does not have the problem of insufficient money, we note the absence of the motif of the struggle for mere subsistence that propels the classic *pícaro* through life. In fact, the characters of Enríquez Gómez's work are quite bourgeois in their appreciation of good living, as witness the judge's lengthy discourse on comfort *(comodidad)*, which is sparked by a feeling of well-being one evening as Don Gregorio, the judge, and several friends get into a coach to visit certain "ladies." Written with characteristic tongue-in-cheek humor, the hedonism of the Judge's observations characterize the entire work:

Por cierto, señor Don Gregorio, que tuvo poca razón Demócrito en poner la felicidad del hombre en reír, Heráclito en llorar, Platón en la virtud, Aristóteles en el honor, Filón en el amor, y otros muchos en diferentes acciones y virtudes. Si ellos dijeran que no hay mayor que la comodidad de cada uno, anduvieran acertados; y no niego haber en el mundo, justicia, razón, virtud, misericordia, amistad, limosna, honra, caridad, templanza, fortaleza, prudencia y sabiduría; pero antes que se ejecuten todas estas morales y políticas virtudes, entra primero la comodidad de cada uno.

Certainly, Señor Don Gregorio, Democritus had little sense when he averred man's happiness to be wrapped up in laughter, likewise Heraclitus in tears, Plato in virtue, Aristotle in honor, Philon in love, and many others in different actions and virtues. If they had said that there is nothing greater than one's well-being, they would have been on the right track. And far be it for me to deny the world truth, justice, reason, virtue, mercy, friendship, alms, honor, charity, temperance, courage, prudence, and wisdom; but before all these moral and politic virtues can be put into practice, the comfort of each individual must be established."

(181–82)

Certainly Don Gregorio enjoys the world, especially its amorous delights. The entire work is suffused with an "un-picaresque" eroticism which, as we have seen, has been credited to the influence of the author's French exile. While there is a heavily satiric, grotesque, and scatological vein, à la Quevedo, apparent in the clinical descriptions of the professional duties of Gregorio's relatives and in the lengthy and grim recounting of the hero's birth, there are also passages of exquisite sensualism as, for example, in the scene in the house of the courtesan of Carmona (chapter 4). The judge's party is ushered into her luxuriously appointed bedroom, and Don Gregorio gives us the following delicately drawn description:

Entramos todos hasta la alcoba, admirados de ver un brazo que corría la cortina haciendo plaza a su dueño; era una dama tan hija de Venus, que parecía haber salido de la espuma en aquel instante. Abrió los dormidos ojos con tal gracia, que nos llenó de luz a modo de relámpago que pasa presto. Sentóse en la cama, arqueó las cejas, tendió los brazos, aderezó la holanda, alentó la vista, armó los ojos, y púsose a matar vidas, diciendo: "¡La justicia en mi cama! Téngolo por imposible, siendo ella el tribunal de los gustos y no de los justos."

We all entered the bedroom and admired an arm that drew back curtains revealing its occupant. It was a lady so much a daughter of Venus that she seemed to have stepped out of the sea foam in that instant. She opened her languid eyes so gracefully that we felt as though we had been hit by a lightning bolt. She sat up in bed, arched her brows, stretched her arms, smoothed the sheets, took aim with her sight, armed her eyes, and set about to finish off her victims saying: "Justice in my bed! I am sure that this is impossible, it being the tribunal of the horizontal and not the upright.

(107–8)

Don Gregorio and the Ladies. *The Life of Don Gregorio Guadaña* consistently presents women whose morality is very much more relaxed than that of the ladies of Enríquez Gómez's *comedia*. The principal female characters are the demimondaines Beatriz and Angela who vie for the attention of Don Gregorio. There is also the aforementioned siren whose chamber he visits in Carmona and who, it turns out, has not one but two gentlemen visitors hidden away. Some idea of the playful eroticism of the work is illustrated in the courtesan's reply to Don Gregorio's question "si había más alacenas" ("If there were any more closets"); "y respondióme que volviese otra noche, y me pondría en la tercera") ("and she responded that I should return another night and she would put me in the third chamber" [113]). We also have the unfortunate adulterous Lucrecia of chapter 10 and the judge's sister pregnant by her servant.[17] All in all, this is a feminine panorama that does not edify by its high moral example.

An important conflict of the story is the competition between Angela and Beatriz to control Don Gregorio's heart and pocketbook. Beatriz is a lively and witty girl whose heart rules her head to the despair of her calculating *dueña*. Angela, equally attractive to Don Gregorio, is the more pragmatic of the two. She knows full well both the necessity and practice of accepting gifts, and in her first meeting with Don Gregorio charmingly relieves him of some two hundred and fifty ducats worth of presents. Angela also has an eye out for her future. When it appears as though Gregorio is not about to marry anyone, she arranges the false breach of promise suit and threatens to send him to jail unless he weds her. The confrontation scene between the two ladies is one of the highlights of the story and a type of scene whose comic potential Enríquez Gómez explored in several plays.[18]

Miráronse las dos a orza, y dijo doña Angela:
—Reina mía, ¿es vuesa merced hermana del señor don Gregorio? porque se parecen.
—Señora, no—respondió doña Beatriz—, soy su cercana deuda por parte de Venus, y vengo a saber de su salud.
—Pues escúselo por ahora—dijo mi ángel—, que está el señor don Gregorio tomado para palacio.
¿Cierto?—replicó dona Beatriz riyéndose.
—Certísimo—respondió doña Angela.
—Y mi sevillana dijo:—Pues crea la señora cortesana tendrá el palacio tan lleno de gente, que no quepa don Gregorio en él.

The two look each other up and down and Dona Angela said: "My dear, is your ladyship Don Gregorio's sister? You look so much alike." "No, Madam," responded Dona Beatriz, "I'm a close relative of his on the Venus side of the family and I've come to inquire about his health." "Well, that's unnecessary now," said Angela, "since Señor Don Gregorio is presently installed in the palace of my heart." "Really," replied Dona Beatriz with a laugh.

"Really," responded Dona Angela. Then my little Sevillian said: "I would
have thought that the Señora Courtesan's palace would be so full of people
that there wouldn't be any more room for Don Gregorio!"

(164)

In sum, the ladies provide a splendid presentation of feminine wiles
for which Gregorio is no match. Although it is obvious throughout the
story of his adventures that he can match wits and swords with men,
when it comes to women Gregorio is irresistibly drawn to the flame.
Gregorio's youth and inexperience leads him to believe that he can
manage multiple affairs without trouble, a judgment he later realizes
to be false: "El daño estaba en la confianza que yo tenía de mi persona,
tanto de galán como de discreto, virtudes que no conocí en mi vida"
("The problem was in the confidence that I had in myself as a gallant
and discreet person, virtues that I never really had in all my life"
[164]). In truth Gregorio is rather inept as a Don Juan, but then,
according to the Enríquez Gómez view of the world, few men have a
chance in the battle between the sexes.[19]

Summary. *The Life of Don Gregorio Guadaña* is noticeably freer
from the heavy-handed didacticism that fills the pages of Enríquez
Gómez's other works written in France. But underlying its overall
lighthearted and anecdotal nature there are many elements of satire.
The satire of the medical professions introduced with Gregorio's genealogy
has already been noted. The idling life at court of the dandies provides
a number of other satirical targets, among them the literary salon that
the protagonist visits in chapter 11 and which presents an opportunity
to parody the rhetorical verse of the day. But by far in *The Life of
Don Gregorio Guadaña* the most sustained satiric consideration is focused
upon the legal and judicial system. From the moment Gregorio steps
into the coach bound for Madrid with the judge, the bailiff, and the
notary, to Gregorio's final march to prison, the total venality of the
system is apparent in a continuing chronicle of arbitrary rulings, favoritism, bribes, and shakedowns. The joy of the citizens of Carmona
on learning of the judge's departure for Madrid testifies to the type of
justice he represents—"salimos todos juntos con harto gusto de los del
lugar que rogaban a Dios los sacase de tanta justicia" ("We all left
together to the intense pleasure of the citizens of the city who were
begging God to spare them from so much justice" [129]).

While *The Life of Don Gregorio Guadaña* is primarily a novel of entertainment, it does have its serious moments. In chapter 5, during the long journey to Madrid, the travelers philosophize on life. The subject comes up from some bantering comments on age and aging that lead to an interesting exposition of ideas. The philosopher laments the negative aspects of life, especially the ultimate mystery that is death. He comments on the irony of our fascination with and, at the same time, fear of death: "Vivimos entre muertos, comemos muertos, vestimos muertos, visitamos muertos, lisonjeamos muertos, y, con tener a nuestra vista tanto cadaver, queremos vivir para siempre" ("We live among the dead, we eat the dead, we dress the dead, we visit the dead, we praise the dead, and in the presence of so many cadavers we want to live forever" [123]). The friar is more positive, as one might expect from a cleric; he says that life is not to be scorned or despised because it is really a series of "escaleras por donde el alma por su merecimiento sube al trono angélico" ("stairs which the soul by merit ascends to the angelic throne" [123]) and, for that reason, our mortal years are allotted to us so that by using our free will we can aspire to be a better state. The politician in turn understands everything in political terms; the soldier relates everything to war. All the conflicting opinions concerning life and its purpose are pondered by Don Gregorio in an interior monologue: "Eché de ver entonces que la sabiduría era un instrumento acordado, cuyas cuerdas sutiles los músicos humanos tocan a tiento, y de aquí me pareció nacía la desigualdad de voces en los maestros, porque cada uno tocaba como le sonaba mejor al entendimiento" ("I then began to see what wisdom was a stringed instrument whose subtle cords human musicians play by ear and from this, it seemed to me, was born the differences in the music of the maestros, because each one played as it best sounded to his way of understanding" [128]).[20]

Nevertheless, the serious moments of *The Life of Don Gregorio Guadaña* are rather the exception than the rule. The narrative is fast-paced and comic as befits the scrapes of a young and inexperienced man making his entry into the *mare magnum* of the court. It is a fairly well-constructed work with its development around characters and relationships that intertwine throughout the course of the narrative into a novelesque creation. It is true, however, that the story line suffers somewhat in the last chapter by a hastily formulated ending that leaves some plot questions unanswered. And while some of the pranks are not so clever as they first promise, there are many other scenes that delight the reader, as much for the action as for the author's mastery of the narrative process. This narrative succeeds, as Hanrahan notes, by allowing the words and deeds of the characters to be sufficiently revealing.[21]

Chapter Six
The Tower of Babylon
Dedication and Prologue

The satiric-moralistic prose work, *The Tower of Babylon,* is dedicated to Henri-Louis d'Aloigne, Marquis de Rochefort. The dedication is dated at Rouen on the tenth of May 1649, a date that, as we will see, may or may not necessarily indicate that Enríque Gómez was in fact still in France. As with other dedications, Enríquez Gómez's choice of the marquis serves at least a dual purpose, first in seeking the protection of a personage with connections to Spain through his travels and, second, in honoring a kindred spirit. The lengthy dedication focuses on the fidelity of the marquis to his royal prince, Gaston d'Orléans (?), and the consequent misfortunes and persecution he shared in this service. In elegant prose Enríquez Gómez harks back to the maritime imagery of *The Moral Academies* to symbolize the marquis as the immovable rock (Rochefort, "roca fuerte") opposed to the waves of adverse fortune and courtly intrigue. For Enríquez Gómez, Aloigne incarnates the highest ideal of nobility, that which combines illustrious birth, heroic stead-fastness, acceptance of adversity, and, of equal importance, the absence of haughtiness.

The dedication also expresses the author's gratitude to the marquis for having obtained Enríquez Gómez's entry into the Order of St. Michel.[1] Enríquez Gómez's proud claims to membership in this order, as well as the titles of counselor and understeward to the French king that appear for the first time in the *Louis God-given* two years earlier, have never been substantiated. It is interesting that these titles were not repeated in *Samson the Nazarene,* produced some ten years later by the same printer, leading us to suppose that his claims of these honors were either premature, withdrawn, or unfounded.

The prologue is a long series of conceits curiously entitled "A los vecinos de esta gran Babilonia del mundo y a las vecinas de la Torre del Oro" ("To the inhabitants of this great Babylon of the world and to the female inhabitants of the golden tower").[2] The charge to the reader—"Lean con cuidado y miren en él, que los que leen con seso

85

tienen ojos, y los que miran sin juicio, antojos" ("Read carefully and
consider it, for those who read intelligently have their wits about them,
and those who consider without judgment are witless")—clearly calls
for a reading between the lines. This suggestion is reinforced by
subsequent cryptic remarks, one in particular that draws an analogy
with inquisitors and the genealogical searches to prove purity of lineage:
"Yo escribo mi *Torre de Babilonia* como algunos su nacimiento que se
les da a los Señores de la censura o tonsura" ("I write my *Tower of
Babylon* as others their birth that they give to the gentlemen censors,
or tonsures"). One possible interpretation of *The Tower of Babylon* is
that the work chronicles in cypher his secret return to Spain. The
Golden Tower he mentions calls immediately to mind the structure that
even today is a Sevillian landmark. The ironic dedication to the female
inhabitants or neighbors of that tower would relate to the strong
antifeminism of the entire work.

Whatever the reader wishes to make of the work's covert messages,
the overt message is clearly stated as that of exposing vice. Drawing
on his experiences and, no doubt, upset by his own recent financial
collapse in France, Enríquez Gómez states that he had in mind "algunos
sugestos que vi y retraté con la pluma" ("Some subjects I saw and
drew with the pen"). He mentions two in particular: the one a Judas,
a traitor, and "almost a *malsín*," (perhaps his son-in-law?); the other
an avaricious usurer who grows fat on the labor of others. The bitterness
of Enríquez Gómez's attacks on his enemies and, in particular, those
ingrates who take advantage of another's misfortunes, indicates that his
problems toward the end of the decade hardened his vision of society
since he wrote *The Pythagorean Century* a few years earlier. In *The
Tower of Babylon* the disillusionment is much more marked, the satire
more biting, and the humor now only thinly covers the underlying
anguish.

Synopsis

Fourteen chapters called *vuelcos* ("turns" as in turning over in bed)
make up the dream the author experiences during one winter night in
which the body rests but the unquiet spirit cannot. The dream commences
as the narrating spirit finds itself wandering through the sumptuous
chambers of a labyrinthine palace, unable to find an exit or trace of
another being. In the midst of this solitary splendor, there suddenly
appears a "venerable" who informs him that the mansion is his to

enjoy as long as he safeguards a diamond-studded jewel. To share with him these luxurious surroundings he is also given a beautiful maiden, whom he finds in the garden. Servants magically appear and the couple settle down to enjoy a life free from every care. This paradise, however, is short-lived. The consort is one day strolling in the garden when a page, "más astuto que las culebras" ("more clever than a serpent") approaches her and asks if she would like to visit other ladies, the harem of a certain prince "que vive en lo profundo de un valle" ("who lives in the depths of the valley" [3]). Through curiosity the woman is enticed into surrendering the jewel in exchange for two rings, one of forgetfulness for her and the other of perdition for the narrator. With the woman's thoughtlessness, the vow is broken, and both the narrator and his companion are ejected from their paradise.

After their expulsion, as the narrator stumbles aimlessly through a dark forest, he is met by a guide, his familiar, who leads him to the Tower of Babylon in which it is his punishment to live. The remainder of the work details all the possible follies of human existence through a tour of the city and its environs.

In chapters 2–4 the narrator is brought to an inn and prepared for his entrance into society. He is set upon by tailors, dancing masters, fencing instructors, idle and dissolute gentlemen, members of the medical professions, and, worst of all, his wife, who reappears demanding cosmetics, clothes, jewels, and extravagant delicacies.

With the exception of chapter 12, the rest of the work takes us on a tour of the city. The narrator and his guide begin their visit at the palace where greedy petitioners swarm about an indifferent *valido*. Bureaucratic schemers (*arbitristas*) hatch crazy schemes to magically set aright the state's economy, soldiers lament the government by civilians, and rumor mongers' sensational fabrications disquiet the populace. A visit to the Temple of Mammon occupies chapters 6–7. In chapter 8 the narrator and guide see the Class of Good Taste where "ladies" receive lessons on chicanery. Chapter 9 tours the Examination and Fair of Honor, in which honor is given as a reward for dishonor and can be purchased and shaped to fit just as cloth is made into a suit of clothes. Chapter 10 takes in the Bazaar of Stupidities where, as benefits a merchant's dream, "llovían compradores y nunca se agotaba la mercancía" ("buyers poured in like rain and the merchandise never gave out" [145]). Chapter 11 takes us on an excursion to Noah's Ark, where the talking animals satirize various elements of society by their form and words. In chapter 12, returning from the Ark, the narrator meets another traveler, the celebrated Marqués de la Redoma (Marquis of the Bottle), Don Marcos de Villena, who alleviates the tedium of the journey by recounting his quasi-picaresque adventures. Chapter 13 has the narrator and the marquis once again in Babylon investigating the state of learning as they visit the Classes of Sciences and witness the absurdities and pomposities of philosophers, mathematicians, theologians, astrologers, and so forth.

The final chapter has the two comrades strolling along the main thoroughfare where they come upon Heraclitus and Democritus, the two philosophers who so often appear in Enríquez Gómez's works since *The Moral Academies*. *The Tower of Babylon* winds up with a lengthy debate between these two that sums up the author's observations and offers a *modus vivendi* for dealing with earthly life. The work ends quite abruptly, promising further "dreams" in a second part that, as far as is known, was never written.

"The Marquis of the Bottle"

As in the case of *The Life of Don Gregorio Guadaña*, incorporated into *The Pythagorean Century*, chapter 11 of *The Tower of Babylon* is merely an envelope for the interpolated tale of the Marquis of the Bottle, which occupies approximately thirty pages. The adventures of this figure are presented as a continuation of the life of the Marquis of the Bottle after he was last seen in one of Quevedo's *Dreams*.[3]

After some three hundred years the marquis regains his freedom, assuming human form as Don Marcos de Villena. As he stands naked on the plain of Barahona pondering his newfound freedom, a stagecoach comes along and picks him up. In the company of two courtesans, a physician, a tailor, a pompous erudite, and a lascivious anchorite, Don Marcos sets off for Madrid. During the first day's journey to an inn at Alcalá de Henares, Don Marcos repays the kindness by rescuing one of the "ladies" from a pursuing angry ex-boyfriend whom she has fleeced. Later that evening, by force of arms, he recovers the money and goods that were extorted from the entire company by the venal authorities of Alcalá.

The next day the party continues on to Madrid. At the stage stop at Viveros Don Marcos runs across Don Julio Bentibolino, who claims to know Marcos from their days in Italy. Don Marcos proceeds on to Madrid with Don Julio in tow and installs him in his mansion. The first danger in Madrid that Marcos faces is the amorous overtures of his host's love-starved sister, who has been kept in such rigorous seclusion that she is ready to pounce upon the first man she sees. Although sorely tempted, Marcos honorably turns aside the invitation. However, he cannot help but become involved in Julio's attempt to elope with his sweetheart. The plan goes wrong as they mistakenly cart off in the dark a mulatto maid instead of the girlfriend and, to complicate the situation, the maid's Berber lover also by mistake carries off Julio's fiancée. This grand mix-up leads to much frantic and comic running about through darkened streets.

Eventually Don Julio is reunited with his fiancée, but their happiness does not last because her father soon arrives with the police. Don Marcos is able to escape with a servant who is a student of the black arts and together and invisibly they visit the boudoir of a courtesan, all of whose lovers appear unfortunately at the same time and begin to fight among themselves.[4] In the final episode of the marquis's tale the two, having fled this melee, visit the quarters of a pious fraud who receives the offerings of his devotees in spartan surroundings and then retreats to his real lodgings where he secretly revels in all the hedonistic pleasures of this world. Here the story ends as the travelers arrive back at the gates of Babylon. Don Marcos, as is usual, promises to continue his tale at a later date.

Major Topics

Hypocrisy, venality, and cupidity in every aspect are the obvious targets of this satire, and in this *The Tower of Babylon* is not very different from many other works of the period. But the composition offers more than merely another dismal litany of seventeenth-century societal and human shortcomings. If we examine closely what at first seems a rather conventional satire, we find a work more profound and original than it first appears. As Enríquez Gómez's last satirical work and one of the last of his French period, *The Tower of Babylon* is a compendium of themes that were introduced into his writings much earlier and developed over the years. Additionally, as a work that puts an end to one era of the author's life, it builds to a conclusion in the final debate between Heraclitus and Democritus that sums up the author's views on life at this crucial point. The following sections present an outline of various themes that underlie and unify not only *The Tower of Babylon* but practically his entire corpus of works to that date.

Adam and Eve Theme

The inclusion of the creation myth in *The Tower of Babylon* represents a continuation of a topic that found its most complete expression in *The First Pilgrim's Guilt*, published five years earlier. The first two chapters of *The Tower of Babylon* are an obvious recasting of the story of Adam and Eve, whose Garden of Eden has been replaced by an enchanted palace suggested by those of the chivalric and sentimental novels.[5] Clearly the mysterious "venerable anciano cuya vista infundía temor y respeto" ("the venerable whose countenance inspires fear and respect" [2]) who assigns the palace to the narrator is to be understood as the Divinity. The narrator is instructed to search the palace garden for "la mayor joya que pudieron formar los cielos" ("the greatest jewel that the heavens could form" [5]), his Eve, as innocent as he. Their union is blessed by the venerable who entrusts them with the diamond-studded jewel guaranteeing their sovereignty over the palace. The penalty for not safeguarding the jewel is also made plain: "Si le guardares serás rey de este dichoso alcázar, ye si le quebrantares, despertarás del sueño y te hallarás algo más que cadáver y mucho menos que nada" ("If you guard it you will be king of this happy palace, and if you break it you will awake from the dream to find yourself a little more than a cadaver and much less than nothing" [6]).

The existence of the narrator and his companion in the enchanted place is the *converso*'s dream of utopia. Despite the lengthy introductory description of the luxuriousness of the palace, the narrator's happiness is more concerned with social harmony than merely the good living to be enjoyed there. Everything that Enríquez Gómez himself must have longed for in his life is here:

Olía todo mi alcázar a quitud. En él no se halló la lisonja ni la tiranía. La mentira no se adornó de mis labios ni la soberbia de mis pensamientos. No supe nunca en qué parte habitaba la guerra; ni de dónde tomó su origen la ambición. No gustó mi corazón del plato de la envidia, ni supe jamás a qué sabía la crueldad. A la justicia llamé madre, y a la misericordia hermana.

All my palace abounded with peace and quiet. In it flattery and tyranny were not to be found. My lips were not adorned with lies, nor my thoughts with vanity. I never knew in what part war was lodged nor where ambition took its origin. My heart did not partake of the dish of envy nor did I

ever taste cruelty. I called justice mother and mercy sister. Tranquillity was
the breath of my spirit and peace the shield of my prosperity.

(4)

The palace of *The Tower of Babylon* expresses life as the author's
dreams would have it. It recalls those idealized views of his youthful
Spanish years, those golden days which the exiled author often remembered with nostalgia and had previously used as the setting for *The
Moral Academies*. Not only did the Adam and Eve story interest Enríquez
Gómez because of its universal application, but it also struck a responsive
personal chord. Quite naturally Enríquez Gómez identified himself with
the Adam-like narrator, who, in Enríquez Gómez's view, because of
his trusting innocence, was expelled into a life of envy, cruelty, ambition,
and lies. Like the disgraced narrator, Enríquez Gómez longed for the
return to tranquillity and stability that would magically put an end to
his trials. This identification with the first man is reprised in a humorous
form at the beginning of the tale of "The Marquis of the Bottle" as
Don Marcos returns to this world and views his situation: "Me hallé
en carnes hecho un Adán . . . y porque no me faltasen Evas, divisé,
cosa de un tiro de piedra . . . dos ninfas" ("I found myself naked,
an Adam . . . and so as not to lack Eves I saw a little distance off
. . . two nymphs [the courtesans]" [176]).

Misogyny and Misogamy

Within *The Tower of Babylon's* general negativism women receive
more than their share of blame. In Enríquez Gómez's interpretation of
the Fall, the most striking feature is the overemphasis upon the woman's
guilt and the portrayal of the man as the naive, bumbling innocent,
too easily manipulated by female wiles. Immediately after succumbing
to the temptation to exchange the jewel for two rings, Eve is transformed
into a wheedling, petulant caricature of a wife who demands that the
narrator also wear one of the rings. Her final argument sums up her
grasping shrewishness: "¿Qué quería su majestad, que estuviese yo
condenada a soledad perpetua, tratando aquí con cuatro criadas tan
simples como él? Engáñase su merced; yo quise ver y ser vista" ("What
does your majesty want, that I be condemned to perpetual solitude
with only four maids as simple as you for company? Your grace is
mistaken; I want to see and be seen" [5]).

The symbolism surrounding the jewel and the rings is complicated, but both the jewel and the rings are related to the man-woman relationship before and after matrimony. The jewel has two manifestations—first, the heaven-sent wife who is identified as "the greatest jewel" and, then, a diamond which the couple is to guard. In both cases the symbolism is that of purity, which insures the blissful innocence of the couple's life in the palace. The diamond-pure innocence is destroyed when the woman visits the evil lord's palace and is all too easily induced to accept the two rings. The inference seems to be that when, at the woman's insistence, the youth dons his ring, it is as if they are conventionally married and, thereby, in the author's view, doomed to unhappiness. The jewel-ring imagery represents the delusion of a dream of happiness that is destroyed by matrimony. Enríquez Gómez's jaundiced view of the whole marriage scenario is repeated more plainly in the final chapter in the lengthy summation of man's life by Heraclitus. The following is the passage describing the wedding:

Consideremos luego la novia ir por sus pasos contados a la iglesia como a la pila, muy a lo vírgen dando el "sí" entre dientes. Dejemos la boda y veamos llevar a la madrina la novia a la cámara de tormento, llorando su virginidad y el novio riendo su necedad. Pasemos en silencio las once mil, considerando la mañana del arrepentimiento, diciendo al menor disgusto aquello de "mal haya quien contigo me juntó."

Let us now consider the bride who with reluctant steps goes to the church as if to be baptized, very virginally whispering "I do." Let us move on from the wedding to see the Matron of Honor conducting the bride to the torture chamber, she lamenting her virginity and the groom grinning foolishly. Let us pass in silence the deflowering to consider the morning of repentance, she saying at the slightest upset that old "Curses on the one who paired me with you."

(246)

In contrast to the narrator who laments at every turn his expulsion from the blissful palace, the wife is totally unrepentant. She appears once more on cue in chapter 4 as the narrator says, " '¡Desdichado de mí! que por una mujer me veo perdido y preso en la Torre de Babilonia.' Apenas dije la última razón cuando veo a la señora mi esposa entrar por la sala diciendo, 'Marido, pues estáis vestido, [vísteme] a mí o me vestiré yo' " (" 'Woe is me; on account of a woman I am lost and a prisoner in the Tower of Babylon.' Scarcely had I spoken the last phrase when I saw my wife enter the salon saying, 'Husband, since you are all decked out, dress me up also or I will do it myself' " [29]). Unlike the husband who is horrified by the excesses of Babylon, the wife thrives in such an atmosphere, demanding all the luxuries society can invent. The portrayal of the wife in *The Tower of Babylon* as grasping, vain, capricious, and shallow but artful differs little from the presentation of the many courtesans whom Enríquez Gómez is so fond of describing. Concerning women in general, as far as the narrator is concerned, "Su mayor bondad es parir, y su mayor virtud enredar" ("Their greatest good is to have children and their greatest virtue is to scheme" [7]).

The negative evaluation of women and matrimony is further developed in chapter 8 when the narrator visits the Class of Good Taste and witnesses a Circe giving lessons in trickery to a multitude of women who come forth with their problems. In almost every case the advice is centered on how to deceive their husbands and lovers. The ladies are taught that with their natural cleverness they can gratify their every desire if they learn to disguise their conduct with feigned innocence and piety.

The rabid antifeminism of *The Tower of Babylon* is somewhat softened in the "Marquis of the Bottle," although the two "Eves" in the coach that rescue Don Marcos are even more blatant courtesans than the types found before in *Don Gregorio Guadaña*. Nevertheless, the narrator is cognizant of the man's role in female misbehavior. Don Marcos is perplexed and amused by the paradoxical character of his host, Don Julio, who insists on the strictest seclusion of his sister but, at the same time, resolves to steal his girlfriend from her father's house. The masculine schizophrenia demanding virginity and faithfulness in the relative and wife, but encouraging indiscriminate seduction in the man is the subject of one of Don Marcos's ponderings on "la locura de los hombres, que queriendo sacar las hijas de los hombres honrados de su casa, querrán que no las sacasen a ellos las hermanas" ("the folly of men, who, wishing to abduct from their homes the daughters of honorable men, at the same time wish that their sisters not be abducted from them" [198]). The pathetic efforts of Don Julio's repressed sister to initiate a romance with Don Marcos are nobly rejected and, instead of condemning her amorous overtures, Marcos recognizes them as desperate attempts to break free from her imprisonment. Marcos observes that denial of education and virtual imprisonment only increases female susceptibility to romances. Their repressed state practically guarantees that they will behave foolishly at the first opportunity: "que las mujeres recogidas por

fuerza son como polvo que con poca lumbre toman fuego; y si como
yo llegue llegara otro, lo mismo fuera, que tales mujeres no miran
(porque no las dejan ver) sino el primero que hallan como sea hombre"
("that women forced into seclusion are like gunpowder that ignites with
the smallest flame. Whether I came along or another it would be the
same since such women do not see [because they are not allowed to]
any further than the first man that comes along, no matter who"
[192]).

Babylon, Babylonia, and Babel

The site to which the narrator and his wife are condemned shows
a symbolism that can shift and combine in a synthesis of the author's
perceptions of his own situation. The evil lord's ring of perdition is the
passport into the city, according to the narrator's guide: " 'Muestra el
anillo, que es tu pecado,' dijo mi compañero. "Mostréle y, respondieron
todos, 'pase el hombre al calabozo eterno de Babilonia, condenado por
todos los días de su vida' " (" 'Show the ring which is your sin,' said
my companion. I showed it and all responded, 'let this man pass on
to the eternal dungeon of Babylon, condemned for all the days of his
life' " [9]). Thus the ring, which earlier was identified with matrimony,
also represents the larger concept of Original Sin, our fatal heritage
from the first man, the first exile.[6]

The narrator is condemned to what at first is clearly the Tower of
Babel with confusion of tongues: "Apenas me coloqué en una de sus
calles cuando me mareó el juicio un mar de voces cuyas oleadas,
compuestas de lenguas diferentes, eran bastantes a derribar de su asiento
todo el cuerpo de la naturaleza" ("Scarcely had I entered one of its
streets when my senses were dizzied by a sea of voices whose waves
composed of different languages, were enough to shake all of nature
from its foundation" [9]). As it so often happens in Enríquez Gómez's
works, combined with the broader application of the story of Babel
and man's impertinence is the author's personal experience. The story
of the Tower of Babel must have seemed quite immediate to Enríquez
Gómez as, with a sensation of confusion and alienation, he entered
various foreign cities in his exile years. The incomprehensible chatter of
the people in the streets would have been disheartening to an author
so involved in the artistic nuances of his native language.

The choice of Babylon instead of Babel for the setting represents the
fusion of the legendary tower with the ancient city of Babylon. Babylon,

famous for its vices and the seductive nature of its luxuries, had long been a symbol of corruption's attractiveness—the city of the sensual and ephemeral delights that serves to distract man from the purity and spirituality of heaven, the city of God. For the author, the city of Babylon and the Tower of Babel merge into the image of earthly existence wherein man is condemned to dwell: "Que la gran Babilonia no acabará en cuando hubiere mundo, ni aún pienso que el mundo acabará en cuanto hubiere Babilonia" ("For great Babylon will exist as long as there is this world and I even think that the world will not cease as long as there is Babylon" [8]). The wandering narrator, forced into this chaos, is Adam, the Wandering Jew, and the *converso* writer himself, who, like so many of his race, roamed the earth. The Tower of Babel *cum* Babylon also suggests the famous Babylonian captivity when the Jews were enslaved and expelled from their land. The biblical lamentations for the lost Zion have struck a responsive chord in many an exiled writer and were a natural motif for Enríquez Gómez, who longed to return to Spain despite the discrimination and persecution he suffered there.

Birth and Rebirth

Because of the stigma attached to *conversos* by their birth we note in Enríquez Gómez an obsession with the topic of birth, a topic that is returned to again and again in this and other compositions, especially, as we have seen, in *The Pythagorean Century*. The biological and physiological process of reproduction are present in *The Tower of Babylon* in various representations of the undignified process by which we are engendered and the suffering attendant on our arrival into this world. Chapter 14 addresses these points quite clearly:

Pues ¿qué diré cuando la madre se queja por echar fuera lo que concibió, no reparando en qué entró con gusto ha de salir sin él? (Quisiera ella no pagar lo que comió.) Pues ¿qué diré cuando la señora criatura se le atraviesa en la garganta del medio día? . . . Consideremos luego la comadre pidiendo pujos y los circunstantes admirados, como si ellos hubieran venido por más limpio camino. Unos diciendo "ya sale," otros "ya viene," y la criatura diciendo con el silencio "nones."

What shall I say when the mother labors to push out that which she conceived, not realizing that what entered pleasurably has to exit painfully?

How she would like not to have to pay for what she took in! What shall
I say when the little one gets stuck in the nether neck? . . . Let us consider
the midwife demanding pushes and the onlookers astonished as if they arrived
by a cleaner road. Some saying "here it comes," others "now it's arriving,"
and the little one saying by its silence "nay."

(243)[7]

Again in the visit to the anatomy class in chapter 13 the narrator sees
the dissection of a woman's womb and hears the following morbid
commentary defining birth in terms of pain and suffering, a passage
from a blissfully unconscious state to miserable earthly life related to
the Fall from Grace: "Este agujero estrecho y rugoso tiene cinco venas,
las cuales se rompen cuando la mujer quiere ser mátir y no virgen.
Este es el puente por donde pasa el género humano. 'Ese es el diablo,'
replicó otro . . . 'ninguno lo pasó que no cayese de puente abajo' "
("This narrow and wrinkled opening has five veins which are broken
when the woman wishes to be a martyr and not a virgin. This is the
bridge through which passes the human gender. 'This is the devil,'
replied another . . . 'no one passes it without falling head first from
the bridge' " [220]).

Enríquez Gómez's constant reminders of the pain and sordidness of
birth leads on to chapter 14 where the innocence of childhood and
adolescence provide our only periods of happiness. But this ephemeral
state unfortunately passes like a dream as adulthood brings responsibilities, failures, and sickness in a constant struggle against opposing
forces. All the negative elements in life that cause pain and suffering
for Enríquez Gómez were particularly identified with the burden of the
Jewish blood of his paternal line. This accident of birth that led to his
victimization was difficult for him to fathom—"¿y qué desméritos puede
tener el que no tuvo voto en su nacimiento?" ("and what demerits can
there be for him who had no vote in his birth?" [259]).[8] His meditations
on the injustices of life comprise the greater part of the last chapter,
the debate between the two philosophers.

Since in reality the *converso* stigma could not be overcome, forgotten,
or escaped, Enríquez Gómez often invented situations that returned the
protagonist to the womb. His subconscious rejection of the *converso* lot
and his desire for a better life could be expressed fictionally by being
born again in a sort of what-if fantasy.[9] This topic had been elaborated
several years earlier in *The Pythagorean Century*, in which a soul
transmigrates from body to body in a vain search for a better existence.

In *The Tower of Babylon* the rebirth device opens the three main sections of the work: first, with the Adam-like narrator who awakens in the Eden-like palace without knowledge of a prior life; second, in the tale of the marquis who compares his release from the bottle with the act of being born only better, for he goes on to express his relief at having a glass mother instead of a real one—"Gracias a Dios que me libró de barriga de mujer" ("Thanks be to God who relieved me from a woman's belly" [173]); and, third, the life history recounted by the philosopher Democritus in the last chapter, beginning with the unpleasant description of birth already cited.

Along with the wish for a new start there is always the sad realization that to be born or reborn into this world makes little difference because of the fundamental evilness of mortal man. The marquis compares his new life to the past and chides himself for expecting anything better: "¿Por qué vienes a un siglo tan caduco? . . . ¿Imaginaste hallar el mundo en el estado que lo dejaste? Pues vienes muy engañado" ("Why do you come into a century that is so played out? . . . Did you think to find the world in the state you left it? If so, you are very mistaken" [174]).

Heraclitus and Democritus

The fantasies of rebirth are failures, just as Enríquez Gómez's youthful illusions fail with his maturity. Given the harsh realities of this life documented in the pages of *The Tower of Babylon,* the question becomes whether man's course is to cry in frustration or laugh at the ridiculousness of it all. *The Tower of Babylon* concludes in chapter 14 with a debate between Heraclitus and Democritus that, as before in *The Moral Academies,* offers a summary of Enríquez Gómez's view of the world. In the choice between tears and laughter we are confronted with equally pessimistic outlooks, both philosophers agreeing as to the essential miserableness of human existence. The fundamental difference is that the weeper despairs of this world, whereas the laughing philosopher recognizes that virtue can exist here, but it is born of suffering, persecution, and degradation. In a topsy-turvy world money and power are always victorious. The final ironic joke is that those who claim to possess honor and virtue are frauds, while the humble and downtrodden, commonly thought not to have these qualities, are actually the virtuous ones.

The laughter versus tears argument leads the author to the comparison of life and theater made by many writers: "Siendo tu vida fábula con voz, farsa con alma, y comedia con tragedia" ("Your life being plot with a voice, a farce with soul, and comedy with tragedy" [241]). Just as we would laugh at the idiocies of a staged farce and cry at the outcome of a tragedy, the lengthy characterization of man's life which Democritus relates in chapter 14 shows that comedy and pathos are a characteristic of our existence. The starry-eyed youth is duped into marrying a maiden who turns into a nagging, capricious harridan; well-beloved children grow into wastrels impatiently awaiting their parents' demise and the chance to squander their inheritance; scholars are forced to toady to the ignorant rich, and so forth. The suffering of the poor are obvious, but even for the wealthy and the powerful history shows that the possibility of ruin and disgrace is ever menacing. As nothing is secure in this world, our only hope of preserving sanity is to laugh, though laughter may be tinged with bitterness and tears. The reason for all this suffering that ends only with death eludes Heraclitus: "¿Para qué concedieron los cielos vida al hombre; siendo la vida jeroglífico de la muerte, y siendo la muerte tiranía de la vida?" ("For what reason did the heavens concede life to man; life being the hieroglyph of death, and death the tyranny of life?" [240]). The author's reply through Democritus is that it is all a grand mystery that we cannot comprehend, but the essential point is to maintain faith in God's love:

Si Dios ordenó con su inmensa sabiduría este gran mundo, y crió al hombre para que lo gozase, ¿por qué lloras con rigor lo que Dios crió con amor? ¿Quejaste porque te dieron una vida llena de miserias sujeta a la muerte? Pues ¿qué querías, vivir eternamente, engendrando cien mil hombres y trescientas mil mujeres? Pues, dime, ¿dónde había mundo para tanta gente, o gente para tanto mundo?

If God in his immense wisdom ordered this great world and created man to enjoy it, why do you weep rigorously for what God created lovingly? Do you weep because you were given a life of miseries subject to death? Well, what do you want, to live eternally, engendering one hundred thousand men and three hundred thousand women? Tell me, where there would be world for so many people, or people for so much world?"

(242)

One thing is clear: to avoid death means a worse penalty, that of suffering eternally the miseries of human life. (In passing we note that

Enríquez Gómez could not resist a last antifeminine comment by compounding the difficulties of eternal life with three times as many women as men.)

The Tower of Babylon and "The Marquis of the Bottle"

The fourteen chapters of *The Tower of Babylon* provide a framework for a composition that was perhaps intended to be the author's final statement on contemporary society. The principal organic divisions of the satire are symmetrically distributed: (1) the introduction—the vision of Eden contained in chapter 1 that outlines what was to be and man's subsequent destruction of paradise; (2) the body—chapters 2–13 detailing the opposite state, symbolized by the city of Babylon, the consequence of man's disobedience; and (3) the summation—the message of hope that is presented by Democritus in chapter 14.

As we have seen, *The Tower of Babylon* develops a message from two perspectives—personal and universal. There are more than enough statements throughout the work to be certain that the author based the satire on the experiences and circumstances of his own life. At the same time, these experiences have largely been depersonalized and universalized through the use of biblical myth (the Creation, Noah's Ark, Babel, and Babylon) and Greco-Roman images (Pecunia, Democritus, Heroclitus) in order to relate the work to the entire history of man.

The tale of the Marquis of the Bottle constitutes a quasi-independent unit of *The Tower of Babylon*. The marquis's story, recounted to pass the boredom of a journey, is interpolated into the larger work after the excursion to Noah's Ark in chapter 11. The inclusion of this story and its content, the roguish adventures of a young man in Madrid, follows a pattern established previously by Enríquez Gómez's *The Life of Don Gregorio Guadaña,* inset into *The Pythagorean Century* (see chapter 5). In spite of its obvious autonomy, the integration of the marquis's story in *The Tower of Babylon* is accomplished with a good deal more artistry than Don Gregorio's in *The Pythagorean Century.* It is joined to the parent work in a more logical and natural manner. There is no abrupt shift from verse to prose and the figure of Don Marcos, the marquis, remains a character in later chapters. The final episodes of the marquis's story, recounting the visit to the courtesan and then to the false saint, do bring it back in line with the satirical structure and tone of the larger composition, *The Tower of Babylon.*

One obvious purpose of the inclusion of the marquis's tale is to provide comic relief from the heavily pessimistic satire of *The Tower of Babylon.* But there are some unusual features of the story indicating that Enríquez Gómez was also communicating in a veiled way an important event in his life. One clue to the autobiographical element is Enríquez Gómez's use of the journey motif between specific geographical locations. Five years previously the author had used this same technique in *The Life of Don Gregorio Guadaña* to recount Don Gregorio's travels from Seville to Madrid. This story was no doubt loosely based on Enríquez Gómez's own youthful experiences dating from the time he left his apprenticeship with his uncle's business to strike out on his own in Madrid, circa 1624. The travels of the marquis appear to be a sequel to those of Don Gregorio, this time relating a journey to Madrid from the North, Enríquez Gómez's route during his clandestine return to Spain in the late 1640s. A clear indication that Enríquez Gómez speaks through his character is the manner in which Don Marcos comments on his years in limbo and his amazement at the changes that have taken place in Madrid during the intervening years. Enríquez Gómez's choice of Quevedo's marquis was probably made for several reasons, but he must have been especially attracted by the aptness to his own situation of one of the marquis's speeches from Quevedo's *Vista de los chistes:* "Sábete—dijo—que mi nombre no fue del título que me da la ignorancia, aunque tuve muchos; solo te digo que escribí muchos libros, y los míos quemaron, no sin dolor de los doctos" (" 'You should know,' he said, 'that my title was not that which is commonly given me, even though I had many titles. I can only say that I studied and wrote many books which were burned in spite of the objections of educated people' ").[10]

Also indicative of the autobiographical nature of the tale is the sudden change from the mythical setting of Eden, Babylon, and Noah's Ark in an indeterminate time frame to specific geographical places, and, most startling of all, the unique inclusion of a specific day, date, and year. The marquis reports: "Salí de ella [la redoma] un martes, veintiuno de julio, año de mil y seiscientos y cuarenta y siete" ("I left my bottle on a Tuesday, the twenty-first of July, in the year 1647" [173]). As with so many aspects of Enríquez Gómez's compositions, a message is obviously left in this bottle, but its decipherment is problematic. The most obvious interpretation of the statement is that Enríquez Gómez supplied the episode of the marquis's return to be inserted in *The Tower of Babylon* after he had returned to Spain to commemorate some facet of his release from the glass bottle of his own exile. (We will see in the following chapter that the last canto of his epic, *Samson the Nazarene,* was also sent to his French printer from Spain.) It is tempting to assume that in this way Enríquez Gómez has announced his return to his homeland. One problem, however, is the date 1647. Both Révah and Amiel, on the basis of solid evidence, report Enríquez Gómez's return as taking place two years later in 1649. An alternative explanation is given by C. H. Rose who has interpreted this obviously decisive date as that of the clandestine publication in France of Enríquez Gómez's *Angelic Politics,* which contains a strong attack on the Inquisition and which caused him problems with the authorities.[11] Until new information comes to light, the importance of 21 July 1647 will continue to be a subject of debate.

The Tower of Babylon and Quevedo

One of the most persistent criticisms of Enríquez Gómez has been that he merely imitated such better authors of his day as Calderón, Góngora, and particularly the famous satirist, Francisco de Quevedo. The connection with Quevedo is especially obvious in the case of *The Tower of Babylon.* It is true that Enríquez Gómez, like others, was impressed with the satiric dream format that Quevedo developed with such success. Enríquez Gómez himself notes this in his prologue—"Si les pareciere que he sido grandísimo soñador, doyles el consejo de D. Francisco de Quevedo: 'Tomen el sueño que gustaren' " ("If it seems to the reader that I have been a very great dreamer, I reply with the advice of Don Francisco de Quevedo: "Choose the dream that pleases you' "). Again, in the opening page of "The Marquis of the Bottle" (173) he acknowledges his debt by having Don Marcos state, "Yo, señores míos, después que el milagroso ingenio de D. Francisco de Quevedo me dejó en su redoma . . ." ("Sirs, after the miraculous ingenuity of Don Francisco de Quevedo left me in his bottle . . ."). In general Enríquez Gómez did not hesitate to borrow words and phrases from Quevedo as well as his folkloristic marquis. However, a comparison of Quevedo and Enríquez shows a strong contrast between the former's rapid and sketchy parade of satirical targets and the latter's more developed succession of theaterlike scenes in *The Tower of Babylon.* Another key point of contrast is the relative clarity of Quevedo's prose as opposed to Enríquez Gómez's ambiguity. Even though Quevedo's *Dreams* abound in puns and conceits, and even though the actual targets of his satires have not all been identified, there are few of Quevedo's passages whose general meaning is not decipherable. But the reverse is true in the case of Enríquez Gómez, whose work is very often so deliberately oblique that practically every page exudes the presence of cryptic messages and comments. Quevedo's hermeticism seems more a literary device, a verbal game, whereas that of Enríquez Gómez has a more personal intent typical of the atmosphere of secrecy with which many New Christians shrouded their lives.

In the end, Quevedo and Enríquez Gómez represent fundamentally different points of view, although as satirists and moralists they often coincide in their targets—doctors, lawyers, notaries, government officials, idle *hidalgos,* and so forth. But as representatives of two opposing social groups, their perspectives on the world could not be the same. In Enríquez Gómez's works we find the constant preoccupations of the New Christian, the merchant, the exile. Consequently almost everything is interpreted from the point of view of the religious persecution and the atmosphere of intolerance he felt. Quevedo's works, on the other hand, as the Old Christian aristocrat, are heavily influenced by his rabid anti-Semitism and xenophobia.[12]

General Observations

Already predisposed toward the satiric and the extravagant as seen in *The Pythagorean Century,* nothing suited Enríquez Gómez's muse better than the "dream" format of *The Tower of Babylon* permitting the author so much latitude. The wildest deformations of place, personages, and actions are possible, scenes can shift from one to another with little need of logical transitions, time can be compressed or extended, and the dream is a natural vehicle for the expression of symbols and portents. Likewise the author can alternate between verse and prose, between the comic and the serious, with perfect freedom.

Enríquez Gómez's delight in his own versatility is once again apparent in the wide variety of types of prose.[13] Chapters 1–2 begin with an allegory of the palace and gardens, the venerable, the jewel, and the evil lord. Later there is the Dantesque guided tour of Babylon with its chaos related in passages conveying the agitated press of the people in their frantic scramble for wealth and honors (chapters 6–7, "In the Temple of Pecunia," are the best examples). For fast-moving comic escapades involving situation comedy as well as verbal wit, there are the adventures of Don Marcos de Villena. Along with the elevated, the satiric, the moralistic, and the comic, as if to complete the gamut of prose, the pathetic is introduced in the final chapter in those passages detailing man's history of sufferings as expounded by Democritus and Heraclitus.

Very characteristic of *The Tower of Babylon* (and typical of Enríquez Gómez) is its theatricality. It seems as though he thought of the work's episodes as scenes of a play with lengthy descriptions of the settings detailing, for example, the architectural grandeur of the Temple of Pecunia of chapters 6–7, the fantastic and elegant palace of chapter 1, or the luxurious sensuality of the bedchamber of the sleeping courtesan in chapter 12. In addition, there is a fondness for spectacle and special effects that Enríquez Gómez himself calls *tramoyas* in the work, employing specifically the Spanish stage term for the dramatic illusions whereby people appear or disappear suddenly, mountains open, and other such impossible things occur. Again, the scenes in the Temple of Pecunia provide the best examples: in one instance the true God descends in a cloud to rebuke the devotees of Mammon; later, in a scene that recalls the elaborate plays staged in the Buen Retiro for the royal court, the nave of the temple is transformed first into "the entire ocean" (78) upon which pirates assault merchant ships, and then into a spacious and prosperous province that is despoiled by four hundred foreign soldiers.

As far as is known, *The Tower of Babylon* is Enríquez Gómez's last large-scale satirical work. Soon after, or perhaps during its composition, he returned secretly to Spain. The fact that *The Tower of Babylon* shows more care in construction and presentation, as compared to previous exile works, as well as its lengthy and cryptic prologue, indicates that Enríquez Gómez commemorates in this work the end of an important epoch of his life. In this composition his prose style reaches a level of maturity and elegance combined with originality of thought that places it among the best of his works. *The Tower of Babylon* is certainly worthy of greater attention than it has been given to date.

Chapter Seven
Samson the Nazarene

Sansón nazareno (Samson the Nazarene) is presumably the last work of Enríquez Gómez's French exile and the last that bears his true name.[1] Although the first and only known edition is that published in Rouen by Maurry in 1656, we know by the printer's statement appended to the prologue that thirteen of the fourteen books of the epic were printed in 1649, according to Révah the year of the author's secret return to Spain. It may be that the unfinished state of *Samson the Nazarene* indicates that his return was undertaken on the spur of the moment. At any rate, the last book dealing with Samson's ultimate release from captivity was supplied to the printer sometime prior to 1656. The dedicatory epistle is missing, either suppressed or lost in transit, but Maurry, the printer, indicates that he knew to whom the work was to be dedicated and that, as in the case of other Enríquez Gómez dedications, it was to a high ranking personage whose problems mirrored those of the poet: "El autor dedicaba este libro a un príncipe tan grande en el nacimiento y en el valor como en la desdicha que tiene de verse en desgracia de su rey" ("The author dedicated this book to a prince as great in birth and valor as he was in the misfortune to be out of favor with his king"). This prince could have been either Gaston d'Orléans or the Prince de Condé, both active participants in the Fronde, the French civil war that took place during the minority of Louis XIV. Since Condé at one point fought for the Spanish in Flanders, he seems the more likely candidate given Enríquez Gómez's penchant to seek a Spanish connection in his dedications. Oelman and A. J. Cid suggest that this involvement in French politics was one of the reasons Enríquez Gómez had to leave France.[2]

The Prologue: Reminiscences of Madrid

The prologue, which seems to have been written about 1649, is Enríquez Gómez's most lengthy and informative.[3] Its listing of his works follows the example of other authors of the day who felt constrained to catalog and publicly claim their compositions because of the unscrupulous practices of the printers.[4] In addition, it is also likely that the list was motivated by the realization that his literary career as Antonio Enríquez Gómez was soon to be terminated by the assumption of an alias for reentry into Spain.

Enríquez Gómez's nostalgic reminiscences of the artistic milieu of the Madrid of his younger days is set against an understandable note of bitterness at his lack of recognition and at the realization of the ephemeral nature of human existence. We sense this author's particular need to gain some measure of immortality through art, especially as life and fortune had not dealt kindly with him. The very first sentence, with its reference to the lost verses of the "Prince of Wisdom" (Solomon), expresses every artist's nightmare, namely, that time will destroy the work as well as the man: "El príncipe de la sabiduría escribió cinco mil versos: y había en ellos tanto que decir por los misterios que ocultaban que pudieron pasar por cinco mil poemas. Careció el mundo de este tesoro por la continua revolución del siglo" ("The Prince of Wisdom wrote five thousand verses: and there was in them so much that for the mysteries they concealed they could pass for five thousand individual poems. The world lost this treasure because of the continuous uproar of the centuries"). The detailed account of Enríquez Gómez's works to date included in the volume of what he obviously considered his crowning literary achievement was to serve as a testimonial to his accomplishments. (The works he claimed are noted in chapter 2 and the bibliography.)

The prologue also expounds Enríquez Gómez's view on epic poetry (which he refers to as heroic poetry). Of the five representative works that he rates as masterpieces, four offer no surprise—those of Homer, Vergil, Tasso, Camões. But for the representative Spanish epic he picks the poem of a fellow *converso*, Miguel de Silveyra's *Maccabean* (Naples, 1638), and expends considerable words of praise on the author of this forgotten work: "Ha sido el más vehemente espíritu que cantó acción heroica por tan levantado estilo" ("His has been the most impassioned spirit to sing heroic deeds with so lofty a style"). This unbounded regard for Silveyra is natural considering Enríquez Gómez's circumstances.[5] For the self-taught writer, the learned Doctor Silveyra, who moved in the highest social circles, was a very admirable figure, an example of the heights to which a *converso* might aspire. Likewise, Silveyra's flight to Italy to escape the Inquisition represented an event with which Enríquez Gómez could certainly sympathize.[6] In addition, Silveyra was a leading practitioner of the baroque style that Enríquez

Gómez found so admirable, and the subject of his epic, the deliverance of Israel by the Maccabees, is very much in consonance with Enríquez Gómez's interpretation of the story of Samson.

Enríquez Gómez includes in the prologue his list of great authors, classical and contemporary. The list of non-Peninsular greats includes seven classical writers—Horace, Persius, Juvenal, Plautus, Terence, Pomponious, and Enius; five Italians—Ariosto, Petrarch, Guarino, Dante, and Marino; and four French—the brothers Corneille, Brébeuf (Georges de), and duBartas (Guillaume de Salluste). His choice of Spanish authors includes Boscán, Herrera, Luis de León, Góngora, the Argensolas, Antonio de Mendoza, Manuel de Faria y Sosa, and Diego de Mendoza. This roster is followed by another concentrating on the famous Spanish dramatists of his earlier days in Madrid (previously reproduced in chapter 2).[7]

Also in the prologue are indications of works he had planned to include: a collection of Doctor Silveyra's writings, a second part of *The Tower of Babylon,* what sounds like the titles of two plays (*Amán and Mardocheo,* and *El caballero del milagro*),[8] another heroic poem entitled *Joshua,* and a work referred to as "los triunfos inmortales en rimas" ("immortal triumphs in rhyme"). The latter work is announced as "el que más presto daré a la estampa" ("the next to be given to the printer"). As far as is known, none of these works were completed or published.

From the listing of his own numerous works, together with the references to those in progress and those planned, and from his comments on literature in general, we note two pervasive elements in the prologue— his pride in his own achievement and in his artistic versatility, and his total dedication to the writer's craft. Enríquez Gómez's reverence for literature shines throughout this prologue and reveals the autodidact's veneration of a profession of which he strived so much to be a part. For him the act of literary creation was akin to obeying a divine impulse, and every creation merited attention: "No me acuerdo de haber leído libro malo, uno mejor que otro, sí" ("I do not recall having read a bad book, some better than others, yes, of course"). Because of the semidivine nature of the act of artistic creation, Enríquez Gómez feigns incomprehension at the horrendous bickering of the leading writers of the day. "La confianza de algunos ingenios gigantes los hace enanos: todo lo censuran, pareciéndoles que califican su juicio con decir mal. Lo cierto es que a pocos le parecen bien los hijos ajenos" ("The confidence of some giant wits makes them dwarfs: they censure everything, seeming to them that they exercise their intelligence by speaking ill of others. It is certainly true that very few of them appreciate works that are not their own"). From the number of times that Enríquez Gómez mentions his rivals *(émulos)* in this and other works, we may well suppose that he was speaking from sad experience.

Forerunners of *Samson the Nazarene*

For a writer as proud of his versatility as Enríquez Gómez the enormous prestige of the epic was an irresistible temptation and challenge. Although the majority of previous religious epics show a New Testament orientation, there were a few on Old Testament figures, the latter generally being the works of *converso* poets.[9] As it is not mentioned in the prologue, Enríquez Gómez seems not to have known Jacob Uziel's *David* (Venice, 1624), but, as we have seen, his enthusiasm for Silveyra's high-flown, style was imitated in *Samson the Nazarene,* although the two works have yet to be compared to see how much *Samson* owes to the *Maccabean.* In addition, in 1649 Diego Enríquez Basurto, Enríquez Gómez's son, also published an epic with his father's printer, Maurry, entitled *Triunfo de la virtud y paciencia de Job* (The triumph of virtue and the patience of Job). It seems logical to think that the father's epic aspirations influenced the son's and that Diego's choice of topic was inspired by his father's "Epistles of Job" included in *The Moral Academies of the Muses* (1642).

Another stylistic model of *Samson the Nazarene* is obviously Luis de Góngora's very influential poem *Fábula de Polifemo y Galatea* (Polyphemus and Galatea) (ca. 1613), which is singled out for praise in Enríquez Gómez's prologue. Aside from the obvious phraseology and vocabulary that influenced so many authors of the period, there is little to connect directly *Samson the Nazarene* with Góngora's work except perhaps for the scene in which Samson discovers Dalestina sleeping by the brook, a situation that seems modeled on Góngora's version of the meeting of Acis and Galatea.

Kirkconnell's catalog of the numerous literary versions of Samson and Delilah indicates the age-old fascination with the story and shows that, apart from the Bible, Enríquez Gómez's choice of the topic for his epic could have been influenced by at least two previous Spanish plays.[10] Of the two the more likely source of inspiration for Enríquez Gómez's poem is *El valiente nazareno* (The valiant Nazarene) of Juan Pérez de Montalbán (1638). *Samson's* prologue, with its praise of Pérez de Montalbán, points in this direction. It has already been noted that an Enríquez Gómez sonnet appears in Pérez de Montalbán's anthology, *Posthumous Fame* (1636). Further, we note that title of the Montalbán play is very close to that of a play of Enríquez Gómez (writing as Fernando de Zárate), *El valiente Campuzano* (The Valiant Campuzano). All in all, it seems certain that Enríquez Gómez knew the Pérez de Montalbán play and that it suggested at least the idea for *Samson the Nazarene*.

Kirkconnell also records another Spanish play about Samson by Francisco de Rojas Zorrilla.[11] According to Kirkconnell, the play was acted in Madrid in 1641 but is now lost and there is no indication of its exact title. Rojas Zorrilla is another playwright that is mentioned in the memoir-prologue to *Samson the Nazarene,* but the lack of information on this work obviously makes its influence an unknown quantity.

Synopsis of *Samson the Nazarene*

Samson the Nazarene is an elaboration of the biblical version (Judges 13–16) that adds details and scenes to flesh out the story and to conform to the epic format. The poem is narrated in 7,224 lines divided into fourteen books (cantos), each of which averages sixty-five stanzas. The meter throughout is the royal octave: eleven-syllable lines in stanzas of eight verses, rhyming *AB AB AB CC*. Each book is preceded by a fine engraving by Daquet *fils* that illustrates the action of the particular canto. The entire work naturally divides itself into three distinct sections as follows.

Books 1–5 deal with the story of Samson and the beautiful Philistine maiden who is unnamed in the Bible but here is called Dalestina. One afternoon Samson encounters Dalestina as she reposes beside a brook. He is smitten at once with her, and determines to marry her. Each set of parents is unhappy at the prospect of a marriage outside their religion but they reluctantly arrange the match. During the wedding feast, when the young Philistine men begin proposing riddles to entertain themselves, Samson presents his celebrated enigma concerning the lion he had killed previously and the swarm of bees that produced honey in the dead lion's mouth: "Yo penetré en el monte, y vi en el llano, / del bravo comedor salir comida, / y del fuerte dulzura conocida") ("I entered the forest and saw in the clearing from the fierce devourer come forth food, and from the strength acknowledged sweetness" [3.30]). The

Philistines, not able to solve the riddle and piqued by the arrogant attitude of the Jewish hero, determine to extort the answer from Dalestina by threatening the life of her parents. She finds out the answer and betrays Samson. Enraged, he retires to the wilds to ponder the situation. After a period of time, unable to forget his love for her, he returns to claim her only to find that his father-in-law, assuming Dalestina to be abandoned, has married her to another. Samson's wrath is not placated by the father's offer of Dalestina's sister. He revenges himself by burning the crops and vineyards of the Philistines, but the vengeance goes awry when an angry Philistine mob attacks Dalestina's house and she perishes in the flames.

The second part of the poem, books 6–10, recounts the military exploits of Samson as he leads the Hebrews in several victorious battles against the Philistine oppression. In book 7 an angel conducts Samson to a grotto where he is shown in a vision a parade of Hebrew immortals beginning with Abraham, passing through Samson's time, and concluding with those heroes yet to come. This section of the poem obeys the general tendency for an epic to have a prophetic component that relates the subject to the destiny of the nation. The visit to the underworld, also a feature of many epics, is incorporated into book 9 with its impressive infernal vision of the pagan temple of Dagon in a cavern near Gaza. In book 10 the desperate Philistines resort to a magic mirror to discover the manner of conquering Samson. An examination of the astrological signs reveals that all are favorable to the hero except for Venus. Acting on this information they attempt to capture Samson employing the courtesan of Gaza. This tactic fails as Samson fights his way through the city streets, then breaks down the city gates and carries them off.

The final and most celebrated portion of the Samson story in books 11–14 detail the meeting of Samson and Delilah, his betrayal and delivery into the hands of the enemy, his blinding and humiliation, and his eventual triumph as he brings down the pagan temple on himself and the Philistines.

Samson the Nazarene is structured around a series of interrelated opposites—man-woman, sight-blindness, secret-revelation, and daring-prudence—discussed in the following pages. These topics are found in greater or lesser degree of elaboration in many of the author's works and are indicative of the conflicts that preoccupied him throughout his life.

The Man-Woman Conflict

Samson's prodigious strength is a divine gift in conflict with the profane, carnal desires that pervert his mission as champion of his people. His uncontrollable desire for the forbidden fruit that are gentile women leads to the threefold transgression (Dalestina, the courtesan, and Delilah) that comprises his amorous career and which ultimately leads to his downfall, as he acknowledges in his palinode: "Tres veces con los ojos he pecado, / grave delito en hombre nazareno. / Tres mujeres sin fe me han engañado; / y tres veces cuarenta me condeno" ("Three times with my eyes have I sinned, a grave crime for a Nazarene [i.e., Nazirite]. Three faithless women played me false, and three times forty do I condemn myself" (14.44).

The antifeminine stance of *Samson the Nazarene* implicit in the biblical story is even strengthened in Enríquez Gómez's version by the omission of the positive figure of Samson's mother, so important in the scriptural text and in Jewish commentaries. Enríquez Gómez composes a progression of incidents in which the three women in the hero's life exhibit increasing grades of perfidiousness. Clearly in *Samson the Nazarene,* as in many of his other works, there is an unrelentingly negative presentation of women that applies not only to the three gentile women, but to all women.

Samson's first love is Dalestina. The attraction between her and Samson is genuine and tenderly related as benefits a first love. Of the three women in his life, Dalestina is the only one who really loves Samson. But in spite of the love that they clearly hold for one another, it is preordained that the match will have a tragic outcome because of the differences of religion and because of the inherent frailty of the feminine nature. Dalestina is "mujer al fin, cuya flaqueza, unida / a la fragilidad de sus antojos, / es sombra errante" ("in short, a woman whose weakness, joined to the caprices of her whims, makes her an errant shadow" [2.20]). The dramatic possibilities of Dalestina's dilemma as she is forced to choose between her husband and her people are explored in two fine speeches—one (3.52–64) in which she ponders her course of action when she is faced with the threats of the Philistine youths extorting the answer to Samson's riddle, and the other (5.41–51), her dying declaration to her people and to Samson.

The second woman to figure in the epic is the nameless courtesan of Gaza. She is paid by the Philistines to entice Samson into her chamber and distract him by lovemaking while the enemy soldiers surround the house. The short episode with the prostitute is only a prelude to Samson's final involvement with Delilah, but it develops the progressive weakening of Samson's ability to resist the temptations of carnal desire, and also darkens the perception of feminine character by removing any motivation by love. Consequently, the potential for disaster is increased. To the already perceived frailty and capriciousness of women, the courtesan adds another dangerous element, that of greed. Unfortunately, even as the dangerous enmity between Samson and the Philistines deepens, Samson's confidence in his own ability to overcome his adversaries increases. At the same time that Samson's self-confidence increases, so also does the resolve of the Philistines to put an end to him by any means. Samson's sarcastic taunts as he places the gates of Gaza on Mount Hebron are too galling for his enemies to swallow without fighting back:

> Subid, subid al templo esclarecido
> si la venganza vuestro pecho inflama.
> No suspendáis el paso, ni el oído.
> Subid al capitolio de la fama;
> bajaréis [a] esta lóbrega caverna
> a sumergiros en la noche eterna.

Climb up, climb up to the noble temple if to vengeance your breasts are aflamed! Stop not your course nor your hearing! Climb up to the acropolis of fame; for you will be hurled down to the lugubrious cavern to be submerged in eternal night!

(10.63)

The description of Samson's first glimpses of Dalestina by the brook and of Delilah bathing in a stream illustrate the author's careful development of Samson's amorous career. At both meetings a water scene serves to contrast the two women, Dalestina the innocent first love and Delilah the ultimate temptress. Samson himself is sensitive to the difference: "Una dormida en cándidas arenas, / y otra despierta en líquidos raudales" ("One asleep on snowy sands and the other awake in the turbulent stream" [11.11]). Both are forbidden women; each dangerous in a different way. The more chaste presentation of Dalestina is set against the intense eroticism of Delilah in her bath. "La vista penetró con sus pinceles, / en los pechos, cercados de alelíes, / botones dos con picos carmesíes" ("His eyes painted the picture—on her breasts,

surrounded by gillyflowers, two buttons with scarlet tips" [11.13]).
Samson's sensual desires are further aroused by contact with Delilah's
all but nude body as he rescues her from drowning.

For Delilah there is no dilemma with regard to the betrayal of the
hero as there was for Dalestina. The fact that she owes her life to
Samson makes all the more heinous her eventual treachery. The equation
that sums up women is now complete: Dalestina contributed weakness,
the courtesan of Gaza added greed, and Delilah supplied the lust for
power (the promise of marriage with a Philistine prince). There is
additionally the perverse desire on Delilah's part to be the one to defeat
by beguilement the hero who cannot be bested by strength. The detailed
narration of Delilah's wiles to discover Samson's secret is one of Enríquez
Gómez's best elaborations of a woman's persuasive powers, a topic that
seems an obsession with him.[12] Coyness, cajolery, feigned wrath, tears,
threats of suicide, protestations of love, and so forth, are the tactics
that Delilah, the consummate actress, employs to break down Samson's
guard and extract his secret.

The situation in *Samson the Nazarene*, in which the Hebrew hero
pays the ultimate price for his uncontrollable fascination with gentile
women, is only one of the several situations in which Enríquez Gómez
expresses a strongly misogynous attitude. We have seen this attitude in
several earlier published works—*The Tower of Babylon, First Pilgrim's
Guilt, The Pythagorean Century* and *Life of Don Gregoria Guadaña*. In
the last book of *Samson the Nazarene* Enríquez Gómez shows that
relationships, not just with gentile women, but with all women are
dangerous. Here the conflict between the sexes comes to its point of
maximum development as Samson identifies his fall with that of Adam.
Samson declares to Balonte, the Philistine prince:

> para rendir a Adán el enemigo
> no acometió su fuerza poderosa
> a escala vista. Dióle por castigo
> la hermosura primera de su esposa.
> Yo de esta suerte, cruel Balonte, digo
> (guiado de mi estrella rigurosa)
> que amor fue el árbol, yo el Adán prendado,
> tú la serpiente, y Dalida el pecado.

To subjugate Adam the Devil did not need to employ his great power in
obvious ways. He used the ultimate beauty of Adam's wife. I, in the same

manner, cruel Balonte, say, impelled by my unlucky star, that love was the tree, I the captive Adam, you the serpent, and Delilah was the sin.

(14.41)

Sight versus Blindness

Related to the man-woman conflict is the sight versus blindness opposition that is constantly in evidence throughout the verses of *Samson the Nazarene*. Most obvious are the poetic conceits of seemingly endless variations on the blind Cupid and the numerous astrological metaphors involving any number of light sources that wax and wane. The sight-blindness motif is worked into the poem in an exceptionally complex fashion. At first the opposition is expressed by conventional literary metaphors—the blind love god's darts strike the susceptible hero who is in turn blinded by love. However, as the story progresses the metaphor eventually becomes real when the Philistines deprive Samson of his sight. Blinded by love, Samson cannot see his obligation to the law of his people. The actual loss of vision comes to symbolize his blindness to understanding, knowledge, and observance of God's requirements. The sight loss is also manifest in the loss of Samson's hair, which, following ancient tradition, is presented as akin to the rays of the sun, the light that in turn stands for the strength that comes from obedience and fear of God.[13]

The process whereby spiritual blindness actually causes the loss of physical sense and then captivity and death—a central message of the work—is summed up in the final speech which Samson delivers to the assembled Philistines (14.35–52). This speech concerns the cycle of sinning, repentance, and restoration to God's favor. Recognition by Samson of his error has cleared his inner vision, the one that in the last resort is the most important. He says in his speech:

> ¡Mas ay! que me dirá la voz divina:
> "Llora Sansón y lava tu pecado,
> que el llanto es la corriente cristalina
> donde quede el delito perdonado."
>
> . . . .
> Ya sé que son los ojos una escala
> por donde sube el hombre al solio puro;
> que aquel humor que el corazón exala
> cristalino vapor taladra el muro:
> pero si este rocío se me tala

otro tengo en el alma más seguro;
que áquel pasó por caños visuales
y éste por arcaduces celestiales.

But oh! the divine voice will say to me, "Weep Samson and cleanse your
sin, for tears are the crystaline current by which the guilt may be pardoned."
. . . Well I know that the eyes are a staircase by which man ascends to
the pure dais; that the humor the heart emits, crystaline vapor, penetrates
the wall; but if they have removed this dew from me I have another more
sure in my soul; for the former passed through visual channels and the latter
through celestial conduits.

                                                                    (14.45–46).

Secret and Revelation of Secret

Inextricably entwined with the sight-blindness opposition is the theme
of secret and revelation. In Samson's disclosure of his secret and his
subsequent suffering and punishment we have a clear indication of the
author's desire to draw a parallel to the experiences of the *conversos*
and *marranos* in general and to himself in particular.

It does not require too close an examination to see that a *converso*
or *marrano* reading the epic could easily identify with a Judaic hero
moving in a hostile milieu, a hero whose superhuman strength was the
result of the divine favor of an ineffable God. The secret and divine
source of his strength is unmistakably an identification with the situation
of the crypto-Jew. In an incautious moment the secret is revealed to a
false friend (like the *malsín,* so ubiquitous in his earlier works), leading
to arrest and torture, to degradation and humiliation before a multitude
gathered in a religious rite that involves the immolation of the hero
(the auto-da-fé). The steadfastness of the martyr and his final act of
bringing down the pagan temple on the heads of his enemies is a
fantasy that every victim could appreciate. And it may be said that
every steadfast martyr's death does open at least symbolically a crack
in the edifice of persecution. This is certainly Enríquez Gómez's interpretation in his ballad on the death of the martyr Lope de Vera (see
chapter 8).

The appropriateness of *Samson* to Enríquez Gómez's times is obvious.
Without a doubt, one of his intentions was to present a parallel of the
biblical Hebrew situation under the forty-year domination of the Philistines with the *marrano-converso* persecution by seventeenth-century Old

Christians. On the personal plane, however, the exactness of the application of Enríquez Gómez's poem to his own life is difficult to ascertain. One can only note that he spent considerable time among the "Philistines," married one, considered himself betrayed at some point by an informer (possibly a woman), and returned incognito to the land of his enemies where he finished the climactic part of his poem and where he, no doubt, expected apprehension at every turn. Oelman, however, sees this epic and the "Romance al divín mártir Judá creyente" (see chapter 8) as two compositions reflecting personal religious crisis and that from pro-*converso* he becomes definitely crypto-Jewish.[14]

Daring versus Prudence

We cannot help but notice the author's ambivalent attitude toward the hero in several sections of the poem. Samson is the personification of daring to the point of rashness. He is all action, courage, and impetuosity. But in the biblical version, as in *Samson the Nazarene,* his hero status is tarnished by a bloodthirstiness and wantonness that seem more akin to vandalism than to justifiable warfare. These result in harm to his wife, to himself, and to his own people. At the other extreme, Enríquez Gómez also draws a rather ambiguous view of the deliberateness of Samson's coreligionists who, although brave in battle, are prone to consider at length the situation before acting. Sensibility, analysis, and caution characterize their thinking throughout the poem, as typified in this excerpt from his fellow Hebrews' response to one of Samson's fiery calls to arms:

> No es cordura, Sansón, precipitarse,
> cuando son nuestras fuerzas inferiores.
> . . . .
> Dejémoslos en vicios anegarse,
> y seremos entonces vencedores.
> . . . .
> Sin legítima causa, no conviene
> romper la paz al enemigo adusto.

It is not prudent, Samson, to be precipitate, when our own forces are inferior. . . . Let them by their own vices themselves annihilate and we then the

victors will be. . . . Without legitimate cause it is not wise to break the
peace with a hardy enemy.

(1.30–31)

Samson's thinking is the exact opposite of the legalistic and even rather
accommodating view of the Hebrew leaders. Yet the pragmatic Jewish
elders are respectfully presented by an author whose previous works
often expressed such a practical view concerning the functioning of the
state. Books 1–2 provide many lines to indicate that Enríquez Gómez
was philosophically in line with the cautious wisdom that the Hebrew
elders expressed, but that he, as well as they, were impressed and
delighted by the brio of the reckless Samson. Regardless of his faults,
in the youthful hero are wrapped up all the aspirations of an oppressed
people: "Todo el pueblo a una voz le señalaban / por ángel del sagrado
firmamento, / esperando que el joven sin segundo, / sujete a sí los
términos del mundo" ("All the people with one voice marked him for
an angel of the holy firmament, hoping that this peerless youth would
subjugate to himself the ends of the earth" [1.34]).

For all his defect, Enríquez Gómez's Samson is a hero whose deeds
bring glory to the Jews and reflect the author's sense of pride in origin
that is evidenced in the cavalcade of Jewish notables presented in book
7. *Samson the Nazarene*, like many of his other works, seeks to exalt
the richness of the *converso*'s ancestry rather than to deny or hide it.

Enríquez Gómez as an Epic Poet

The single edition of *Samson* indicates that it was not as popular as
his other works, but its oblivion was also the fate of the majority of
the later seventeenth-century epics. Whether *Samson the Nazarene* is a
good epic in large measure depends upon the predisposition of the
reader. In general, as with other epics of its day, it has been assessed
in a negative light. The problem is that for a good deal of seventeenth-
century Spanish literature, refinement and elegance were synonymous
with conceits, startling similes, a Latinized vocabulary and syntax, and
a liberal use of hyperbole. In this regard, Enríquez Gómez certainly
followed the pattern acceptable to his day and on occasion outdid
Góngora, according to some critics. Menéndez Pelayo, for example,
wrote that "the *Samson* and *The First Pilgrim's Guilt* were the most
perverse, extravagant, and hyperbolic poetry that one finds in the Castilian
language."[15] It is not surprising, then, that eighteenth-century neoclassic

critics regarded Enríquez Gómez's compositions as an abomination, examples of all that should be avoided in literature. For the modern reader, the sheer length of most epics and the monotonous regularity of their construction are almost insurmountable obstacles, but for the devotee of seventeenth-century literature *Samson the Nazarene* contains much more to praise than to censure.

Considering first the negative side, the most tedious aspect of the epic is overuse of certain "elegant" words and phrases so unrelentingly frequent that one wonders how the author failed to notice their repetition. Particularly annoying is the author's infatuation with the word *parasismo* ("paroxysm"), a word whose overuse dated from Enríquez Gómez's first plays. Almost invariably it appears rhymed with *mismo* and/or *abismo* ("the same," "the abyss"). Similarly, the old chestnut *fatigar selvas* or *montes* ("to ride long and hard") is overly evident, as well as the cliché-ridden identifications of female body parts with certain flowers— roses, jasmine, carnations, and orange blossoms, among others.

There is also a tendency to metaphoric repetitiveness, particularly those involving Mars and Venus and the astrological elements that symbolize the planets of these gods. This paucity of inventiveness becomes especially apparent in a poem of such extension. In fact, the grafting of so much Greco-Roman mythology on an Old Testament root seems a bit ludicrous, if not blasphemous. But for Enríquez Gómez, as well as for other poets of his day, the idea of an epic was so closely identified with the classical tradition that this mésalliance not only seemed natural but even required in his attempt of such a consecrated art form as the epic. Even so, Amador de los Ríos regarded Enríquez Gómez's mythological references as excessive by any standards.[16]

To sustain poetic beauty in each of the 7,200-plus lines of *Samson the Nazarene* would have been an impossible task for anyone. Thus it is that many times the verses lapse into the prosaic, particularly in the ennumerative sections such as the roll call of the Jewish heroes (book 7) and the battle deeds of the Hebrew and Philistine warriors (book 8). In addition, the love scenes tend toward the mechanical and trite, and the several passages of architectural description, although not without some interest, soon grow tiresomely hyperbolic in their effort to express grandeur.

Amador de los Ríos found the principal defect of *Samson the Nazarene* to be the lack of a truly epic intonation in all but the last canto.[17] Indeed, the apparent conflicts are of less than epic proportions since Samson's armed struggles with the Philistines, even though related in

heroic style, are certainly unequal contests in which the outcome is never
seriously in doubt. Failing an epic struggle between contending forces,
it might be expected that there would be an interior one—his sensual
inclinations battling the obligation imposed by his God-given strength.
But this is not the case either. Enríquez Gómez's hero is the man of
action and reaction who does not recognize his errors until the final
moment. With his independent and semioutcast existence, irascibility,
sensual nature, titanic strength, and ill-starred career, he seems to combine
aspects of the honor-bound hero of the seventeenth-century drama with
those of the nineteenth-century romantic hero. With some reason it
might be said that Enríquez Gómez's Samson, with his unthinking
approach to life and his enormous self-confidence, has more the makings
of a tragic hero than of an epic hero. But the epic nature of *Samson
the Nazarene* resides not so much in the person of Samson as in the
people he symbolizes. Samson's punishment for his failings is to fall
into the hands of his enemies. His fate mirrors that of the Hebrews
who have been castigated for their sins by the forty-year domination
of the Philistines: "Que reino que pecó tan libremente / ni fuerzas
tiene, mi socorros siente" ("For a kingdom that has so willfully sinned
has no force nor expects any rescue" [1.28]). The epic quality of *Samson*
may be read in the broadest sense, that of a nation struggling to observe
the commandments of a jealous God.

Whatever the defects of *Samson the Nazarene,* Enríquez Gómez
reworked a curiously enigmatic biblical episode to produce a credible
cycle of sinning, captivity, repentance, and redemption that not only
tells a good story but also is pertinent to the *converso* existence. Although
some artistic license is to be expected, in the main the biblical information
concerning the deeds of Samson remains as a skeleton to be fleshed
out by Enríquez Gómez's brush. The poet gave his characters personalities, motives, and feelings. Samson, Dalestina, and Delilah, as well
as other less central figures, become people instead of shadowy, sche-
maticized demigods of a primeval myth.

The best examples of the humanization process are the female figures,
always so strongly conceived by Enríquez Gómez. The contrasting roles
of Dalestina and Delilah are excellently delineated. Dalestina is innocent,
virginal, vulnerable, pathetic in her dilemma, and, at last, heroic in the
face of death. Although the character of Dalestina may be the more
complex, it is the fascinating Delilah that captures the attention and
imagination. The episode concerning Samson and Delilah, culminating
with the destruction of the pagan temple (books 11–14), displays the

poet's talent at its best. The lengthy process by which Delilah pries out Samson's secret is composed with great subtlety and theatricality, reminding us that Enríquez Gómez's abiding love was the stage. One of the author's greatest challenges was to make plausible the biblical version whereby Samson reveals his secret to a woman who has three times proved herself false. In this effort Enríquez Gómez excels, composing what is easily his most dramatically effective confrontation between a trusting man and the ultimate scheming woman.

The martial deeds of Samson are set down in energetic verses that capture the frenzied qualities of conflict—the rushing to and fro of the contending armies, the valiant efforts of the soldiers, and the uncertainties of the battle. Samson's speech to the Philistines from Mount Hebron (book 10) is a magnificent presentation of self-confidence that mingles boastfulness, scorn, and taunts. This is Samson at the apex of his career, secure in his divine favor, fearing nothing, triumphing single-handedly over his foes. The most impressive moment of the poem is his final speech delivered to the Philistines in the Temple of Dagon. Samson has passed from the zenith of his career to the nadir of degradation, yet his spirit is unbroken. This passage, which even Menéndez y Pelayo found praiseworthy, expresses the essence of the noble captive who, although physically humiliated, glories in the superiority that the knowledge of the true God permits.[18] His affirmation of faith, his acknowledgment of guilt, and his supplication for one last show of strength to redeem by his death himself and the people of Israel are presented in verses of great feeling:

> Dios de mis padres, dice, autor eterno,
> de los tres mundos soberanos atlante,
> incircumscripto, santo y abeterno;
> Dios de Abraham, tu verdadero amante;
> Dios de Isaac, cuyo altísimo gobierno
> en la divina ley vive triunfante;
> Dios de Jacob, de bendiciones lleno;
> oye a Sansón, escucha al nazareno.
>
> Unico criador incomprehensible,
> Señor de los ejércitos sagrado,
> brazo de las batallas invencible,
> por siglo de los siglos venerado,
> causa, sí, de las causas invisible,
> perfecto autor de todo lo criado;

pequé, Señor, pequé; yo me condeno;
misericordia pide el nazareno.

God of my fathers, he says, eternal author, Atlas of the three sovereign
worlds, infinite, holy, and eternal; God of Abraham, your true lover; God
of Isaac, whose most high rule lives triumphant in the divine law; God of
Jacob, who enjoys your blessing; hear Samson, listen to the Nazarene. Unique
and incomprehensible Creator, holy Lord of the armies, invincible arm of
the battles, venerated century after century, very cause of all causes, perfect
author of everything created; I sinned, Lord, I sinned; I denounce myself;
the Nazarene begs for mercy.

                                                          (14.58–59)

In sum, *Samson the Nazarene* is a sustained and well-conceived effort.
It shows a continuity and development of theme and imagery not always
so evident in Enríquez Gómez's previous large-scale compositions. In
this epic it appears that its author set out to produce a work of great
personal significance in the most accomplished style of which he was
capable because he knew that this poem would be the last he would
be able to acknowledge openly.

Marranism and *Samson the Nazarene*

The two extant literary works of Enríquez Gómez that most openly
suggest the author's Marranism are *Samson the Nazarene* and "The
Ballad to Judah the Believer" (see chapter 8). From the verses cited
above, obviously *Samson the Nazarene* contains many indications of the
author's Judaic inclinations, if not crypto-Judaism. One important indication is the total absence of any Christian figures specifically foretold
or prophesied. Likewise Marranistic are the continual references to the
one God, omitting any indication of his threefold nature as propounded
by Christianity, and the exclusive restriction of God to the Israelites.
Given Enríquez Gómez's personal involvement in his other exile works,
Samson's stirring final confession of faith to the God of Israel may
well be an expression of the author's own sentiments at the time. On
the basis of this work and "The Ballad to Judah the Believer" Oelman
has called attention to the author's " 'Jewish intentions' . . . the
manifestation of the 'will to Judaism.' "[19]

Yet Oelman admits that certain elements of *Samson* also bespeak the
influence of the Christianity with which Enríquez Gómez was even more

familiar than with Judaism. One curious aspect of *Samson the Nazarene*
is Enríquez Gómez's very choice of this figure as the subject of his
epic. The traditional Jewish interpretation of Samson is disdainful. Samson
is viewed as physically strong but morally weak, a person who breaks
his special covenant with God and thus wastes his talents and lets
down his people.[20] Enríquez Gómez's interpretation of Samson does
have some elements of the traditional Christian versions that tended to
read into the story a prefiguration of Christ.[21] In *Samson the Nazarene*
the redemptive lesson through a process of suffering and death is
specifically noted in several passages: "Baja Sansón de la soberbia cumbre,
/ y redime tu pueblo por que seas / en la pira del sol, divina lumbre"
("Come down, Samson, from the proud heights and redeem your people
so that you may be a divine flame in the sun's pyre" [8.33]); and
especially in his last speech, "Yo me ofrezco a la muerte porque sea
/ redimido mi pueblo en este día / de la dura potencia filistea" ("I
offer myself to death to redeem my people this day from the onerous
Philistine hegemony" [14.62]).

In spite of the strong indications of Marranism in *Samson the Nazarene,*
the whole of Enríquez Gómez's works reveal a religious ambiguity that
is fascinating and probably insoluble. At times it seems that he wishes
to disguise his Jewishness from the Catholics, but, on the other hand,
there are often indications that he was reluctant to totally commit
himself to Judaism. Enríquez Gómez clearly suffered confusion, drawn
as he was by compelling reasons to both religions. While throughout
the corpus of his works we can cite passages to indicate his crypto-
Jewishness and others to indicate his Christianity, we can also find those
reflecting indecision as to religious belief, as for example the words of
Dalestina as she ponders where her allegiance lies:

> De modo, en fin, que de cualquier suerte,
> ni espero vida, ni me falta muerte.
> Así deben de estar los que apetecen
> morir viviendo, no creyendo nada.
>
> . . . .
>
> En este mar, de confusión terrible,
> Choco con un escollo a cada paso.

So it is that whichever way I turn, I expect not life nor lack for death.
Thus it must be for those whose choice is the living death of not believing
anything. . . . In this sea of terrible confusion, with each step I founder
upon a reef. (3.57–59)

Chapter Eight
Various Works

From a literary standpoint, the few years that Enríquez Gómez spent in exile in France were very productive. During these years it is obvious from the number and scope of his compositions that he was ceaselessly at work, his mind teeming with subjects for his pen. Whereas previous chapters have been devoted to Enríquez Gómez's more lengthy works, this chapter considers in chronological fashion his compositions on a smaller scale: *El triunfo lusitano* (The Lusitanian triumph), *La culpa del primer peregrino* (The first pilgrim's guilt), *Luis dado de Dios* (Louis God-given), *La política angélica* (The angelic politics), and "Romance al divín mártir, Judá creyente" (Ballad to the divine martyr, Judah the Believer).[1] The discussion of these shorter works together in one chapter is not to suggest that they are all minor works. In fact, several, particularly *The Angelic Politics* and "The Ballad to Judah the Believer", have to be considered among his most important. Each work, in its way, illustrates a facet of the surprising literary ability of Antonio Enríquez Gómez.

Enríquez Gómez and the Portuguese Restoration

In 1580 Philip II of Spain was crowned king of Portugal after the quixotic King Sebastian died without succession in the battle of Alcazarquivir. For the next sixty years Portugal was loosely incorporated into the Spanish Empire through the joint monarchy of both countries. The historic enmity between the two nations, however, guaranteed the eventual restoration of a Portuguese monarch, which came suddenly in a *coup d'état* on 1 December 1640 that placed the duke of Braganza on the throne of John IV.[2] To legitimize his rule, the new Portuguese king sent an important mission to France seeking the support of the French in maintaining the nation's newly regained autonomy. The restoration of the Portuguese monarchy was actively supported by the numerous Portuguese *conversos* in France who hoped to gain reform of the Holy Office under the new king. Apparently Enríquez Gómez became involved in propagandizing the Portuguese cause through the efforts of his ill-fated friend, Manuel Fernándes de Villareal, the Portuguese consul in Paris, who was later to contribute the *apologia* to Enríquez Gómez's *Moral Academies.*[3]

The Lusitanian Triumph

The Lusitanian Triumph appeared in Paris and Lisbon in 1641, the first composition of Enríquez Gómez to be published during his exile.[4] Apart from its revealing Enríquez Gómez's activities at the time and its serving as an example of the propagandistic uses of seventeenth-century verse, the poem has little to recommend it now. Written in the heroic mode, in just over one thousand lines, the entire panoply of contemporary rhetoric is poured into verses that pile hyperbole upon hyperbole and cultism upon cultism: "Sea tu nombre heroica colocado / en el anal azul libro sagrado. / Don Juan, cuarto planta, has renacido / entre rayos y soles admitido" ("Let your heroic name be placed in the sacred annals of the heavens. Don Juan, the fourth planet, have you been reborn amid thunderbolts and suns" [224]).

Here, as in later extensive compositions, Enríquez Gómez's metrical choice is the *silva,* which allows a maximum of flexibility in terms of rhyme and rhythm. The work is divided into two parts. The first and shorter section is an introduction to the topic and a dedication to the three estates—nobility, clergy, citizenry—whose unified efforts in support of the king have gained the nation's independence from tyranny. The heroic nature of the Portuguese is noted in a brief mention of the nation's historic accomplishments and the first part closes praising John IV. The second and lengthier section is directed to the king and is, in effect, a poetic report detailing the activities of the diplomatic mission from the time they leave Lisbon to their arrival in Paris and subsequent receptions by King Louis XIII and Cardinal Richelieu.

The poet-painter device, so frequent in Enríquez Gómez's verse, forms the basis of this work—"pintaré su jornada" ("I will paint his journey" [228]). The poem devotes a number of lines to fulsome praise of the most important members of the diplomatic team and to the exquisite courtesies accorded them by the French in numerous receptions and banquets. The poem ends with the announcement of a pact among the French, Dutch, and Portuguese and the prophecy of a marvelous future for King John, whose gloriousness is attested to by a series of no less than twenty-one adjectives.

Artificial and propagandistic as it is, the poem does incorporate some elements that were serious concerns for Enríquez Gómez. The shaking

off of the tyrannical Castilian yoke, the liberation from captivity, is, of
course, a natural topic for an exiled poet for whom captivity had
personal significance. His references to Spain are quite condemnatory,
calling it the "tiranía del siglo ("the present day tyranny"), and *tiránicos
Babeles* ("tyrannical Babels"). Likewise the emphasis that is placed on
the wise counsel of the Portuguese representatives reflects the author's
continuing interest that those close to the throne should be of the
highest caliber. In this respect the poor example of Philip IV's advisors,
specifically the Count-Duke of Olivares, contrasts with that of the all-
powerful Cardinal Richelieu to whom Enríquez Gómez dedicates many
lines celebrating his intelligence, prudence, and dedication to the state—
"Aquel casi divino / príncipe del estado y de la ciencia, / aquella de
los cielos eminencia" ("That almost divine prince of statecraft and
science, that eminence of the heavens" [242]).[5]

The First Pilgrim's Guilt

Description and Synopsis.   The year 1644 saw the first appearance
of two of Enríquez Gómez's works, both printed by Laurent Maurry
in Rouen. *The Pythagorean Century,* the more extensive of the two,
proved to be the more popular as evidenced by its many later editions.
The other was *La culpa del primer peregino* (The first pilgrim's guilt),
which Enríquez Gómez later classified in his introduction to *Samson the
Nazarene* as his theological work. *The First Pilgrim's Guilt* was reprinted
only once almost a century later (1735) by the Spanish printer García
Infanzón, who had published earlier the fourth Spanish edition of
Enríquez Gómez's popular *Moral Academies of the Muses.* Despite the
fact that *The First Pilgrim's Guilt* had been overshadowed by the
lengthier and more sprightly *Pythagorean Century,* it does have considerable merit as a poetic work and incorporates many topics that became
characteristic of the author's works. Following the dedication and one-
page introduction is a lengthy poetic composition of one hundred thirty-
seven pages in its first edition.[6] The same variety that characterizes the
composition of *The Moral Academies* and *The Pythagorean Century*
appears in *Pilgrim,* which seems almost a compendium of poetic genres,
each determined by the flow of the central theme as it passes from
one modality to another. *Pilgrim* is divided into seven sections of varying
versification, ranging through the narrative, lyric, satiric, didactic, and
heroic. The metrical schemes include ballads, royal octaves, *décimas,*
and tercets knit together, as is usual, by *silvas.* The seven sections

comprise three well-defined divisions. The first division consists of the first two sections, "The Prosperous Fortune" and "The Adverse Fortune." The second contains the four "Dialogues between Divine Wisdom and Human Nature." The third is the final section of the work entitled "True Moral Philosophy."

The First Division. "The Prosperous Fortune" recounts in Gongoristic style the creation of Adam and Eve and their idyllic existence in the Garden of Eden. "The Adverse Fortune" begins with a powerfully drawn vision of Satan in Hell that contrasts effectively with the brightness of Eden of the previous section. "The Adverse Fortune" continues with the temptation, the disobedience, and the expulsion from the Garden. The second section does not end with the expulsion, but rather progresses into a lengthy moral satire in which the expelled Adam, now called the Pilgrim or Wanderer, is instructed by Father Time in the consequences of his disobedience.

Father Time begins by showing the Pilgrim in a mirror all the kinds of sinners typical of the satires of the period—the ambitious man, the proud man, the tyrant, the seducer, the hypocrite, and others.[7] There is also a seemingly endless list of the different civilizations that have flourished and died, followed in turn by a list of celebrated villains. Before he takes his leave, Father Time leads the Pilgrim on a tour to view firsthand the injustices that man's first sin introduced into the world. The device of the ingenuous youth instructed by a guide in the evils of the world was a favorite of Enríquez Gómez's. In previous chapters we have seen it employed in both his great satires, *The Pythagorean Century and Life of Don Gregorio Guadaña* and *The Tower of Babylon.*

The Second Division. Following "The Adverse Fortune" comes the most extensive portion of the work, the four dialogues that form the basis for Enríquez Gómez's classification of the work as theological. Each dialogue consists of the questions of mortal man as to the meaning and purpose of life, followed by the responses of Divine Wisdom. The several references to another writer of Judaic background, Leon Hebreo, points to his famous *Dialogues of Love* as a source of inspiration for this section.[8]

The pessimistic view of earthly existence shown to the Pilgrim in Father Time's mirror sets the tone for the questions that are put to Divine Wisdom. The first of these asks the purpose of being born, why is the immortal soul linked to a mortal body destined only to pain and death: "¿Qué vine yo a ganar del nacimiento? / sino un

pesar que nunca se ha gastado" ("What did I stand to gain from birth
except a sorrow that has never worn away?" [56]).⁹ The Wanderer also
has difficulty understanding the rationale for the fall from Grace. Since
the first man was scarcely equipped to struggle against so great an
adversary as Satan, why then did God not save him from this error if
he loved man: "Dime, ¡por qué razón es poderoso / el imperio diabólico
maldito?" ("Tell me, for what reason is the diabolic empire so powerful?"
[75]). Moreover, why is there a need for Satan at all? If God knows
all things past, present, and future, does not then man come into the
world predestined? Why does there have to be so much misery connected
with this life and so little reward for good? Conversely, he questions
the disproportion of punishment to the crime. Why is there eternal
suffering dealt out for finite sins: "Cien años de sacríligos pecados, /
¿cómo pueden tener eterna pena?" ("How can even a hundred years
of sacriligious sins merit eternal pain?" [104]). Other no less fundamental
questions ask what the soul is, what it is made of, what happens to
it after death, and, finally, what hope there is for man?

The replies of Divine Wisdom to the Pilgrim are founded upon
several points of Catholic dogma that are frequently elaborated in the
seventeenth-century Spanish literature so closely attuned to theological
speculation. Man's earthly misery is his lot due to the disobedience of
the first man. With our finite minds we cannot expect to fathom the
intentions of the Almighty, thus what we must do is have faith and
patience in the face of all adversity, live virtuously, and take advantage
of God's Grace with the certainty that God will determine just pun-
ishments and rewards in the next world. Thus, while man will never
cease being a wanderer, a seeker of peace and justice in a very imperfect
world, the "pilgrimage" is in effect a process of purification that can
lead to heaven—"hasta que al cielo / el espíritu vuelva acrisolado"
("until the spirit returns purified to heaven" [131]). As is the case in
many Calderonian works, the doctrine of free will is strongly affirmed.
Original Sin and free will are the two poles anchoring the responses of
Divine Wisdom.

The Third Section.   The four dialogues bring the reader to the
final section of the *Pilgrim,* the discourse of "Perfect Moral Philosophy,"
that offers the rules of conduct by which man can live virtuously. The
lengthy listing of correct and incorrect actions echo other enumerations
that Enríquez Gómez included in, for example, *The Pythagorean Century*
and in *The Tower of Babylon,* all of which can be summed up by one

line, "Aprueba la virtud, reprueba el vicio" ("Approve virtue, reprove vice" [136]).

An interesting feature of this work is its advice of a pragmatic nature that differentiates it from the aristocratic, Old Christian outlook embodied in the majority of the Spanish moralists of the period. As befits a man of the merchant class, there is a good deal of emphasis on the "work ethic": "Trabaja cuando mozo con consejo, / porque descanses cuando fueres viejo" ("Work when young with diligence, so that you may rest when old" [133]). There are also passages advising a practical response to danger that recall the language and antiheroic stance of many Spanish proverbs: "Cuando vieres un reino alborotado, / sal de Chaldea; acógete a sagrado. . . . Cuando tu corazón te dice huyamos, / en el camino le responde vamos" ("When you see a kingdom in turmoil, leave Chaldea, get you to safety. . . . When your heart says 'flee,' respond 'let's go' as you run down the road" [137]).

Along with this sort of practical approach to life, the moral philosophy contains here and there thoughts and warnings that are clearly the result of the author's experiences as a *converso*. Among other things, we are told: "No espíes no. . . . No descubras del prójimo el secreto" ("Don't spy. . . . Don't try to discover the secrets of your neighbor" [131]), and "A él que niega su sangre, no le nombres" ("He who denies his blood is not even to be mentioned" [137]). But for any *converso* the greatest menace was the Inquisition. Enríquez Gómez's lament on the unfortunate integration of the Holy Office and the state is uncharacteristically clear:

> Triunfar por tiranía
> es ruina de la propia monarquía.
> ¡Ay de los tribunales imperfectos!,
> adonde los delitos son secretos;
> salas donde se mira
> en espejo de sombra la mentira,
> y andan los vicios y maldades
> rebueltos en fingidas sanctidades.

To triumph by tyranny is the ruin of a monarchy. Beware the imperfect tribunals where the crimes are secret! Salons where one sees lies in the shadowy mirrors, and where roam vices and evils disguised with false sanctity.
(140–41)

These verses anticipate the detailed attack on the Inquisition that a few years later form the substance of the *Louis God-given* and particularly of *The Angelic Politics.*

The Creation—Adam and Eve. *Pilgrim* introduces in Enríquez Gómez's opus the topic of Adam and Eve that five years later was to be again employed by him in much the same fashion, although perhaps even more allegorically, as the starting point and basis of *The Tower of Babylon.*[10]

Although *Pilgrim* begins with what promises to be only a retelling of the story of Adam and Eve, once the expulsion from Eden is reached the figure of Adam takes on both a universal and personal dimension. The protagonist is now not Adam but the Pilgrim, the Wanderer, Everyman, whose experiences are the sum total of all the succeeding generations that are viewed in Father Time's mirror. As ever, lying just under the surface of this presentation of the Pilgrim is the personal story of the author himself. Enríquez Gómez draws attention to this identification in the very first line of his preface, "La culpa del primer hombre sale publicando las mías en este pequeño volumen" ("The first man's guilt comes out publicizing my own in this little volume"). The personal quotient is especially apparent in the four dialogues and in the final portion, the discourse of moral philosophy. *Pilgrim,* which like several others of his compositions seems at first reading a jumble of genres and verse forms, disjointed and episodic, shows a thematic progression centered about the first man's downfall. This primeval incident affects the whole of mankind and in particular determines the tribulations of one man, the author. The blending of the abstract and symbolic with the concrete and personal we have seen to be a feature of the writings of Enríquez Gómez, and especially of those works written during and after his exile.

Enríquez Gómez's interpretation of the biblical story fleshes out the personalities of Adam and Eve in line with the general view of the man-woman relationship that is elaborated throughout his works. Adam's character is that of a naive youth who aspires only to peace and the enjoyment of a harmonious life, but who, because of outside forces or poor choices, is made to suffer.

In opposition to the guileless Adam, the first woman is presented as very complex. She is grasping, self-centered, beguiling, shortsighted, curious, and ambitious. From the moment of her creation, amid all the praises of her surpassing beauty, there enter discordant notes that point to her guilt in the disaster to come: "y dulce de los hombres homicida,

/ pues primero mató que tuvo vida" ("And sweet homicide is she, for first she killed that which had life" [7]). At first she is deeply in love with Adam, and their love poems to each other are among the best that the poet wrote in any composition. The inspiration for these verses is clearly the Song of Songs attributed to King Solomon:

> Eve—Tu voz y tus requiebros
> castamente he escuchado,
> en tus dulces acentos
> halló mi amor descanso.
>   Como de selva en selva
> viene saltando el gamo,
> así a tu voz ha ido
> al corazón llegando.
>   De amor estoy enferma,
> y del alto collado
> de la gracia divina
> por ti voy preguntando.

Chastely have I listened to your voice and words of love; my love found repose in your sweet sounds. As the hart comes leaping through grove after grove, so too your voice has come to my heart. I am sick with love, and from divine grace's heights I search for you.

(15)

But Eve's jealousy is soon aroused by the fact that Adam's first attention is to God. She easily succumbs to Satan's blandishments and then uses all her arsenal of persuasive powers to convince Adam to join in the sin. In a scene that the author incorporates into many compositions, Eve tempts him with the God-like power he will supposedly attain, she professes her love, she threatens, and then, the final weapon: "Lloró, gimió, la cautelosa fiera, / y enternecióse el corazón de cera" ("She cried, she moaned, the calculating beast, and his heart of wax became soft" [29]). As is the case in so many of Enríquez Gómez's works, the man is no match for the woman who wants something.

   The Marranism of *Pilgrim?* The Pilgrim's doubts about Original Sin, Free Will, the need for Satan to exist, the existence of Purgatory, and other theological concerns create for him a state of confusion. He finds himself in a sort of no man's land that obviously mirrors the author's own dilemma:

Si rezo, soy hipócrita de estado;
si no rezo, me llaman ataísta,
y de cualquier suerte soy culpable.
. . . .
Si acuso al malo, dicen que me vengo;
si no lo acuso, cómplice me llaman,
y todos dicen que verdad no tengo.

If I pray, I am a great hypocrite; if I do not, they call me atheist; and so either way I am guilty. . . . If I accuse a wrongdoer, they claim I seek revenge; if I do not, an accomplice they call me; and everyone says I know not the truth.

(114)

The Pilgrim expresses confusion over the reason why God permits the existence of several religions if there is really only one true faith. There is concern as to how man with his limited intelligence, born into error, can select correctly—"El que nació de nacimiento ciego, / mal puede conocer varios colores" ("He who was born blind can scarcely distinguish various shades of color" [75]). Caught in this middle ground, it is no wonder that the Pilgrim despairs: "Aquí de Dios, quien vive de esta suerte" ("God help him who lives in this manner" [115]).

All these doubts are gradually settled by the discourses of Divine Wisdom in the four dialogues. And so it seems that these fundamental doctrines of Catholicism are accepted by the author. But this is a rather unique Christianity, expounded and supported in a Judaic envelope. Indeed, the Marranistic flavor of the work is particularly strong in its overwhelming reliance on the Old Testament. The poet's marginal reference to his sources that accompany the major poems do include citations to Christian writers—St. Augustine, St. Thomas Aquinas, Duns Scotus, St. Bonaventure, and St. Paul—but in a work that purports a Catholic orientation, the total lack of reference in the verses themselves to any Christian Saint, to the Virgin, to the Trinity, or to salvation through Jesus Christ is quite suspect. While the "Divine Moses" is mentioned, the essential Christian figures are never directly named or prophesied or even hinted at. Like the God of *Samson the Nazarene*, the ineffable deity that is presented throughout *Pilgrim* has a definite Judaic cast. Moreover, the numerous references to the *"one* true God" recall the Sephardic rejection of the Trinity and pantheon of Saints as idolatrous.

With all this, we might well question Enríquez Gómez's purpose in writing this work. Was this self-proclaimed "theology" an attempt to slyly pass off disguised Judaism and undermine Catholicism? Is this a work intended to tweak the church's nose? It seems hardly likely that the work would have passed the censors to be printed in France and Spain if this were the case. Some, no doubt, would find here merely another example of Enríquez Gómez's Marranistic casuistry.[11] However, lacking evidence to the contrary, *Pilgrim* has to be regarded as a sincere exposition of Enríquez Gómez's religious beliefs at the time. *Pilgrim* appears to attempt to integrate the two religions by implying the continuity of the two in the evolution of Christianity from its Judaic origins. The message to *conversos* and Old Christians alike appears to be that rather than rejecting and abhorring all things Hebraic as the inquisitional climate demanded, *conversos* could be Catholics and still be mindful of their ancient heritage. This line of thinking is later more fully developed in the Zárate religious plays (see chapter 9).

Louis God-given

The full title of this prose work is *Luis dado de Dios a Luis y Ana, Samuel dado de Dios a Elcana y Ana* (Louis God-given to Louis and Anne, Samuel God-given to Elkanah and Hannah). It exists in only one edition, that of René Baudry (Paris, 1645).

Here, as before, Enríquez Gómez looks to the Old Testament for parallels with contemporary history. In this case the birth in 1638 of a son to Louis XIII of France and Anne of Austria after twenty years of marriage is compared to the birth of Samuel as recounted in the chapters of 1 Samuel. The comparisons that Enríquez Gómez draws are, of course, very flattering to the French royal family. The author particularly devotes attention to his fellow Spaniard, Queen Anne, noting in her all the virtues of a modern day Hannah. The queen's role in the politics of the day was crucial because of the death of King Louis XIII in 1643. Because of his age Louis XIV did not assume full powers for sixteen years. During these years the queen mother and Cardinal Mazarin did their best to keep the country together in the face of domestic and foreign troubles. Enríquez Gómez's work propagandizes the regency of Anne, finding in her all the attributes of the ideal woman.[12] In particular, she is shown as embodying prudence, a feminine virtue that for Enríquez Gómez was all-encompassing as he shows in his earlier play, the *Prudent Abigail* (discussed in chapter 2).

The chief purpose of *Louis God-given* is to extrapolate lessons from
the biblical source to provide a handbook for the enlightenment of the
young king during the period of his minority. In that respect, besides
the portion of the work dedicated to establishing the analogy between
Samuel and Louis XIV, a major section consists of advice as to how
a king should govern. Of primary concern to Enríquez Gómez is the
selection of ministers who will aid the king in his government. The
corruption and decline of the Spanish monarchy, directed as it was by
incompetent royal favorites, no doubt was present in Enríquez Gómez's
mind as an example of what not to do.

Enríquez Gómez specifically recognizes that the nobility have by birth
a preeminent claim to honors and high offices, and that the monarch
has the right and even the obligation to look to the nobility for support
and service. But Enríquez Gómez also makes clear that the noble
birthright is not the only qualification for these honors; they must be
weighed against talent and virtue: "Señor, los reyes bien pueden, como
señores soberanos, repartir bienes, hazer mercedes y favorecer validos,
pero todos estos favores se deben fundar sobre la base de la razón"
("Sire, as lords and sovereigns, kings are well within their rights to
distribute goods and honors and favor their advisers, but all these honors
ought to be based on reason" [88].[13]

An even more important lesson, again based on the Spanish experience,
is contained in the advice concerning the relationship between state and
church. The biblical lesson that Enríquez Gómez finds to illustrate the
potential for evil in this marriage of the secular and the religious is
that of King Saul's persecution of David. Enríquez Gómez discourses
at length on the crimes committed in the name of religion, taking as
his text Saul's murder of Ahimelech and the other priests for harboring
the fugitive David (1 Samuel 22). In this work and others the Old
Testament Saul is a prefiguration of the persecuting officials of the
Inquisition and his attack on the Holy Office is uncharacteristically
transparent:

> ¿De qué sirve celar la fe para matar al
> inocente? No se contentan estos Saúles con
> afrenta, quieren sangre, devorando como
> lobos crueles las ovejas inocentes.
> Aconsejan a los reyes que salgan a ver en
> públicos teatros lastimosas tragedias.
> Lloran ruinas y foméntanlas. Pésales el

daño y execútanlo. Y últimamente, quieren
que pase plaza de piedad la tiranía.

What has preserving the faith to do with the killing of innocent people?
These Sauls are not content with humiliation, they want blood, devouring
like cruel wolves the innocent sheep. They advise kings to appear in public
spectacles to see shameful tragedies. They deplore ruination, but they foment
it. They are so sorry for the suffering, but they carry it out. Ultimately, they
want tyranny to pass for piety.

(57–58)

Obviously these ministers, these Sauls, are the officials of the Inquisition.[14]
Through their immense power they have perverted religion and even
manipulated the king who, by attending the autos-da-fé gives official
sanction to these bloody displays. Enríquez Gómez hoped that the tragic
lesson of Spain would serve to forestall the spread of religious intolerance
to France. The criticism of the Inquisition in *Louis God-given* is later
developed in much more detail in Enríquez Gómez's *Angelic Politics*.

In spite of its intensity of feeling, its ingenious analogies, and the
elegance of its prose, *Louis God-given* is one of Enríquez Gómez's less
readable works today because of its unrelenting didacticism. The very
form of the work is indicative of its sermonlike content as each division
begins with a text from 1 Samuel. The text is then commented upon,
compared with other authorities, and applied to the French political
situation of the 1640s. As in the case of *The First Pilgrim's Guilt,* the
work is given a scholarly appearance by the many citations that fill its
margins. The sources are generally Old Testament, but here and there
we find New Testament references, citations from St. Augustine's *City
of God* and rare occasional mention of Christ, as if to acknowledge at
least perfunctorily the official Catholicism of the French monarchy.

The Angelic Politics

Background. The mismanagement and malfeasance of the royal
ministers and the corruption of the Spanish governmental system became
a common seventeenth-century topic, especially as the economic and
political failures of Spain became more and more apparent. Numerous
authors of the day discussed the problems facing the state and offered
solutions in treatises on government. One of the most famous was
Quevedo's *La política de Dios y gobierno de Cristo* (God's politics and

Christ's government, 1626).[15] Quevedo's example invited others, for example, that of Enríquez Gómez's friend and political mentor, Fernándes de Villareal, *El político cristianísimo* (The most christian politics, 1642). No doubt both these works suggested the form and title of Enríquez Gómez's *Política angélica* (Angelic politics) which appeared in 1647.

Contents. The complicated printing history of the two parts of *The Angelic Politics,* an analysis of the work, and a reprinting of the second part have been included in the lengthy and oft-cited article of the late I. S. Révah that also revised Enríquez Gómez's biography.[16] The second part of *The Angelic Politics* is so rare that its existence was unknown until Révah's investigations into the matter.

The first part of *Politics* is a treatise on governance in dialogue form, the classic question and answer format that Enríquez Gómez used in *First Pilgrim's Guilt* and in the dialogues of Heraclitus and Democritus in *The Tower of Babylon* and other works. *The Angelic Politics* concentrates on what should be the harmonious workings of a state in which all the various functions from king down are performed by diligent and dedicated people. The "angelic" portion of the title is suggested by titles of previous *políticos* and reflects the author's statement that the Christian nation should be founded on Christian principles, the very type of government that the king's favorite rejected so disdainfully in *The Pythagorean Century.* Enríquez Gómez's brief prologue sets forth his plan: "Desando con piadoso celo dar un medio sobre el gobierno riguroso que se ejecuta en algunos reinos sobre los delitos de religión, di a luz estos dos *Diálogos* con título de *Política angélica,* valiéndome de la doctrina de Cristo y de sus Apóstoles, de los sacros concilios, y de todos los doctores sagrados que trataron esta materia" ("Desiring with pious zeal to give a counter plan to the rigorous treatment of religious crimes carried out in some kingdoms, I brought to light these two *Dialogues* with the title of *Angelic Politics,* basing myself on Christ's doctrine, that of the Apostles, the sacred councils, and all the sacred doctors that concern themselves with this matter" [115]).

Naturally a state based on true Christian doctrine would be a just, and therefore tolerant, one. The presentation of the ideal of tolerance and justice allows the introduction of fairly subtly presented topics that Révah identifies as Marranistic preoccupations. Above all, *The Angelic Politics* criticizes the national policy that foments religious prejudice in every way. The practice of demanding affidavits of blood purity *(limpiezas)* for eligibility for honors, according to Enríquez Gómez, has the effect of discriminating against numbers of people for reasons that cannot be upheld by Christian teachings. A state that calls itself Christian and practices this type of injustice is immoral and can come to no good end.

Second Part. The path of very oblique criticism of the Inquisition made in the first part of the *Politics* is discarded in the second, which not only exposes the injustices of the Inquisition, but also has the temerity to offer a plan to correct its blatant abuses. The existence of the second part in only one extant copy is due to the fact that the Portuguese ambassador, being advised of the open attack on the Inquisition in the original work combining both parts, obtained an order from the French government to suppress the work as libelous to the Portuguese Inquisition. Curiously the person instrumental in bringing the work to the ambassador's attention was Enríquez Gómez's old friend, Fernándes de Villareal. Although the order from the French crown authorized the destruction of the original manuscript and all copies, the ambassador was not too thorough, and Enríquez Gómez evidently was able to have some copies printed of the work separated in two versions—one edition containing what Révah terms the "relatively anodyne" dialogues of the composition, and another incorporating the violently anti-inquisitional dialogues (numbers 3–4). The "safe" edition is dedicated to Jean Louis Faucon, president of the Parliament of Normandy, while the "subversive" text is defiantly directed to "All the Christian Princes, Pillars of the Militant Roman Church." Furthermore, according to Révah, Enríquez Gómez had the temerity to send a copy of the latter work to one of the inquisitional tribunals in Spain.[17]

Except for perhaps its denunciation of the Inquisition, the orientation of the *Politics* gives no overt declaration of Marranism, or crypto-Judaism. However, for Révah it is "a literary and intellectual exercise typically Marranistic: a Judaizer tries to place himself as a Catholic and looks for arguments that the latter would use to oppose the inquisitorial methods and the religious racism at the time in Spain and Portugal" (101). This fiction would be made necessary because, although a more tolerant land, officially France proscribed Judaism. It is also to be supposed that arguments against a religious institution would be more telling if they were made by employing the precepts of that religion against itself. Révah, of course, considered Enríquez Gómez a secret Jew all his life. While his premise has not been shared by everyone, it does seem that at certain periods of Enríquez Gómez's life he inclined toward Judaism more than toward Catholicism. This appears to be the case especially during the years in France and particularly during the latter portion of his exile, when his political and economic problems increased.

Enríquez Gómez's arguments against the inquisitional methods and proceedings are founded on numerous passages from both Testaments, on the Church Fathers, and on Spanish Catholic writers (to their credit not all the opposition to the Inquisition was voiced by Jewish and *converso* writers). The general proposal is to demonstrate that while the state has a vital concern in maintaining its established religion—"Todo el grave peso de una monarquía consiste en la religión, y toda la conversación del estado consiste en que la religión se conserve intacta y sin mancha alguna" ("The whole weight of a monarchy consists in religion, and the whole conservation of the state depends on religion conserved intact and spotless" [119])—there are various ways of going about it, some methods being more productive than others. Obviously for Enríquez Gómez the secretive and even terroristic practices of the peninsular Inquisitions were not only counterproductive, but at the same time denied the very principle of the religion it was established to protect. The model for correct proceedings against heterodoxy Enríquez Gómez found in the pragmatic policies of Cardinal Richelieu, who recognized that the higher interest of the nation demanded forgiveness for the vanquished—Richelieu's generous treatment of the defeated Huguenots being a case in point.

One important item in the criticism of the Inquisition concerns the total secrecy with which it cloaked its actions. The barbarous practice of withholding from the accused the charges and identity of his accusers made response to the accusations well-nigh impossible. As Enríquez Gómez puts it: "Política de 'adivina quién te dio o te acusó' no puede ser cristiana, y vuelvo a decir que no es posible que semejante crueldad se use en reino católico" ("A policy of 'guess who accused you' cannot be Christian, and I repeat that it is impossible that such cruelty could be used in a Catholic kingdom" [124]). Equally outrageous was the secrecy imposed on the prisoners who were held incommunicado for extensive periods of time. Enríquez Gómez's comments on this practice reveal both the geniality with which he wrote and his keen perception of human nature: "Si . . . en la secreta cárcel o calabozo le tienen cuatro, seis, y doce años en justificar la causa, ¿qué se puede esperar de este hombre, sino una desesperación diabólica, teniendo la imaginación tan sujeta a las tentaciones del enemigo común de nuestra flaqueza? . . . ¿Quién duda que el preso, por verse libre de un calabozo eterno, deje de confesar que es chino, moro, y luterano y cuanto gustare la parte contraria?" ("If . . . they hold him four, six, even twelve years in the secret prison while his case is pending, what can one expect for man except a diabolic desperation since our imagination is so subject to the temptations of the common enemy of our own weakness? . . . Who doubts but that the prisoner, to get out of his eternal prison, would confess that he was Chinese, Moor, Lutheran, or whatever would please his captors" [150–51]).

Another aspect of the workings of the Inquisition that particularly bothered Enríquez Gómez was the effect it produced on the victim's family by loss of the family's possessions. The accused's assets were immediately embargoed by the Holy Office to be held for confiscation upon conviction. This unjust procedure seemed to guarantee abuses and made suspect the Inquisition's claim to be concerned solely with the purity of the faith, as Enríquez Gómez sarcastically comments through his mouthpiece, "Si vos decís que los jueces que acrisolan estas causas son espirituales, ¿qué parentesco tendrán los bienes del mundo con los del cielo?" ("If, as you say, the judges that examine these cases are so spiritual, what relationship could the wordly goods possibly have with heavenly good?" [131–32]). The topic was a sore point for Enríquez Gómez, who in about 1624 had initiated a suit to recover goods that the Inquisition confiscated when his father was arrested, goods Enríquez Gómez claimed belong to his Old Christian mother and that were never recovered.

Even worse than the immediate financial losses to the family, which might very well be left destitute, was the opprobrium that was heaped upon the family of the accused. That the innocent should suffer for the crimes of others is inconceivable, especially at the hands of a religious institution. Enríquez Gómez speaks particularly of the libels, or posters, hung in the parish churches identifying heretics and exposing their family to shame and dishonor for years and even generations to come. The practice of visiting the sins of the fathers upon unborn generations not only deprived them of any possible positions of honor or power, but also deprived the state of potential talent. As far as Enríquez Gómez was concerned, the guilty must suffer, but "Sólo el delito de Adán, como pecado original, tocó a toda la especie humana; pero, los demás delitos, al que los comete" ("Only the crime of Adam, as the Original Sin, was apportioned to everyone, but the rest of the sins are the responsibility of those who commit them" [138]).

Summary. *The Angelic Politics* is a beautifully written and historically relevant document that gives a blistering indictment of the hypocrisy of the Holy Office and its ministers. It clearly shows that Enríquez Gómez was conscious of a racial discrimination fostered by the state through this institution and that the infection spawned by the Inquisition would spread to the state that supported it and bring it down. In his estimation, the disease would have a twofold consequence— the undermining of morality, and the destruction of the financial bases of the nation. The latter consequence would be due to the ruination of commerce (a *converso* forte): "Pues es fuerza que, en faltando las columnas del comercio, ha de dar en tierra el edificio de su tesoro, y sin él ni hay quien provea las armadas, ni quien aliente el orgullo de la guerra, ni aún quien repare los accidentes más débiles de la fortuna" ("For it is obvious that lacking the pillars of commerce, the whole financial edifice will collapse, and without it there will be no one to provision fleets or feed the pride of war or even repair the most elementary reversals of fortune" [155]).

The *Politics* is not merely a theoretical condemnation of the Inquisition. Enríquez Gómez's practical side asserts itself in the final portion, which presents a point-by-point plan to reform the injustices of the Holy Office. It would strip away the secrecy surrounding the proceedings, accelerate the progress of cases, discard the practice of confiscation, and protect the rights of the innocent family members. Underlying all the proposed reform is an attack on the fundamental point that forced conversion is prejudicial to the national interest and is anti-Christian.

"Ballad to the Divine Martyr Judah the Believer"

Don Lope de Vera y Alarcón, "Judá creyente." In 1644 Don Lope de Vera y Alarcón was burned at the stake in Valladolid by the Inquisition for openly espousing Judaism and proselytizing. Among the many cases of those who went to their deaths at the hands of the Inquisition none is more remarkable than that of Don Lope, particularly because he was a convert to Judaism. Don Lope was descended from pure Old Christian antecedents. He became attracted to Judaism through his Hebrew studies at the University of Salamanca and was arrested in 1635, shortly before Enríquez Gómez's escape to France. Although the Catholic authorities sought diligently to bring him back to the church, Don Lope persisted in his new found Hebraism until his death. The case was, of course, a marvelous subject for Jewish and *marrano* propagandists and was widely commented upon throughout the *converso* communities where Don Lope was included among the roll of martyrs to the Holy Office.

The Ballad. There are only three manuscript copies of the "Romance al divín martir, Judá creyente" (Ballad to the divine martyr Judah the Believer) according to Timothy Oelman.[18] The fact that the poem was never printed (insofar as is known) leads to the conclusion that the author felt its subject and expression were too pro-Jewish. The inference is then that the poem represents the poet's innermost thoughts and, as such, points to an identification with Judaism that he could not reveal publicly in print. "The Ballad to Judah the Believer" and the epic *Samson the Nazarene* have both been pointed to as proof of the author's true religion.[19] Nevertheless, Oelman downgrades somewhat Enríquez Gómez's crypto-Judaism by assuming that had he wished to be Jewish he would have gone to Amsterdam and declared himself. Indeed the fact that he did not and returned to Spain would indicate a less than convinced attitude toward the religion. Perhaps, as in the case of Samson, the admiration Enríquez Gómez felt for Don Lope was for the courage he had in proclaiming aloud his innermost faith: "No se halló engaño en su boca, / pue iba a voces diciendo: " '¡Viva el Nombre de Adonai, / sacro autor del universo!' " ("No false words were upon his lips, for he went calling aloud, 'Long live the name of Adonai, Holy Author of all that is' " [vv. 27–29]). Oelman describes Enríquez Gómez's attitude during the last part of his French exile as that of a "committed messianist hopeful of the imminent coming."[20]

The date of the "Ballad" cannot be before Don Lope's death in 1644 and, according to Oelman, probably was composed prior to returning to Spain, ca. 1649, when the poet was also occupied with *Samson Nazareno*. The composition dates from a time of difficulties for Enríquez Gómez, a period of financial reversals and a strained relationship with the French authorities caused by the publication of *The Angelic Politics* and perhaps some involvement with the rebel forces of the French civil war.

The longest of the two versions of the "Ballad" contains 550 lines in the traditional Spanish ballad meter, the same assonance being maintained throughout. It is composed of two parts of unequal length. The verses of part one are devoted to Don Lope's imprisonment and his efforts to maintain his adopted religion in the face of constant efforts by the inquisitors to dissuade him. The second part, from verse 19 to the end of the poem, is Don Lope's speech from the stake. His words begin with a recognition of God's eternal law as declared to the Jews from the time of Moses. Much of the argument is based on the concept of unity—one God, one law, one truth—which Don Lope considers contradicted by the idolatry of the Catholic doctrine of the Trinity:

> Quererme tú reducir
> a tres distintos sujetos,
> multiplando deidades
> con sus festivos desvelos,
> es decirme que la causa
> se iguala con los efectos,
> y lo propio es para mí
> dividirla en tres que en ciento.

To try to force me to believe in three separate individuals, multiplying deities, each with their festive observances, is like trying to tell me that the cause is equal to its effects; thus I might as well divide it into a hundred as into three!

(vv. 155–63)

Since Don Lope rejects the divinity of Christ, the redemption offered through Jesus and the escape from Original Sin cannot be accepted: "Comió Adán una manzana, / y, para salvar su yerro, / ¿queréis vosotros formar / quién le beba este veneno?" ("Adam ate the apple, and now, in order to expunge his sin do you wish to find another [Christ] to drink this poison for his sake?" [vv. 247–50]).

Don Lope's declaration of faith is simply but defiantly stated: "¡Judío soy, castellanos! / La ley de Moisés confieso / dada en el monte Sinaí / por el autor de los cielos" ("I am a Jew, Castilians! I profess the Law of Moses, which was given on Mount Sinai by the author of the heavens" [vv. 295–98]). As the flames spring up about him the hero's words are directed to the "Dios de Abraham, Dios de Isaac, / Dios de Jacob, Rey eterno" ("God of Abraham, God of Isaac, God of Jacob. Eternal King" [vv. 323–24]), and he accepts joyously the martyrdom as proof of his fidelity to the Law. He welcomes the flames as purifying agents.

The final hundred or so verses of the second part are again directed to the onlookers and deliver an obscurely worded prophecy, beginning "¡Ay de ti! pueblo sin Dios, / aquél que idolatras ciego" ("Woe betide you, godless people, you that blindly worship idols" [vv. 389–90]). As analyzed by Oelman, this section is based on the Book of Daniel and in part on the cryptic *Trovas* of Gonçalo Annes Bandarra, published at Nantes in 1644. Here the martyr predicts the destruction of his vile persecutors, "que con ignorante celo / reducir quieres al sol / en un círculo pequeño" ("who blind through your misguided faith seek to confine the sun within but a tiny circle" [vv. 43–44]), and announces the coming of the Messiah after an epoch of general destruction. In spite of the Jewish character inherent in the poem's messianism, Oelman notes that "its lack of overall coherence in terms of Jewish tradition and its extensive reliance on Biblical sources"[21] gives it more a "Jewish direction" than it reveals an extensive knowledge of Hebraic thought. Oelman's analysis finds that Enríquez Gómez was not well versed in "Talmudic, Kabbalistic or other Jewish sources."[22] This observation supports the conclusion that Enríquez Gómez's years in France were not spent in the study of Judaism, and that, at best, his Judaism was superficial.

The "Ballad" is one of Enríquez Gómez's most successful compositions in its uniting of subject matter and artistic expression. The relative brevity of the composition evidently allowed the poet the luxury of polishing it, a process that seems not to have taken place in longer works. The choice of the shorter ballad line, the traditional oral meter, accords well with the oral nature of the content in the address of the martyr to the public and to God and the report of the proceedings as if it were to be recited in public. At the same time, the elevated tone and phraseology of the poem casts it along heroic lines as befits the subject matter; this is especially the case in the final prophecy with its obscure and mysterious note.

Chapter Nine
The Zárate Plays

Antonio Enríquez Gómez Alias Fernando de Zárate

The suggestion that Fernando de Zárate y Castronovo was an alias of Antonio Enríquez Gómez was first made by Adolfo de Castro in the last century. In the ensuing polemic a majority of eminent investigators maintained the contrary, and the matter was viewed as more or less settled until 1962 when Révah was able to document the correctness of Castro's contention. Since Révah published his findings all scholars have come around to accept his discovery as to Zárate's true identity.[1] For convenience and for contrast, in this chapter the plays of the last period of Enríquez Gómez's life are referred to as the Zárate plays as opposed to the first plays, the Enríquez Gómez plays.

Unfortunately, for the final period of his life Enríquez Gómez was not able to leave a list of play titles as he had done earlier for his Madrid series. To compile a list of the Zárate plays is thus much more difficult and must be done on the basis of catalogs and reports of performances that are often erroneous, confused, or incomplete. An examination of these sources gives a list of twenty-eight titles that are solely attributed to Fernando de Zárate (see appendix for titles), but that does not necessarily mean that Enríquez Gómez (alias Zárate) actually wrote them. The authenticity of all these plays is a question that awaits much further study. There are also seven other plays (listed in the appendix) that at one time or another have been attributed to Zárate, but over the years have also been assigned with varying degrees of certainty to other authors.

The dating of the Zárate plays is even more problematic than that of the Enríquez Gómez plays. Prior to 1660 we presently have reference to only one Zárate composition, *La loa de los siete planetas* (The seven planets), composed as a short introductory piece *(loa)* for a staging of a Calderón play in Seville in 1658.[2] From 1660, the year before his arrest, there exists or there are references to three manuscripts, two Zárate plays staged in Madrid, and the printing of five of the Zárate plays and shorter works.[3] However, the majority of the Zárate plays appear in print in various collections *(partes)* from 1661 to 1678. Rose has called attention to the inventory of items confiscated when the dramatist was arrested to include a bundle of manuscripts of plays and *loas*.[4] Obviously these were sold to printers by inquisitional officials and began to find their way into print even before the death of the dramatist in 1663. It is ironic that the works of the man the Inquisition wished to silence continued to appear because of the greed of the institution itself. It is, of course, entirely likely that there were more Zárate plays that have been lost or have not yet been identified. In addition, given the facility with which the dramatist adopted new identities as the need arose, the works of Antonio Enríquez Gómez are quite likely still extant under other aliases besides Fernando de Zárate y Castronovo.[5] He was, after all, in Spain for close to ten years before we have the first reference to a Zárate work.

Classification

Of the twenty-eight plays that seem likely authentic Zárate works, three were not available for consideration for this study.[6] The remaining twenty-five can be put into three major categories: the cape and sword plays, the adventure plays, and the religious plays.

There are more cape and sword plays in the Zárate group than in the Enríquez Gómez group, but they still form the smallest category of the playwright's production. The plays are: *Antes que todo es mi amigo* (My friend above all), *La palabra vengada* (The pledge avenged), *La presumida y la hermosa* (The presumptuous lady and the beauty), *Quererse sin declararse* (Love undeclared), and *Mayor mal hay en la vida* (There is worse evil in life).

The adventure plays are divisible into two types, first those dealing with historical personages—*La conquista de México* (The conquest of Mexico), *Los dos filósofos de Grecia* (The two Greek philosophers), *El maestro de Alejandro* (The tutor of Alexander), *Vida y muerte del Cid Campeador* (The life and death of the Cid), *El primer conde de Flandes* (The first count of Flanders), *Las tres coronaciones del emperador Carlos V* (The three coronations of Emperor Charles V), and *El valiente Campuzano* (The valiant campuzano)—and, second, those plays that are based on fictional main characters—*La defensora de la reina de Hungría* (The queen of Hungary's defender), *Los hermanos amantes* (The sibling lovers), *Mudarse por mejorarse* (To change for the better), and *Quien habla más, obra menos* (Actions speak louder than words). In both cases the adventures are of heroic proportions, generally involving royal or noble protagonists and having an intrigue that threatens the peace and security of a state. Usually there are included the standard comic relief sections provided by the *graciosos* and at least one love interest. At times the love story may be an integral part of the play, as in *The Sibling Lovers,* or it may be more an accessory action, as in *The Three Coronations* and *The Valiant Campuzano.*

The plays on Christian religious topics in the Zárate group comprise a new category, the major difference between the Enríquez Gómez plays and the Zárate plays. They are *La conversión de la Magdalena* (The conversion of the Magdalene), *La escala de la gracia* (The stairway of grace), *Mártir y rey de Sevilla, S. Hermenegildo* (St. Hermenegild, martyr–king of Seville), *El médico pintor, San Lucas* (The doctor-painter, St. Luke), *Las misas de S. Vicente Ferrer* (The masses of St. Vincent Ferrer), *El obispo de Crobia, S. Estanislao* (St. Stanislaus, bishop of Crobia), *S. Antonio Abad* (St. Anthony Abbot), *Santa Pelagia* (St. Pelagia), and *El vaso y la piedra* (The chalice and the rock).[7] As we have seen, the biblical plays of the Enríquez Gómez period were concerned with Old Testament subjects viewed in an historical perspective rather than a religious one. The New Testament, Christian orientation of the Zárate religious plays, however, transcends the merely historical presentation by their fervent avowals of Christianity, their concentration on the Christian mysteries, and their miraculous happenings. The religious plays in fact very often seem a blending of *auto* and *comedia.*

Zárate Heroines and Heroes

The presentation of the Zárate heroines follows generally the same pattern established earlier in the Enríquez Gómez plays. There are several representatives of the manly woman *(mujer varonil)* who is adept at the use of arms as portrayed in the brawling Catuja of *The Valiant Campuzano* and by the Moorish warrior women of *The Life and Death of the Cid* and *St. Hermenegild.* Like their earlier counterparts, these ladies are as bellicose and courageous in battle as any man. Less openly Amazon-like but as resolute are others such as Nise, the errant sister of *St. Vicente Ferrer,* who entices the Moor, Mulay, with the promise of her charms, then stabs him and leaves him for dead.

Decisiveness and forcefulness continue to be as characteristic of the Zárate ladies as of the Enríquez Gómez heroines. The one situation in which these traits come to the fore is that of their selection of a husband, a process ever complicated by opposing forces such as a father, a brother, or another figure of authority. Very often the ladies are quite forward in their desires, as in the cases of Alfreda of *The First Count of Flanders,* Leonor of *Campuzano,* and Dorotea of *The Pledge Avenged.* And very often the heroines must resort to guile to gain the object of their desire, as do Violante of *The Three Coronations* and Porcia of *To Change for the Better.*

However, in spite of these similarities of type with his earlier feminine creations of the Madrid period, there is a very noticeable lessening of the strident misogamy and misogyny apparent in the plays of his more youthful period and especially frequent in his exile literature. In this regard the sonnet in praise of women in *The Conquest of Mexico* comes as quite a pleasant surprise after the antifeminine jeremiads of *The Tower of Babylon, The Pythagorean Century,* and *Samson the Nazarene.* A portion of the sonnet reads:

> Una mujer leal no tiene precio
>
> . . . .
>
> y hombre que en poco sus consejos tiene
> llora después arrepentido y necio.
> Si daños han venido por mujeres,
> por ellas tantos bienes han vendio,
> que son lo menos bueno sus placeres.[8]

A loyal woman is priceless. . . . And a man who little values her advice later weeps in repentance. If women have occasioned harm, also have they produced so much good of which enjoyment of their pleasures is the least important factor.

The overall impression of a more flattering presentation of women in the Zárate plays is no doubt due to the number of religious plays. All the forcefulness and vigor of character of his secular women is also apparent in many of his saintly ones, such as in the case of Francisca, the sister of St. Vincent Ferrer, who murders her rapist, commits suicide, and then is miraculously pardoned; or in the case of the falsely accused queen of *Queen of Hungary's Defender,* whose special and fervent devotion to the Virgin restores her sight and regains for her the king's favor. The topic of a woman's restoration to good repute is apparent in the poet's fondness for the repentant woman as exemplified by Mary Magdalene, who has a central role in two plays—*Conversion of the*

Magdalene and *Chalice and the Rock.* Another Magdalene-like heroine is St. Pelagia, the rescued courtesan of the play of the same name. This is a work that is especially interesting for its blending of eroticism and religious fervor.

Of course, the ideal of Christian femininity is to be found in the various representations of the Virgin from the play dedicated to her, the *Scale of Grace,* to the several other works in which she appears or is important—*Queen of Hungary's Defender, Doctor-Painter St. Luke,* and *Chalice and the Rock.*

Because of a general softening of criticism of matrimony and a less strident antifeminism as compared to earlier plays, there is a tendency in the Zárate plays away from the generalized presentation of males as dupes and befuddled fools. However, there are still some Zárate works in which the males are taught a lesson by the ladies—Violante (of *Three Coronations*) gets back her philandering boy friend by a clever ruse; the womanizing prince of *To Change for the Better* is taught his lesson by Porcia in what seems the comic version of the earlier Enríquez Gómez tragedy, *What Honor Obliges;* and, finally, the guilty males of *Queen of Hungary's Defender* are punished as a result of the queen's divinely inspired scheme. Still, the Zárate plays have some of the stereotyped *galanes* who alternate between lovelorn and jealous and are as quick to whisper sweet nothings as they are to fight. But among them there are also some male roles remarkable for their originality. One of these is the *valentón,* Pedro Campuzano (discussed at the end of this chapter), a figure that both repels and attracts, and upon examination may not be the hero that he seems.

Another intriguing play is *Sibling Lovers,* which presents a father-son conflict that is as audacious in its sexual implications of potential double incest as it is for its rather ambiguous presentation of a monarch. In this work Prince Fadrique and his father both fall in love with Margarita. To further complicate matters the king learns that she is his long lost illegitimate daughter. Both the prince and Margarita, however, refuse to accept that they have the same father, believing the story to be an invention of the king to separate them. *Sibling Lovers* is an exceptionally interesting play for many reasons, one being the development of the king's character from a self-centered libertine, whose past threatens his realm with civil war, into a responsible monarch who strives to reestablish contact with his estranged son.

An exceptional Zárate hero is Martín Peláez of *Life and Death of the Cid.* The young Martín is to be sent to Valencia by his father to learn soldiering at the side of the Cid. But Martín resists the idea, explaining to his chagrined father that he is not at all attracted to military life:

> Filósofo soy, que busca
> la quietud entre estos robles.
> . . . .
> No a todos, señor, nos suena
> bien las militares voces,
> ni los laudes de Marte
> animan los corazones.[9]

I am a philosopher who seeks the quiet of these groves. . . . Not to all of us, sir, sound well the martial cries, nor do the instruments of Mars animate our hearts.

Having been raised in a pastoral setting and knowing little of war, Martín is full of self-doubt about his ability to become a soldier. Consequently, the suspicion on the part of the Cid and his knights, portrayed as rather a bloodthirsty lot, that he is a coward clouds his relationship with them. Gradually Martín's trepidations are overcome and he becomes a brave knight, ending all doubts as to his manliness.

Worthy of note in the Zárate plays are two minority male roles— that of Muley of *St. Vicente Ferrer* and Hazan of *Pledge Avenged*. Muley is a black man. As a child he is sold into slavery but is later rescued and converted by a Christian hermit. After the death of his mentor, he becomes a renegade Moslem pirate only to be shipwrecked, wounded, and again rescued by a Christian gentleman to whom he enslaves himself in gratitude. Enríquez Gómez has created an excellent dramatic role here as Muley struggles against his passionate desire for the wife of his rescuer. The tragic outcome of the play (as far as he is concerned) is caused in large measure by his color.[10] A somewhat similar situation is built about Hazan, the Morisco, who, with the majority of his people, was expelled from Spain by the Christians and consequently desires to avenge his past ill treatment on them all.

Interest in Government

Enríquez Gómez's abiding interest in government and governing remains an important element in the Zárate plays. We would expect this, given the political orientation of much of his exile literature. And so, with the exception of the cape and sword plays that concentrate on the amorous intrigues of the gentry, almost every Zárate play has a political message. This interest in the correct and just functioning of the state has all sorts of variations: the play may be laid in an historical setting such as *First Count of Flanders, Three Coronations, Life and Death of the Cid,* and *Tutor of Alexander;* or in fictional settings such as that of *Queen of Hungary's Defender, Sibling Lovers,* or *To Change for the Better.* The historical setting may be altered to include supernatural forces of opposition such as in *The Conquest of Mexico,* in which the pagan gods vainly attempt to prevent the introduction of Christianity during the Spanish conquest. Even many of the religious plays are vitally concerned with the topic of governance because of the close connection of church and state. This is especially the case when the religious conflict concerns the royal family, as in *St. Hermenegild* and *Queen of Hungary's Defender,* in both of which the struggle is against the Arianism of the monarch; or in *St. Stanislaus,* in which the bishop struggles against the sinful nature of the king of Poland. The errant nature of the monarch or of persons close to the throne, usually involving lust for an unattainable woman or desire for power, is a matter of national interest because of the effect the errors may have on the nation. The king's lecture to his son in *To Change for the Better* draws attention to the special obligation the royal family has to set the example: "Disponerte a reinar es mi cuidado, / que se obra indignamente si se ignora, / y es civil ruina un necio de su estado" ("My task is to prepare you to reign, for he who comports himself unworthily is the ruin of his state").[11]

One change from the Enríquez Gómez plays that is obvious in the Zárate plays is that whereas in the earlier plays correct governance of a state depended upon adherence to a universal code of morality that mixed justice and mercy, the later works obey the same precepts in the name of Christianity. The addition of the Christian factor also leads to a broader concern in many of the plays in that the field of battle is not merely limited to the confines of one or more kingdoms but instead is a contention for men's souls—the political is transcended by the spiritual. With this elevation of the struggle to the spiritual level, we see the introduction in many plays of a villain who did not appear in the Enríquez Gómez period—the devil. The devil's concern is always to prevent the spread of Christianity by fomenting pagan opposition, by seeking to subvert the potential for saintliness, or by minimizing the effect of a saint's good works.

Final Christianity?

The introduction of the Christian component to the Zárate dramaturgy is the single most important factor that sets these plays apart from the earlier plays. The Christian orientation of the Zárate plays was for many years the major element that scholars relied upon to disprove Castro's judgment that Zárate was an Enríquez Gómez alias. Now that we know that Zárate and Enríquez Gómez were one and the same person, the startling turnabout from the suspected Marranism of Enríquez Gómez's earlier compositions to the flag-waving Christianity of his Zárate plays is remarkable and curious. Is this conversion an expedient that enabled him to continue to write when he secretly returned to Spain? Is it merely a red herring to confuse inquisitional investigators accustomed to the Old Testament flavor of the earlier plays? If Enríquez Gómez-Zárate was a crypto-Jew until the end, why did he write so many plays that contain a Christian content so fervid as to merit admiration three centuries later?[12] If the author did not really share his expressed devotion to the Virgin, Jesus, and the saints, why did he not dedicate his pen to more historical plays or to more comedies, both areas in which he excelled?

Sincerity is difficult to gauge in an author speaking through his creations, but several critics have identified a veritable profession of Jewish faith in the last book of *Samson the Nazarene* and in "The Ballad to Judah the Believer." Can we then say that the following lines from *Chalice and the Rock* that Enríquez Gómez wrote for St. Paul's confession of Faith are any less sincere?

> . . . y yo desengañado
> de la soberbia que truje,
> entré en la ciudad, a donde
> el sacro bautismo pude
> recibir, y a esta montaña
> la soledad me conduce,
> en cuyas lóbregas peñas
> de los errores que tuve,
> arrepentido confieso;
> que aquel nazareno ilustre,
> hombre y Dios es el Mesías.[13]

And I, disabused of past haughtiness, entered the city where the Sacred Baptism I could receive, and to this solitude I came, in whose gloomy rocks

I repent and confess my past errors; for that illustrious Nazarene [Jesus], man and God, is the Messiah.

If we are inclined to accept all passages concerning religion at face value, we must conclude that Enríquez Gómez in the last period of his life settled his religious dilemma in favor of Christianity. If we do not accept the sincerity of his ultimate Christianity, then we must regard Enríquez Gómez as one of the most convincing dissimulators of his age and might very well question the sincerity of his previous "Jewishness."

Enríquez Gómez's final turning to Christianity seems supported by the dynamic evangelistic nature of the religious plays of the Zárate period. With few exceptions they are set in epochs and areas of confrontation between Christianity and other religions, be it with Judaism, Islam, Arianism, or paganism. In all cases the Christianity is proselytizing and, as such, generously forgiving of past errors of understanding as it receives joyfully its converts into full communion. In this regard we note an implicit criticism of the Christianity of Enríquez Gómez's own day, which was more concerned with punishment of backsliders and with the annihilation of heterodoxy.

The representation of Judaism in the Zárate plays is carefully differentiated from Arianism, Islam, or paganism, which are presented as the devil's traps to snare the unsuspecting. Judaism is never criticized or presented negatively; rather, it occupies an honored place in the Zárate plays as the basis for Christianity, the first step, as it were, toward the true religion. Over and over the parallels between the Old and New Testaments are drawn—the Virgin is presented as a latter-day Abigail (*the* model of womanhood in his earlier plays), the Old Testament heroes are cited in comparisons with Catholic figures (Cortez is a second Moses, a new David; his Catholicism unites the Ark of the Covenant with the Cross). This syncretistic presentation of Judaism and Christianity is particularly obvious in those areas in which the fundamental doctrines of Catholicism are adduced from Old Testament sources. One example is the play *Stairway of Grace,* which is vitally concerned with prophecies that support not only the messianic nature of Christ, but also the Immaculate Conception of Mary and the doctrine of the Trinity.[14]

The optimistic and joyful nature of the religious plays is a contrast to the depressed atmosphere that is embodied in the exile literature, so centered about the topic of Adam's Fall and Original Sin. The doubts, fears, and confusion that are such a part of the French works are settled (at least literarily) in the Zárate plays. Unless these plays have no relations whatsoever with the author's own beliefs, the religious struggle was finally decided in favor of a loving and accommodating Christianity: "La fe de Cristo profeso, / ésta ensalzar imagino, / ésta adoro, ésta confieso" ("Faith in Christ I profess. This I intend to propagate. This I adore. This I confess").[15] The amount of critical attention that has been devoted to the Zárate plays is perhaps even less than the little accorded to the Enríquez Gómez plays; which is to say that the total dramatic production of Enríquez Gómez offers an original area of investigation yet to be explored. The remainder of this chapter contains a closer look at three representative plays of the Zárate period: *The Presumptuous Lady and the Beauty*, *The Chalice and the Rock*, and *The Valiant Campuzano*.

The Presumptuous Lady and the Beauty

Synopsis. Don Diego de Peralta y Guzmán is ransomed from Moorish captivity and released in Naples. He decides to return to his native Seville for the first time after twenty years of soldiering to visit his sisters Leonor and Violante, but before he returns home he must honor a vow he made during his captivity to make a pilgrimage to Santiago. The following scene shifts to Don Diego's house in Seville where the action is to remain during the rest of the comedy. Don Diego's comrade, Don Juan, and his servant, Chocolate, have been in Seville a week, and during this time Juan has fallen love with Leonor who, they find out, is Don Diego's sister. Assuming that Diego is still being held prisoner, Chocolate comes up with a plan to impersonate Don Diego and then introduce Don Juan into the household as his friend, thus facilitating Juan's courtship of the wealthy Leonor.

As neither sister nor their uncle, Don Pedro, have seen Diego for many years, Chocolate easily passes himself off as the wandering brother and sets about to arrange his master's marriage as well as feather his own nest. Leonor, as inordinately proud of her wit as Violante is of her beauty, has declared her intention to enter a convent rather than marry. She regards all men as dull-witted and unworthy of her intellect. Naturally Chocolate's scheme eventually brings Juan and Leonor together after many of the requisite spats and reconciliations.

Chocolate himself falls for the servant, Elena, who becomes unbearably haughty on receiving his attentions, imagining herself future mistress of the house. To finance their wedding Chocolate accepts "loans" from Don Carlos and Don Gaspar, two local gallants who are seeking Violante and Leonor in marriage and who are duped by Chocolate into thinking that he favors their suits.

There are the usual scenes of mistaken identity in dark gardens, jealous tiffs, and people hiding in neighboring rooms. The situation becomes more complicated at the beginning of the third act when the real Don Diego returns home after his pilgrimage and Chocolate must try to keep him away from his own house. When the plot is strained to a hopeless degree of confusion, all the characters come together in a reconciliation effected by the uncle, Don Pedro, who marries off the ladies to everyone's satisfaction.

Characterization. *The Presumptuous Lady* is a sprightly comedy that occupies the same bright spot in the Zárate period that *Love is Proof Against Deceit* did in the Enríquez Gómez's plays. One of the most conspicuous differences is the change in the presentation of the female characters. In the earlier play they completely dominate the stage, but in *The Presumptuous Lady* quite the reverse is true, with the two sisters assuming the more conventional positions about which the action and interest revolve. The quality that the later creations have lost is that of the ability to scheme in order to control their own fate by manipulating their fathers, brothers, and boy friends.

But if the ladies have lost a bit of their accustomed astuteness, there remains a good bit of the Enríquez Gómez heroine in their forwardness. Both sisters enjoy a state of greater independence than that of the usual *comedia* heroine. The fact that they live by themselves, their guardian and tutor Don Pedro occupying another house, does not seem to surprise anyone, though it is quite an unusual situation. Thus as wealthy orphan sisters they enjoy the protection of their Uncle Pedro with no immediate familial tyranny to put a stop to the letters and visits of their *galanes*. Chocolate professes to be shocked by their freedom and by the boldness of the visits of Gaspar and Carlos. However, he manages to overcome his indignation when he realizes that he can profit from the visits of the two.

A hint of the skeptical and cynical Enríquez Gómez attitude toward women lingers on in this play. The title refers to the comic nature of the two sisters whose respective vanities are the sources of a good deal of the play's humor. Violante's narcissism is mindlessly charming but she exasperates the intellectual Leonor, who regards her sister's flirtations as undignified. She rebukes Violante for receiving a would-be lover's note, and Violante replies, "Si Dios me hizo tan hermosa, / ¿qué he de hacer?" ("If God made me so beautiful, what can I do?"),[16] and confesses "Solemos ser las hermosas / muy tiernas de corazón" ("We beautiful people are wont to be very tenderhearted" [517, a]). However, Leonor's pretensions to intellectualism are just as risible. When she receives her love note the shoe is on the other foot. Leonor's indignation at such nonsense is considerably tempered by her suitor's praise of her wit. Violante impishly urges her to tear up the note, but Leonor demurs, "Algo le he de perdonar, / porque me llama discreta" ("I have to pardon him a little since he calls me clever" [517, c]). This is quite a change from her statement made a few moments earlier, "Viven los cielos, / que si algún hombre intentara / quererme, que le matara" ("Heavens above, if some man dared to love me I would kill him" [517, a]). The comic presentation of the two sisters is enhanced by their competitiveness—each wishing to outshine the other for Don Juan. While their conflicts do not have the malicious undertone of a Leonor and Juana of *Love is Proof Against Deceit,* Leonor and Violante do take obvious delight in discomfiting each other.

With the exception of the *gracioso,* Chocolate, the male roles in this play show very little development from those of the author's earlier days. The gentlemen-suitors are very conventional, their minds being occupied first and foremost by amorous attention to wealthy and attractive ladies, a game played out in rather stylized steps. Thus, the three gallants, the brother, and the uncle function mechanically with no spark of originality or individuality. Indeed, a good deal of the play's humor is a result of these automatons being set in motion at cross purposes by Chocolate.

Chocolate is the culmination of all the many Enríquez Gómez *graciosos* and the vindication of all the Enríquez Gómez servants who have been bullied, brow-beaten, and even beaten by their masters. His assumption of nobler status is rather a subversive act but one that does not set society entirely on its ear as his master does not assume the servant's role. Nevertheless, there is involved a clever satire on the conventional theatrical representation of upper-class values. As a *gracioso* Chocolate is quite uncommon. Although not a valiant person, he is certainly more daring than most Enríquez Gómez's *graciosos* in inventing the ruse and urging it on his reluctant master with the statement, "O tienes amor o no" ("Either you are in love or you're not" [516, c]). After coming up with the general scheme and a vague plan to overcome Leonor's disinclination to marry by playing on her jealousy, he improvises the majority of his subsequent deeds as the situation presents itself. Part of his charm is his inability to pass up any opportunity for chicanery,

particularly if it is a chance to swindle money from foolish gentlemen.
All the conflicting accommodations he makes soon lead to confrontations
that he manages to forestall with more and more difficulty until the
final scene in which the situation is so confused by his doings that the
uncle must be brought in deus ex machina to resolve the contending
claims to the ladies. Until that happens, however, his stratagems provide
a number of genuinely comic moments.

   Satire of Pretentiousness.   The human frailty that is satirized in
this play is that of pretentiousness. The ladies' pretenses are their claims
to beauty and intellect and their protestations of maintaining decorum.
Then there are the gallants, Carlos and Gaspar, who, attracted by the
wealth of the ladies, attempt to court them with hackneyed methods
and trite phrases. Chocolate's blustering speeches in which he affects
concern for the honor of his house, his bravado, and his ridiculous
posturing complete the none too flattering satire of the upper class.
Chocolate's hyperbolic assessment of Don Juan's worthiness is a case
in point: "Don Juan / es y fue de los primeros / nobilísimos caballeros
que descendieron de Adán" ("Don Juan springs from the very first
noble gentlemen to descend from Adam" [518, a]). But the gentry
have no monopoly on pretense. The servant, Elena, is another whose
pretensions to a higher station are made fun of in the absurd airs she
affects once Chocolate, alias Don Diego, convinces her that he will
marry her and elevate her on the social scale. The fictitious genealogy
he invents for her, which she is all too pleased to believe, traces her
back to the Visigothic Christians from the mountains of Asturias.
Chocolate tells his incredulous "sister" Leonor that the servant girl is
really Doña Elena de Mendoza y de Peralta, "su padre vino de Cangas
/ a conquistar a Sevilla" ("her father came from Cangas to reconquer
Seville from the Moors" [525, a]). The absurdity is made all the more
humorous by the fact that her father would have to have been four
hundred years old to accomplish this deed. In this way the dramatist
pokes fun at contemporary Spaniards who claimed nobility on just as
insecure grounds. Enríquez Gómez must have relished this touch since
he wrote the play under the alias Zárate, a name connoting descent
from the same northern mountains. The masquerade device on which
the play is based is given deeper significance when we realize that
Chocolate's masquerade is the product of a *converso* who in real life is
masquerading as an Old Christian gentleman. There are a number of
passages throughout the play that allude to this irony, slyly hinting
that things are often not as they seem.

General Observations. There is in *The Presumptuous Lady and the Beauty* a good deal to recall Enríquez Gómez's skill in earlier plays in inventing complicated comedy plots, only perhaps raised to a higher degree of excellence. With three *galanes,* a brother, and an uncle, plus two *damas,* the possibilities of humorous confusion is already great enough. But to muddle things a bit more, Chocolate also invents an extra identity for himself, that of Don Diego, and he also invents a fictitious lady, Doña Ana, with whom Don Juan is supposedly involved.

Enríquez Gómez, however, is in control of his comedy, which moves briskly along from one entertaining situation to another. The comic situations of the play provide a good measure of the work's humor, but another major comic element is the author's skill in creating clever dialogue, a talent that was evident as early as his Madrid period. The repartee between the two fatuous sisters in the first act has already been noted; equally amusing is a scene in the second act in which, as Leonor praises the beauty of a friend and Violante lauds the wit of another lady, each maliciously pricks at the balloon of the other's vanity. Of course, Chocolate being the principal wit of the piece, has many fine opportunities for clever lines.

The Chalice and the Rock

Synopsis. The first act of this play opens with Saul pursuing Mary Magdalene and a band of Christians who are preparing to embark for Europe. Just as he has them at his mercy we have the first of the play's many miracles: Saul finds himself suddenly powerless to strike down the Christians and they escape. The second scene introduces another story line, that of St. Peter and his servant-companion, Zabulón (the *gracioso*). St. Peter is seeking to counteract the growing influence and fame of the apostate, Simon the Magician. Simon, the personification of false pride and pagan magic, is attempting to gain the support of the Emperor Nero. The emperor maintains an open mind in the conflict between Peter and Simon and proposes a duel of miracles when he returns to Rome. The third major story line shifts the action to Europe and concerns the king and queen of Marseilles who, as they prepare a pagan sacrifice, witness the miraculous rescue of Mary Magdalene's band of Christians from a storm at sea. This miracle and another involving the appearance of the infant Jesus convert the monarchs to Christianity. As a result they set off on a pilgrimage to the Holy Land. Act 1 closes

with another miraculous conversion, that of Saul as he is on his way
to persecute the Christians of Damascus.

In the second act Peter and Zabulón come across Saul, who has
taken the Christian name Paul and has been living as a hermit after
his conversion. Together the saints set out for Jerusalem to spread the
faith. In the meantime, the kind and queen of Marseilles have arrived
in the Holy Land, but the queen dies shortly before they reach Jerusalem.
The remainder of the second act involves a tour of the holy places
during which Peter guides the king and Mary Magdalene guides the
spirit of the queen, which is not visible to her husband.

At the opening of act 3 Peter and Zabulón are miraculously delivered
from Herod's prison. Upon their release, Paul brings them the news
that Simon is in Rome practicing his pagan spells and preaching against
the church. Both saints determine to proceed to Rome to combat Simon's
maleficent influence. At the same time, the king and queen of Marseilles
are reunited as she is returned to life through the intercession of Mary
Magdalene. They both make a vow to live as Christians and to return
to their land via Rome. The monarchs arrive in Rome in time to
witness a debate between Simon and Peter which becomes a disquisition
by Peter on the mystery of the Trinity as foretold from Old Testament
sources. Naturally Simon is confounded by Peter's truths, but the
ultimate test of their powers is to see which can raise the dead. When
a cadaver is brought in it only raises one hand at Simon's command;
for Peter the corpse arises and proclaims Christ. Clearly Peter wins the
day, but Nero's fears are aroused by the display of Christianity's power
and he orders the execution of both Peter and Paul. Although Peter
has an opportunity to escape, a vision of Christ deters him, and he
goes joyously to his death. The play ends with angels and the others
exalting the martyrdoms of saints Peter and Paul.

Unity of the Play.   As is very often the case with Spanish classical
drama, the unifying element of this play is definitely not its action.
The action is divided between three interrelated but contending story
lines that are introduced in turn in the first act: Paul's story and his
conversion; Peter's struggle against the apostate Simon; and the conversion
of the rulers of Marseilles. By the end of the work all three actions
have been interwoven into a whole. Nevertheless, the impression is that
the play is needlessly episodic and much too fragmented by the presence
of five or six main characters plus a strong *gracioso* role. Also obvious
is that the unities of time and place are unimportant as the scene shifts
back and forth between Europe and the Near East. The helter-skelter

nature of the play has a good deal in common with the earlier Enríquez Gómez plays which often have the appearance of being pieced together out of material sufficient for two or three works.

But there is unity in *The Chalice and the Rock;* it is found in the theme that threads together each story and each character. On examination, the underlying preoccupation of all the characters and their actions is seen to be rebirth, a topic that we have seen so obsessively employed in the works of Enríquez Gómez's French period. In *The Chalice and the Rock* rebirth comes about by acceptance of Christianity and is presented in both a religious and a literal sense. The theme is introduced in the first scene as Mary Magdalene introduces herself with reference to her brother:

> Lázaro mi hermano es éste,
> él que durmiendo a la sombra
> de la muerte, al cuarto día,
> por la virtud milagrosa
> de Cristo resucitó.

Lazarus is my brother. He who sleeping the sleep of the dead, on the fourth day, by the miraculous virtue of Christ was resurrected.

(74)[17]

In a similar sense Mary Magdalene herself was reborn into a virtuous state from a previously wicked existence. The other great sinner of the play to be reborn from a state of pernicious ignorance is Saul, whose glorious conversion on the road to Damascus provides the climactic finish to act 1 and is recounted again in a Gongoristic version in act 2.

Other instances of the theme involve Pedro's resurrection of the cadaver in act 3, a feat he had already performed before, according to Zabulón. Additionally, the conversion of the pagan monarchs of Marseilles is strengthened by the death and resuscitation of the queen, made all the more symbolic by the fact that the reborn Mary Magdalene is the agent of this miracle and is the queen's guide to the holy places of Jerusalem. In fact, so all pervasive is the topic of rebirth that even the *gracioso's* comedy plays around such a serious subject. Practically the first descriptive words concerning Peter are Zabulón's admiring, and humorous, comments concerning his ability to raise the dead.

> Como un santo ha predicado,
> gentiles con beneficio
> ha convertido, que es juicio:
> pero me dejé admirado
> que, sin ir a Josefa,
> resucitase anteayer,
> padre mío, una mujer.

Like a saint he has preached and he has converted gentiles with much benefit. But I was astonished the day before yesterday to see him resuscitate a corpse without waiting for the Last Judgment, that—God help us!—was that of a woman.

(76)

Zabulón's fascination with the process leads to the comic scene in which he tries in vain to call forth the dead queen from her tomb.

The power to resurrect is here a specifically Christian attribute and the touchstone of a true religion, as the pagan Emperor Nero himself acknowledges when he tests Simon and Peter by requiring them to raise the dead. The play's message is quite clear—in the resurrected Christ alone there is life. The several passages concerned with Jesus' authenticity as the Messiah and the various sections explaining and upholding the Trinity give this play a unique flavor. Rather than addressing those already secure in their faith, *The Chalice and the Rock* seems directed toward people outside Christianity, specifically the Jews or *marranos*. The setting of the work on the chronological dividing lines between Judaism and the earliest Christianity allows the author to demonstrate the ties between the two religions. Thus Judaism is presented as the precursor of Christianity and, as such, there is a continuity that, for example, permits Peter to find the basis of the Trinity in Abraham's vision of three angels. Before the advent of Christianity, according to this play, Judaism was correct, the true path. Mary Magdalene's, Paul's, and Peter's previous Jewish existence is not denigrated, but they have evolved by recognizing and accepting Jesus. Those in error are those who remain obdurate in their nonacceptance, like Simon, whose rejection of Christianity makes him a greater villain than even Nero, who is merely ignorant of the truth.

General Observations. In a work so totally dedicated to a spiritual message it is not surprising that character development is nonexistent. The overall presentation of the personages is akin to that of medieval religious paintings in its rigidness and unidimensionalness. In a dramatic sense, the only really interesting figure is that of the hypocritical *gracioso* Zabulón, whose very human, fearful reactions to danger provide the comic antics to brighten the essentially grave tone of the work.

One point of continuity between *The Chalice and the Rock* and the earlier Enríquez Gómez plays is a certain emphasis on the feminine roles. There is also the same agitated pace maintained as in earlier works, and the usual fondness for the spectacular theatrical moment that in *The Chalice and the Rock* reaches unprecedented frequency, culminating in the final miraculous vision, that of Christ bearing his cross. This final supernatural scene ends a series of appearances and references to Christ, whose Resurrection is the supreme moment of Christianity. The fervent Christianity that sets *The Chalice and the Rock* apart from Enríquez Gómez's first group of plays is summed up by Peter's prayer affirming his dedication to Christ: "Salvador mío, / mi Jesús, mi Dios, mi amparo . . . que si mil vidas tuviera, / las entregara al suplicio" ("My savior, my Jesus, my God, my refuge. . . . If I had a thousand lives, I would gladly deliver them all up to torture for your sake" [100]).

The Valiant Campuzano

Synopsis. The play opens in Granada, where Leonor and Don Pedro are exchanging pledges of love. They wish to marry, but the match is vigorously opposed by Leonor's brother and guardian, Pedro de Alvarado y Campuzano, on the grounds that Pedro is tainted by the Moorish blood of his father and grandfather. Campuzano is a man of irascible temperament with a hair-triggered sense of honor. He has two comrades who accompany him in his escapades—his servant-*gracioso* Pimiento, and the formidable Catuja de la Ronda. The lowborn Catuja is as attractive as she is violent, and her skill is brawling equals that of Campuzano himself. Although it is never made absolutely clear, she seems to be both Campuzano's lover and his fighting companion.

Because of a street fight with some ruffians and later with the police, Campuzano, Catuja, and Pimiento have to leave Granada to avoid arrest. They return when Campuzano learns that Pedro is courting his sister and that marriage is a possibility. Campuzano rejects Pedro's request to marry his sister in terms so insulting that he begins another fight with Pedro and his friend Alvaro. The police surround the house but Campuzano and his comrades manage to fight their way out and escape.

In act 2 Campuzano, Pimiento and Catuja take refuge at an inn on the outskirts of the city. The innkeeper, whom Campuzano believes to be a friend, informs the police of their presence and a squad of officers led by a magistrate arrives to capture Campuzano. However, in the struggle Campuzano and Catuja manage to disarm the officials and proceed to kill the informing innkeeper. Campuzano secures a pardon from the intimidated magistrate on the condition that Campuzano leave Spain to join the army in Italy. Before he leaves the country, once again Campuzano returns to his house because he has received word that Leonor is to be married that evening. Campuzano, Catuja, and Pimiento, all masked, sneak into his house and mingle with the wedding guests. In a dramatic scene they suddenly reveal themselves, extinguish the lights, and carry Leonor off to a convent.

As act 3 opens all the principal figures of the first act have made their way to Italy. Campuzano and Pimiento are reunited with Catuja who stayed behind for a time in Granada. She brings the news that Leonor escaped from the convent to rejoin Pedro, but Pedro now refuses to marry her until he has avenged the insults he has suffered from Campuzano. Soon after we learn that Pedro has also arrived in Italy and that Leonor has followed him seeking restoration on her honor. In the military activity of the Siege of Vecelli, Leonor, Pedro, Campuzano, and Catuja cross each other's paths.[18] During the complicated movement of the battle scene, Campuzano and Catuja distinguish themselves. Immediately after the battle Campuzano kills Pedro, is pardoned by his general, the marquis of Leganés, and then is promoted to captain. Campuzano remains with the army in Italy, but Leonor has no other recourse than that of returning home to reenter the convent. For reasons that are not well explained, Catuja also decides to return to Granada.

A Play of the *Valentón*. Campuzano is at once an example of an Enríquez Gómez play of fictionalized adventure and a *comedia de valentón*. The term *valentón* is difficult to translate into one English word; the augmentative suffix produces something akin to "hyper-valiant," with both positive and negative aspects. The *valentón* is more than brave, he is rash, a quality of most *galanes* of the seventeenth-century stage, but here carried to even greater extremes. The *valentón* is a total law unto himself, recognizing only his own will which is entirely involved in maintaining his personal honor. This attitude, of course, brings instant conflict with any other person or agency that attempts to contradict in the slightest the desire of the *valentón*. Thus there are the inevitable clashes with the law that lead to his outlaw status.

The egotistical, bullying, and swaggering nature of the *valentón* is redeemed only by the intensity of his patriotism and his willingness to put all of his considerable bellicosity at the service of his king. Also, in his defense, it should be noted that the *valentón's* outlaw status is partially the fault of unscrupulous local officials and a corrupt judicial system, and that when the *valentón* does come into contact with a leader of character and ability (such as the marquis of Leganés in this play) he does not hesitate to serve in a subordinate position.

The *valentón* is no stranger to Enríquez Gómez's dramaturgy nor to Golden Age drama in general. His play *The Valiant Diego de Camas,* as the title indicates, is an early example of the author's interest in the type, dating from before 1633.[19] Others of Enríquez Gómez's heroes also come close to filling the *valentón's* mold, such as David of *The Prudent Abigail,* and certainly Samson of his epic poem. It is also possible that his lost play *El rayo de Palestina* (The thunderbolt of Palestine), with its typically *valiente* sounding title, is another work in the same vein, possibly a play about Samson.

Judging from the large number of extant *sueltas,* we can say that *The Valiant Campuzano* was a very popular play. In fact, Ada Coe has found records of the play's performance as late as 1788.[20] The popularity of this play seems to have been exceeded only by Enríquez Gómez's *Tutor of Alexander* and *Life and Death of the Cid.*

Characterization. The public's long-lasting acceptance of this play was, no doubt, due in large part to the swashbuckling actions that fill each act. In Pedro Campuzano and Catuja de la Ronda Enríquez Gómez dramatizes two characters that, by the strength of their personalities, are quite memorable considering the usual stereotyped *comedia* roles. Like many *valiente* plays the hero is based on an historical personage whose daring exploits elevated him to folk hero status.

Pedro de Alvarado y Campuzano is pure, raw, masculine ego, unencumbered with regard for any concerns other than his own. He is the very synthesis (or perhaps caricature) of the *hidalgo's* attributes in his disdain for manual labor, his exaltation of his pure and noble lineage, and his willingness to maintain the *status quo* even if his family starves—"pobre nací, pero limpio / de la mancha tenebrosa / que introdujeron a España / álarbes banderas moras" ("I was born poor but of ancestry unblemished by the dark stain that the Moors introduced into Spain" [577, a]).[21] All these qualities are obvious in his speech

to the captive judge in act 2, in which he defends himself for all the
troubles he has been involved in over the past several years. All of his
exploits resulted from acting as befits an *hidalgo*—rescuing ladies from
mistreatment, avenging his father's honor, aiding friends, and other
deeds. In spite of several murders that he admits having committed,
he is able to say with pride: "En mi vida robé a nadie, / ni dije mal
de persona; / por dinero a nadie he muerto" ("I have never robbed
anyone, / nor spoken ill of anyone, / nor murdered anyone for money"
[577, c]).

Campuzano's vision of himself is slanted to say the least. While it
may be true that his honor has kept him from killing for money, it
has certainly never kept him from associating with the low types with
whom he is constantly carousing. His honor is also perfectly content to
ruin his sister's chances for marriage with the man she desires. His
claim to have never spoken ill of anyone is contradicted by the gross
insults based on hearsay evidence that he delivers to Leonor's suitor:
"¿Quién os dijo a vos que yo / quiero perro con cencerro / en mi
linaje?" ("What makes you think I'd allow such a flagrant mongrel in
my bloodline?" [573, b]). Pedro's reply to Campuzano's libels sum up
what was obviously the dramatist's reaction to the *valentón:*

> Que sois hidalgo confieso;
> pero no lo parecéis
> en el lenguaje grosero.
> Porque siempre las palabras
> fueron luces de su dueño.

That you are an *hidalgo* I do confess, but you do not act like one when
you use such gross language. The words a man uses indicate his character.
(573, b)

Campuzano, constrained as he is by the straightjacket of honor,
contrasts with the freedom that his companion, Catuja, enjoys by virtue
of her low class origin. Of all the memorable female roles that Enríquez
Gómez created, that of Catuja is his best in that she seems to sum
up the forcefulness that characterizes his ladies since his first play, *To
Deceive in Order to Reign.* Her manner is as gruff and aggressive as
that of Campuzano and her appearance is just as intimidating as she
struts about in her rough clothes, brandishing her dagger. The servant,
Pimiento, finds his master's attachment to her incomprehensible even

though he admits she is good-looking. But Campuzano responds to
Pimiento's objections by stating that high-born ladies cannot compare
with her in any way and, in truth, Catuja seems the perfect companion
for the wandering Campuzano in his street existence as they pass from
one fight to another. In fact, Catuja's display of her ability to use her
dagger introduces the action of the play as the police try to arrest her
for wounding a man who lewdly alluded to her relationship with
Campuzano. In matters of violence Catuja always takes her place alongside
Campuzano even though his masculine ego would rather see her in a
less aggressive role. She constantly has to remind him of her worth, as
for example in act 2, when she says to him:

> Pues, ¿qué vales tú sin mí?
> ¿Te ensanchas porque te nombran
> el valiente Campuzano?
> Pues nada, amigo, te sobra;
> que en el gasto de la muerte
> yo soy tu ayuda de costa.

What are you worth without me? Are you puffed up because they call you
Campuzano the Valiant? Well, friend, you are not unique, for in passing
out death blows I am your principal aide.

(578, c)

Catuja's penchant for action and adventure is well brought out in
the play. She is as brave as Campuzano or any man, but her one
frustration is that she finds little recognition because of her sex. Men,
including Campuzano, while they are impressed by her resourcefulness,
tend not to give her full credit. Campuzano mirrors the male ambivalence
toward her. Her services as a fighter are invaluable to him, but he
accepts them reluctantly, feeling that her deeds are not appropriate for
a woman. "Repara que eres mujer" ("Remember that you are a woman"
[582, c]), Campuzano says to her when she asks the marquis of Leganés
for the same permission to join his forces that has been granted to
Campuzano. And while she is Amazonian in valor—"[soy] Catuja
Pantisilea, / segunda Palas de Ronda" ("I am Catuja Pantasilea, a
second Pallas from Ronda" [580, a])—she does not share the Amazonian
distaste for men. Free from constraints of family honor, Catuja is
sympathetic to Leonor's problems, urging Campuzano to allow his sister
to marry the man she wishes and, in the last act, serving as intermediary

between brother and sister to effect a reconciliation. As for her own sentimental feelings, she admits to being inextricably linked to Campuzano while at the same time insisting on her own identity and sense of self-worth. She is not one to endure just any sort of treatment from her boy friend, as she plainly tells him:

> Si estimares mi fineza,
> amor te lo pagará.
> Y de no, yo tengo pies
> y sé el camino real.
> Yo soy tuya, ya lo sabes.
> Para mí la guerra es paz,
> que este negro querer bien
> nos hace querer muy mal.

If you esteem my qualities, you will be rewarded with love, and if not, I have feet that know where the highway is. I am yours; you know that. For me war is peace, and this damned love makes us have these quarrels.

(581, b)

The Question of Honor.   The question of honor, the obligations it imposes, and the response to the obligations provide the theme and variations for this play. In every one of the characters Enríquez Gómez has examined a different aspect of the honor problem, and we are left to surmise if the punctilious observation of the code is indeed rewarded.

Campuzano is born an *hidalgo* and, in accordance with the code of society, defends his honor at all costs. His personal valor and disregard of physical danger is a positive quality, even if he may be said to overreact in some of these situations. Noteable, however, is his almost hysterical concern for racial purity that causes all the problems and results in the death of Don Pedro, the enforced spinsterhood of Leonor, and his separation from Catuja.

In the character of Don Pedro, Enríquez Gómez gives us the *converso* dilemma thinly disguised under the label Moorish. As a suitor Don Pedro is acceptable in every way—in his good manners, his affection for Leonor, and his wealth. He is, moreover, an attractive person, and comports himself as a *hidalgo*. Truly Don Pedro is a gentleman except for one thing over which he has no control—his blood line, his descent from Moorish (read *converso*) ancestors. The play's paradox, and very likely the author's covert message, is that Don Pedro, the one man who really seems a gentleman, is a New Christian doomed to humiliation and death at the hands of the bigoted ruffian of an Old Christian, Pedro Campuzano.

With regard to Leonor and honor, her birth, like that of her brother, condemns her to a style of life over which she has little control. Her struggle to marry the man of her own choosing outside of her social class is against the conventions that the seventeenth-century theater upheld. Because she proceeds contrary to decorum in her attempt to evade her brother's prohibition against marrying Don Pedro, her rebellion is frustrated. On the other hand, while we sympathize with her complaint against her brother's tyranny, Leonor's motives are not totally based on love. In a conversation with her cousin Ana, Leonor reveals that her desire to marry Pedro is based on reasons perhaps more economic than sentimental. However much Campuzano may disdain money, for his sister the prospect of genteel poverty is not attractive. She says:

> Don Pedro es rico y me fundo
> en que si tiene dinero,
> es el blasón verdadero
> que hoy estima más el mundo.
> Si no es tan noble que pueda
> con mi linaje igualarse,
> bien puede sobrellevarse
> esta falta con la rueda
> de la fortuna, que iguala
> la más noble calidad
> con la mayor cantidad.

Don Pedro is rich and I would say that if one has money, that is the coat of arms that the world most esteems. If he is not noble enough to equal my lineage, his fortune will make up the difference, for that makes quality equal quantity.

(571, c)

Of the four main characters—Pedro, Leonor, Campuzano, and Catuja—it is ironic that true honor, that nobility of spirit which comes from within, is best exemplified in Catuja, the camp follower, who, according to convention, is doubly void of honor as a woman and as a person of low class status. Nevertheless, she is brave, always honest in her advice, and unfailing in her support for Campuzano even if she believes his course to be wrong. At the same time she is broad-minded and sympathetic to the problems of Pedro and Leonor, feeling that their desire to wed should be sufficient.

A Final Observation. *The Valiant Campuzano* is a play that was intended by Enríquez Gómez to be understood in two ways. On the most obvious level it is a work that affirms the Old Christian order. Campuzano's killing of Don Pedro is forgiven and, as a result of his bravery, he is recognized by his commander and promoted to captain. But there are enough discordant notes to indicate that Enríquez Gómez intended the play as an implicit criticism of Old Christian domination of society. The lack of a genuine love interest on the hero's part makes the play rather unusual and leads to a very uncommon denouement notable for its lack of marriages that so often characterize the ending of seventeenth-century plays. This lack of such a harmonizing note indicates that the killing of Don Pedro and the frustration of Leonor's desires have only satisfied Campuzano's personal affront and have not really restored order to society in a larger sense. The play poses some intriguing questions concerning Enríquez Gómez's views on honor. Are the *valentón's* actions really to be applauded as, no doubt, they were by contemporary audiences? Could a *converso* with such a background of persecution as Enríquez Gómez seriously present a bigoted type as Campuzano as a hero? Is it possible that the real play here concerns the tragedy of the *converso* Don Pedro, and that it is disguised as a *comedia de valentón,* ostensibly exalting Old Christian values?[22]

Notes and References

Chapter One

1. Antonio Domínguez Ortiz, *Los judeoconversos en España y América* (Madrid: ISTMO, 1971), 13. For an informative article outlining the work that has been done on Iberian *marranos,* see Gérard Nahon, "Les marranes espagnols et portugais et les communautés juives issues du marranisme dans l'historiographie récente (1960–1975)," *Revue des Etudes Juives* 136, nos. 3–4 (1977):297–367. Unless otherwise noted all translations in this and other chapters are my own.

2. See *Encyclopaedia Judaica* (New York: Macmillan, 1971), 11:1018, for a review of the various theories on the derivation of *marrano.* At one time or another Hebrew, Árabic, and Spanish have each been advanced as the origins of the word.

3. In this I follow the practice of Yosef Hayim Yerushalmi, in *From Spanish Court to Italian Ghetto: Isaac Cardoso A Study in Seventeenth-Century Marranism and Jewish Apologetics* (New York: Columbia University Press, 1971), xv.

4. L. García Iglesias, *Los judíos en la España antigua* (Madrid: Cristiandad, 1978), 40–41.

5. Ibid., 69–70.

6. García Iglesias writes (ibid., 35–36) that although the term "Sepharad" mentioned in Obadiah 20 was taken by medieval Jews to refer to Spain, the biblical identification was really with the city of Sardis in Asia Minor.

7. Arianism; the heresy established by the fourth-century A.D. Alexandrine theologian Arius. Arius taught that Christ the Son was not consubstantial with God the Father. See entry in *Encyclopaedia Britannica,* 11th ed. (Cambridge: Cambridge University Press, 1910).

8. García Iglesias, *Los judíos* 199–202. Bernard S. Bachrach has written that historians have overestimated the effectiveness of Visigothic anti-Jewish policies and underestimated the importance and strength of the Jewish community. See his "A Reassessment of Visigothic Jewish Policy, 589–711," *American Historical Review* 78, no. 1 (1973):11–34.

9. Julio Caro Baroja discusses the various ghettos of Spain in *Los judíos en la España moderna y contemporanea* (Madrid: Ariel, 1961), vol. 1, chaps. 1–2.

10. The Sephardim played a considerable role in the politics and commerce of the United States. A popular work outlining their contribution

and aristocratic nature is Stephen Birmingham's *The Grandees: The Story of America's Sephardic Elite* (New York: Dell, 1972).

11. Domínguez Ortiz, *Los judeoconversos,* 151: "The majority of converts wound up assimilating because there was in them a real will to integrate themselves into the surrounding society."

12. For the conflict between Jews and *conversos* see Stephen H. Haliczar, "The Castilian Urban Patriciate and the Jewish Expulsion of 1480–92," *American Historical Review* 78, no. 1 (1973):35–58.

13. Domínguez Ortiz, *Los judeoconversos,* 44–45.

14. Benzion Netanyahu, *The Marranos of Spain From the Late XIVth to the Early XVIth Century According to Contemporary Hebrew Sources* (New York: Kraus Reprint Co., 1973). According to Yerushalmi (*From Spanish Court,* 21–31) Netanyahu bases his work on the *responsa* of rabbis outside the peninsula which tended to view anything less than strict adherence to all practices of Judaism as non-Jewish. Yerushalmi argues that, given their circumstances, the Iberian *marranos* did the best they could to keep alive their Judaism, and it is absurd to write them off as Christians, especially if in their hearts they did not consider themselves such.

15. Domínguez Ortiz, *Los judeoconversos,* 66–77.

16. Ibid., 69, n. 13.

17. "Lusitanian Jewry had not suffered the slow debilitative process of erosion which their Hispanic brethren had endured from 1391 to 1492" (Yerushalmi, *From Spanish Court,* 4). Moreover, Yerushalmi observes that since the Portuguese community was converted entirely and at once by a decree of King Manoel, there was no long period of Jews and *conversos* living together as in Spain: "Portuguese Jewry thus evaded the corrosive intracommunal and intrafamilial ruptures which conversion had brought to Spanish Jewry, and which had plagued the latter through much of the fifteenth century" (ibid., 6).

18. By the late sixteenth century, in the numerous cases cited in Caro Baroja's *Historia,* the vast majority of the accused were identified as Portuguese.

19. Three widely cited works dealing with this institution are Henry Charles Lea, *A History of the Inquisition in Spain* (New York: Macmillan, 1906); Henry Kamen, *The Spanish Inquisition* (New York and London: Weidenfeld & Nicolson, 1965); and Cecil Roth, *The Spanish Inquisition* (New York: Norton, 1964). Paul J. Hauben, *The Spanish Inquisition* (New York: Wiley, 1969), offers a bibliography and selections from the various interpreters of the Inquisition.

20. Roth, *Spanish Inquisition,* 131. Although for most of its history the Inquisition was primarily concerned with heresy, it also dealt with other crimes—homosexuality, bigamy, fornication, witchcraft, blasphemy, sacrilege, and others.

21. See Bartolomé Bennassar, *L'Inquisition espagnole, XVe—XIXe* siècle (Paris: Hachette, 1979). This collection of essays based on statistical studies of archives proposes that, after its initial period of establishment, the Inquisitional methods and proceedings were not nearly as harsh as has been portrayed.

22. See Caro Baroja, *Historia,* 1:328, citing Sebastián de Horozco: "In 1538 when the *sanbenitos* that were in the cloister of Toledo Cathedral and that corresponded to persons penanced during the first days of the Inquisition became faded and worn, they were ordered renovated and placed in the parish churches of the quarters where the reconciled had lived and where their descendants were still. This reopened past shame and a large number of families changed their name."

Chapter Two

1. From the unpaginated prologue to *Sansón Nazareno* (Rouen: Maurry, 1656). I have modernized the spelling and punctuation of the Spanish texts for the sake of readability.

2. Among other New Christian writers active during the seventeenth century were Mateo Alemán, Felipe Godínez, Miguel de Silveyra, Juan Pérez de Montalbán, the two Cardosos, Vélez de Guevara, and perhaps Rojas Zorrilla (there are some doubts about his ancestry). For a good portion of their lives these writers were active in Spain. Other New Christians wrote in Spanish and Portuguese in various exile locations. For the Low Countries see Henry V. Besso, *Dramatic Literature of the Sephardic Jews of Amsterdam in the XVIIth and XVIIIth Centuries* (New York: Hispanic Institute, 1947). A. Domínguez Ortiz discusses the impact of *conversos* on literature in *Los judeoconversos,* 193–217; he states: "No one can deny that an important percentage in quantity and quality of our writers in the Golden Age were *conversos*" (215).

3. Before Révah the standard source for the life of Enríquez was the much cited article on him in Barrera y Leirado, *Catálogo del teatro antiguo español* (Madrid: Rivadeneyra, 1890), 135–42.

4. The remark is a pun difficult to translate. The phrase has a proverbial meaning something akin to "I don't give a damn; I couldn't care less." Its literal meaning is "Let them give me everything [their worst] there."

5. I. S. Révah, "Un pamphlet contre l'Inquisition d'Antonio Enríquez Gómez: La seconde partie de la *Política angélica* (Rouen, 1647)," *Revue des Etudes Juives* 131 (1962):81–168. I have relied heavily on this article for the dates and facts of Enríquez Gómez's life. Additional information is included from the introduction to Charles Amiel's edition of Antonio Enríquez Gómez, *El siglo pitagórico y vida de don Gregorio Guadaña* (Paris: Ediciones Hispanoamericanas, 1977), and from other sources as cited.

6. C. H. Rose, "Las comedias políticas de Enríquez Gómez," *Nuevo Hispanismo* 2 (1982):45–56.

7. Caro Baroja, *Inquisición, brujería y criptojudaísmo* (Barcelona: Ariel, 1974), 82–83.

8, Révah, "Un pamphlet," 138.

9. Ibid., 143.

10. Although he does not discuss the Spanish academies, an informative account of the type of literary activity that took place in similar associations is found in Irving A. Leonard, *Baroque Times in Old Mexico* (Anne Arbor: University of Michigan Press, 1966), chaps. 9–10.

11. For more on Febos, see Caro Baroja, *Inquisición*, 60–62. A lengthy article by Cecil Roth discusses crypto-Jewish activities at Rouen: "Les marranes a Rouen: un chapitre ignoré de l'histoire des Juifs de France," *Revue des Etudes Juives* 88 (1929):113–55.

12. In Timothy Oelman's introduction to his edition of the *Romance al divin mártir, Judá Creyente* (Rutherford, N.J.: Fairleigh Dickinson University Press, 1986), he discusses Enríquez Gómez's relationship to Febos.

13. From the prologue to *Samson the Nazarene*.

14. Caro Baroja, *Inquisición*, 61.

15. Révah, "Un pamphlet," 122. The italics are mine.

16. For more on this figure see I. S. Révah "Fernándes de Villareal: Adversaire et victime de l'Inquisition portugaise," *Iberida, Revista de Filologia* (Rio de Janeiro) 1 (April 1959):33–54; 1 (December 1959):188–207. Concerning the relationship between Enríquez Gómez and Fernándes de Villareal, see Michéle Gendreau-Massaloux and C. H. Rose, "Antonio Enríquez Gómez et Manuel Fernándes de Villareal: Deux destins parallèles, une vision politique commune," *Revue des Etudes Juives* 136, nos. 3–4 (1977):368–88. See also for this period of Enríquez Gómez's life, C. H. Rose, "Portuguese Diplomacy Plays a Role in the Printing of Some Peninsular Works in Rouen in the Seventeenth Century," *Arquivos do Centro Cultural Português* (Fundação Calouste Gulbenkian) 10 (1976):523–41.

17. Amiel, *El siglo pitagórico*, xix.

18. Gendreau-Massaloux, Rose, "Antonio Enríquez Gómez," 376.

19. Amiel, *El siglo pitagórico*, xix.

20. Ibid., xx.

21. See, for example, the remarks of Ramón de Mesonero Romanos in his introduction to *Dramáticos posteriores a Lope de Vega, Biblioteca de autores españoles*, 47:xxxii–xxxiv.

22. Jesús Antonio Cid, "Judaizantes y carreteros para un hombre de letras: A. Enríquez Gómez (1600–1663)," in *Homenaje a Julio Caro Baroja* (Madrid: CSIC, 1978), 291. Not everyone is so certain, however; Caro Baroja in *Inquisición* (154–55) feels that Enríquez Gómez was probably a Christian at least during the final portion of his life. Another investigator who strongly

maintains Enríquez Gómez's Christianity throughout his life is José García Valdecasas, *Las "Academias morales" de Antonio Enríquez Gómez* (Seville: Anales de la Universidad Hispalense, 1971).

Chapter Three

1. The dates for *Diego de Camas, Fernán Méndez Pinto,* and *Captain Chinchilla* are established by H. A. Rennert's report of play presentation in his "Notes of the Chronology of the Spanish Drama," *Modern Language Review* 2 (1906):331–41; 3 (1907–8):43–55. The date assigned to the *Overweening Pride of Nimrod* is taken from Barrera's report of a manuscript in the library of Lord Holland that included the notation that the play was presented at the Prado Theater on 5 August 1635. The year 1642 is the first printing of Enríquez Gómez's *Moral Academies* which includes the four plays cited. Finally, J. A. Cid's "Judaizantes y carreteros," 273–74, cites a document of ca. 1649 that contains a reference to a play of Enríquez Gómez whose title is given as *King Solomon,* no doubt the play, *The Throne of Solomon,* in the author's listing of 1649.

2. The *valiente* play was increasingly popular during the seventeeth century. Both Campuzano and *The Valiant Diego de Camas* deal with the exploits of this particular *comedia* type, and the title of the lost *Thunderbolt of Palestine* indicates a possible third play along this line.

3. Quevedo in particular vacilated between friendship and enmity toward Olivares. For more detail see D. W. Bleznick, *Quevedo* (New York: Twayne, 1972).

4. See, for example, a summary of the characteristics and elements of the Spanish *comedia* in Everett W. Hesse, *Calderón de la Barca* (New York: Twayne, 1967).

5. For more on this most interesting and possibly first play of Enríquez Gómez see Glen Dille, "The Originality of Antonio Enríquez Gómez in *Engañar para reinar*," in *Renaissance and Golden Age Essays in Honor of D. W. McPheeters,* ed. Bruno M. Damiani (Potomac, Md.: Scripta Humanistica, 1986), 49–60.

6. *The Prudent Abigail* (Valencia: Orga, 1762), 7.

7. J. Amador de los Ríos, *Estudios históricos, políticos y literarios sobre los judíos de España* (Madrid, 1848), 555.

8. *To Deceive in Order to Reign* (Valencia: Orga, 1762), 12.

9. Ibid., 31.

10. Ibid., 31.

11. *Fernán Méndez Pinto,* ed. L. G. Cohen, F. M. Rogers, and C. H. Rose, Harvard Texts from the Romance Languages, no. 5 (Cambridge, Mass.: Harvard University Press, 1974), 2.457.

12. Melveena McKendrick, *Woman and Society in the Spanish Drama of the Golden Age: A Study of the Mujer Varonil* (Cambridge: Cambridge

University Press, 1974), 142. See also Glen Dille, "Notes on Aggressive Women in the *Comedia* of Enríquez Gómez," *Romance Notes* 21 (1980):1–7.

13. *Fernán Méndez Pinto*, 1.53–60.

14. *To Deceive in Order to Reign*, 5.

15. *What Jealousies Oblige* (Barcelona: Escuder, n.d.), 7.

16. Amador de los Ríos, *Estudios*, 555.

17. See C. H. Rose's comments on the poetics of *Fernán Méndez Pinto* in her portion of the introduction to the play, 65–73.

18. Leandro Fernández de Moratín. *La derrota de los pedantes*, ed. John Dowling (Barcelona: Editorial Labor, 1973), 90.

19. *Dramáticos posteriores a Lope de Vega*, BAE 47, 1:xxxii–iv.

20. Marcelino Menéndez y Pelayo, *Historia de los heterodoxos españoles* (Madrid: Biblioteca de Autores Cristianos, 1956), 2:259.

21. H. Graetz, *Volkstümliche Geschichte der Juden* (Lepzig, 1923), 219.

22. This play is discussed in more detail in Glen Dille, "Antonio Enríquez Gómez's Honor Tragedy, A lo que obliga el honor," *Bulletin of the Comediantes*, 30, no. 2 (1978):97–111. There is a critical edition of *What Honor Obliges* done as a University of London M.A. thesis in 1953 by Silvia Wynter. Wynter concludes that the play was written about 1640.

23. It is interesting to note that Amador de los Ríos, the only critic to pay much attention to Enríquez Gómez's plays, suggested that his tragedy was written first and inspired those of Calderón (*Estudios*, 558–59). Amador based this suggestion on the mistaken idea that Enríquez Gómez was twenty years older than Calderón, when actually they were the same age. Unfortunately, neither the tragedies of Calderón nor that of Enríquez Gómez can be dated with enough accuracy to establish precedence. The notion that Calderón might have turned to Enríquez Gómez for inspiration is not so farfetched. C. H. Rose has suggested that the second part of *La hija del aire* (The daughter of the air) was Enríquez Gómez's and not Calderón's. See her controversial article "Who Wrote the *Segunda Parte* of *La hija del aire*," *Revue Belge de Philosophie et d'Histoire* 54 (1976):797–822. At least two other Enríquez Gómez plays were at times attributed to Calderón—*Jealousies Cannot Obscure the Sun* and *To Deceive in Order to Reign*. On the other hand, Calderón's *La española de Florencia* (The Spanish lady of Florence) was at least once attributed to Enríquez Gómez—see Ada Coe, *Catálogo bibliográfico y crítico de las comedias anunciadas en los periódicos de Madrid, 1661–1819, Johns Hopkins Studies in Romance Literatures and Languages*, vol. 9 (Baltimore, 1935), 89.

24. *What Honor Obliges*, in *Dramáticos posteriores a Lope de Vega*, BAE, 47:511.

25. *Contra el amor no hay engaños*, in *Las academias morales de las musas* (Bordeaux: Pedro de la Court, 1642), 304–5.

26. *The Prudent Abigail*, 2–3.

27. J. A. Cid notes this trait in "Judaizantes y carreteros," 288.

Chapter Four

1. José Sánchez's work on seventeenth-century literary academies includes excerpts of fictitious academies in Enríquez Gómez's *Moral Academies* and the *Pythagorean Century*. See his *Academias literarias del siglo de oro español* (Madrid: Gredos, 1961), 187–91.

2. See chapter 2, n. 16.

3. García Valdecasas, *Las "Academias morales,"* 42, comments that "Danteo and Albano are two very different ways of understanding the world, but so entwined that perhaps they represent two postures of the same soul in a bipartite soliloquy."

4. All citations to the Academies are made from the first edition (Bordeaux, 1642). I have modernized the orthography for convenience.

5. It is interesting to note that this retelling of the Dinah story ends with her dishonor and does not then include the subsequent bloody massacre with which her brothers take their revenge.

6. Other sonnets beginning with variations of this verse are presented by B. W. Wardroper in his *Spanish Poetry of the Golden Age* (New York: Appleton-Century-Crofts, 1971), 49–53. Except for his adoption of the famous first verse, Enríquez Gómez's poem is entirely independent in form and content from all the other versions.

7. Silvia Wynter (*A Critical Edition*, 44) calls attention to the fact that the index of the *Moral Academies* announces the play *No hay poder contra el honor* (No power prevails over honor) and suggests that *What Honor Obliges* was a last-minute substitution for some unknown reason.

8. In his introduction to his edition of the *Pythagorean Century* (xix–xx), Charles Amiel indicates that this was in fact Enríquez Gómez's plan when he did return to Spain several years later.

9. Judith Rauchwarger, "Antonio Enríquez Gómez's *Epístolas tres de Job*: A Matter of Racial Atavism?," *Revue de Etudes Juives* 138, nos. 1–2 (1979):69–87. Among other studies of works on Job, Rauchwarger has considered his son's epic: "A Seventeenth-Century Epic: Diego Enríquez Basurto's, *El triumpho de la virtud y paciencia de Job*," *Sefarad* 40 (1980):99–120.

10. Rauchwarger, "Gómez's *Epístolas*," 85.

11. Ibid.

12. The *Polyphemus and Galatea* is mentioned by Enríquez Gómez in the introduction to *Samson the Nazarene*, and its influence is clear in several passages of that work. See chapter 7.

13. In addition to its appearance several times in the *Academies*, we find examples of the sleeping beauty motif in *Gregorio Guadaña*, in *Samson the Nazarene*, and in several plays. Whether it has any special meaning for

174 ANTONIO ENRÍQUEZ GÓMEZ

Enríquez Gómez, or simply interested him for its poetic possibilities, is a matter for further study.

14. Cid, "Judaizantes y carreteros," 284–85, notes the predilection for the topic in various works of Enríquez Gómez: "The topic is a commonplace that appears in other authors. But no one has used it with more insistence than Enríquez, nor given it so many meanings." A detailed analysis of Enríquez Gómez's presentations of the topic is to be found in Angel M. García Gómez, *The Legend of the Laughing Philosopher and Its Presence in Spanish Literature (1500–1700)*, 2d ed. (Córdoba: Universidad de Córdoba, Servicio de Publicaciones, 1984), 192–223. I am grateful to Michael McGaha for supplying a copy of this work.

15. This seems to suggest that Enríquez Gómez left Spain in 1636.

16. Yerushalmi (*From Spanish Court,* 110) observes this same reticence in Isaac Cardoso. Even after he attained the safety of Italy and returned publicly to Judaism, Cardoso's voluminous writings reveal extremely little about his family history. The dread of compromising oneself and one's family was strongly and early ingrained into *converso* children and even more so in the case of *marrano* families.

17. Juan Luis Alborg, *Historia de la literatura española* (Madrid: Gredos, 1967), 3:491.

18. Guillermo Díaz Plaja, *Historia general de las literaturas hispánicas* (Barcelona: Spes, 1953), 3:382–85.

19. Marcelino Menéndez y Pelayo, *Historia de los heterodoxos españoles* (Madrid: BAC, 1956), 261.

Chapter Five

1. All citations in this chapter refer to page numbers in Charles Amiel's edition of the *Pythagorean Century,* previously cited. The introduction to this edition includes a detailed examination of the various editions of this work and reveals a spurious edition of 1682. Amiel's notes and appendixes are an invaluable mine of information on this and other Enríquez Gómez works.

2. Other dedications that show this same sort of sympathetic admiration of a victim of adversity are that of the *Tower of Babylon,* dedicated to the Marquis of Rochefort (see chapter 6), and that of *Samson the Nazarene* to an unnamed magnate, probably the Prince de Condé (see chapter 8).

3. The terms *soberbio* and *arbitrista* are difficult to translate succinctly. The *soberbio* is the man of overweening, sinful pride. The *arbitrista,* so often a satiric target of seventeenth-century literature, was a person proposing plans and projects to pull the country out of its financial morass. The *arbitrista's* schemes often involved wildly irresponsible methods of taxation that promised instant alleviation for the state's chronic lack of funds. Amiel (*Pythagorean Century,* 322–32) gives a bibliography of works pertaining to the *arbitrista.*

4. Caro Baroja, *Inquisición,* 61. See also Amiel, *Pythagorean Century,* 320–21, on the Hebraic origin of the word.

5. J. H. Elliott, *The Count-Duke of Olivares: The Statesman in an Age of Decline* (New Haven: Yale University Press, 1986).

6. Ibid., 646.

7. Amiel, *Pythagorean Century* 56, n. 16. Gendreau-Massaloux and Rose, "Antonio Enríquez Gómez" (381–85), discuss in detail Enríquez Gómez's views on the choices of the king's ministers.

8. Even though Enríquez Gómez treats the idea of rebirth as a literary device, it is a fact that for cabalists the doctrine of transmigration was very important. B. Netanyahu's book, *Don Isaac Abravanel: Statesman and Philosopher* (Philadelphia: Jewish Publication Society of America, 1972), illustrates this belief in Abravanel's works: "God offers a possibility of rehabilitation even to souls which leave the body contaminated and full of sin, that is, without repentance. They are given the opportunity to purify themselves and get rid of the material sin which clings to them by being returned to another body where they can repent and achieve this aim" (117).

9. J. H. Silverman, "Los 'hidalgos cansados' de Lope de Vega," in *Homenaje a William L. Fichter, Estudios sobre el teatro antiguo hispánico y otros ensayos,* ed. A. David Kossoff and José Amor y Vázquez (Madrid: Castalia, 1971), 693–711.

10. In his edition Amiel notes the passages that were expurgated in subsequent editions.

11. *Tesoro de los mejores autores españoles,* 60 vols. (Paris, 1838–70); vol. 38 is *Tesoro de novelistas españoles antiguos y modernos con una introducción y notas de don Eugenio de Ochoa* (1847).

12. W. Atkinson, in "Studies in Literary Decadence: The Picaresque World Novel," *Bulletin of Spanish Studies* 4 (1927):19–27, is totally negative: "Don Gregorio . . . is an unprincipled and undesirable individual who is drawn to vice and foppishness by heredity and he fails to hold our interest or to attract our sympathy on a single count" (26). Ticknor is a little more kind: "A book of little value [the *Pythagorean Century*] . . . except for the *Gregorio Guadaña* which is occasionally pleasant and interesting because it evidently gives us sketches from the author's own experience" (*History of Spanish Literature* [Boston: Houghton, 1872], 3:128).

13. R. O. Jones, *Historia de la literatura española,* vol. 2, *Siglo de Oro: prosa y poesía,* (Barcelona: Ariel, 1974), 212.

14. Juan L. Alborg, *Historia de la literatura española* (Madrid: Gredos, 1970), 2:491–92. The most recent and lengthy look at *Don Gregorio* is M. J. Thacker's "Gregorio Guadaña: Pícaro-Francés or Pícaro-Galán," in *Hispanic Studies in Honor of Frank Pierce,* ed. John England (University of Sheffield: Department of Hispanic Studies, 1980), 149–68. Thacker debunks the idea of French influence on the novel, noting instead a natural evolution of the

picaresque genre along lines of the *novela cortesana* especially as developed by Castillo Solórzano.

15.   Peter N. Dunn, *The Spanish Picaresque Novel* (Boston: Twayne, 1979), 111.

16.   See, for example, Edward Nagy, "El anhelo de Guzmán de 'Conocer su sangre': Una posibilidad interpretiva," *Kentucky Romance Quarterly*, 16 (1969):75–95.

17.   Amiel, *Pythagorean Century*, 154, n. 3, compares the incident of Lucrecia to chapter 17 of Castillo Solórzano's *La niña de los embustes, Teresa de Manzanares* (1637).

18.   For example, *To Deceive in Order to Reign, What Honor Obliges,* and *Brains versus Beauty.*

19.   Thomas Hanrahan disagrees. He writes in his *La mujer en la novela picaresca* (Madrid: Porrua, 1967) that "Enríquez is impartial" (363) with regard to the battle of the sexes and that Gregorio "is not necessarily condemned to defeat" (363).

20.   Gendreau-Massaloux and Rose note that Enríquez Gómez's imagery involving a finely tuned instrument is inspired by the emblems of Andrea Alciati; they cite other examples in *The Angelic Politics* and in *Louis God-given.* See their "Antonio Enríquez Gómez," 380, n. 30.

21.   Hanrahan, *La mujer,* 358.

Chapter Six

1.   The Order of St. Michel was founded by Louis XI at Amboise in 1469. Information from the *Grand Larousse Enciclopédique* (Paris, 1964), 9:528.

2.   The Golden Tower is a Sevillan landmark. Whether the reference is to this particular structure or to the Tower of Babylon of this work (or to both at once) is not clear. The dedication to the female inhabitants is also cryptic but not unusual considering the antifeminine tone of the work. All page references to the *Tower of Babylon* are to the edition of 1649.

3.   Francisco de Quevedo, *Obras completas,* ed. Felicidad Buendía (Madrid: Aguilar, 1961). The marquis appears in *La visita de los chistes,* 232–48.

4.   A somewhat similar situation was employed before by Enríquez Gómez in *Don Gregorio Guadaña* when Gregorio goes on patrol with the judge in Carmona; see 109–13 of Amiel's edition.

5.   Both this work and the earlier *First Pilgrim's Guilt* are not noted in Kirkconnell's catalog of European versions of the Creation. See Watson Kirkconnell, *The Celestial Cycle* (Toronto: University of Toronto Press, 1952).

6.   In effect, this work as well as others of Enríquez Gómez are lengthy variations on the concept of Original Sin. The same has been noted

with regard to another *converso's* work, Alemán's *Guzmán de Alfarache*. See Jones (*Historia,* 192) citing the finds of Enrique Moreno Báez.

7. A similar passage relating the difficult birth of Don Gregorio Guadaña is to be found in Amiel's edition of the *Pythagorean Century,* 87–89.

8. This topic is a continuation of an idea present in the *Angelic Politics* which is particularly concerned with the prejudicial treatment of innocent children of guilty parents. See chapter 8.

9. C. H. Rose discusses in detail the expression of the exile's fantasies in "Antonio Enríquez Gómez and the Literature of Exile," *Romanische Forschungen* 85 (1974):63–77. This article is an elaboration of her portion of the introduction to an edition of *Fernán Méndez Pinto.*

10. Quevedo, *Obras completas,* 234.

11. See the article of Gendreau-Massaloux and Rose, "Antonio Enríquez Gómez," 376, n. 21.

12. For information concerning Quevedo's life and works see Bleznick's *Quevedo.* Chapter 3 (41–69) discusses the *Sueños.*

13. There are also a number of verse passages in a variety of meters in the *Tower of Babylon,* but these are quite uniformly burlesque and satiric.

Chapter Seven

1. "Nazarene" is used as the translation following the lead of J. H. Parker who, in his *Juan Pérez de Montalbán* (Boston: Twayne, 1976), 57–58, translates *El valiente nazareno, Sansón* as *The Valiant Nazarene, Samson.* Actually, Samson was not a Nazarene "from Nazareth" but a Nazirite: "For the child shall be a Nazirite to God from the womb to the day of his death" (Judges 13:7). *The Expositor's Bible* by W. S. Robertson Nicoll (New York, 1909) has a lengthy section on Nazirites: "The Nazirite's life partook of the nature of the priestly as well as of the prophetic office; it was a protest against the self-indulgent habits of the surrounding nations; and something of the warrior and the judge was also inherent in the service which the Nazirite rendered for God and His people, as in the case of Samson in his exploits against the Philistines" (259). The *Samson The Nazarene* had been edited in a University of London M.A. thesis (1976) by Timothy Oelman: "Two Poems of Antonio Enríquez Gómez: Romance al divín mártir, Judá Creyente and Sansón Nazareno." Portions of the epic have been translated by Oelman in *Marrano Poets of the Seventeenth Century* (Rutherford, N.J.: Fairleigh Dickinson University Press, 1982). See also Oelman's "Tres poetas marranos," *Nueva Revista de Filología Hispánica* 30 (1981):184–206.

2. Cid, "Judaizantes y carreteros" (271–300), and Oelman, *Marrano Poets* (212), suggest the Grand Condé, and that Enríquez Gómez's involvement with the Fronde caused his departure from France. All citations to *Samson*

refer to book and stanza of the only known edition, that of Maurry at Rouen, 1656.

3.   The prologues to the *Tower of Babylon* and the *Samson* are fully reprinted in A. Porqueras Mayo's *El prólogo en el manierismo y barroco españoles* (Madrid: CSIC, 1968), 137–39, 213–17. An introductory study and critical edition of the Prologue to *Samson nazareno* has been published by M. G. Profeti in "Un esempio de critica 'militante': il prologo al *Sansón nazareno* di Enríquez Gómez," *Quarderni di lingue e letteratura* 7 (1982):203–12.

4.   Pérez de Montalbán, for example, made a similar list as Parker notes (*Juan Peréz de Montalbán*, 69–70).

5.   Frank Pierce regards Enríquez Gómez's praise of Silveyra as "bordering on dementia," but then notes that the *Samson*, as well as Usiel's and Silveyra's works, "merit and need" further study. See his *La poesía épica del siglo de oro* (Madrid: Gredos, 1968), 314–16.

6.   For a résumé of Silveyra's life, see J. Caro Baroja, *Inquisición*, 125–233.

7.   This type of catalog recalls, among others, two such roll calls at the end of Pérez de Montalbán's miscellany, *Para todos* (1632). Parker, *Juan Pérez*, 106–9, reproduces the table of contents of this work.

8.   Enríquez Gómez was probably inspired by an earlier play of another *converso* writer, Felipe Godínez, whom he certainly knew in Madrid. As early as 1613 Godínez had written *La reina Ester* (Queen Esther), subtitled *Amán y Mardoqueo*. See Carmen Menéndez Onrubia, "Hacia la biografía de un iluminado judío: Felipe Godínez (1585–1659)," *Segismundo* 25–26 (1969–71):89–130.

9.   See Pierce's catalog of epic poems in *Poesía épica*, 327–75.

10.   Watson Kirkconnell, *That Invincible Samson* (Toronto: University Toronto Press, 1964). Kirkconnell was evidently not aware of *Samson the Nazarene* of Enríquez Gómez as it does not appear in his list.

11.   Ibid., 177. A. Domínguez Ortiz indicates that there is some doubt concerning the Old Christian status of Rojas Zorrilla (*Los judeoconversos*, 210). As for Pérez de Montalbán, there is little doubt of his New Christianity.

12.   See, for example, the Eve of the *First Pilgrim's Guilt* and the Eve figure in the *Tower of Babylon*. There are also examples of the cajoling woman in his plays; one previously discussed comic treatment is that of Juana of *Love is Proof Against Deceit*.

13.   A. S. Palmer examines the myth of Samson and the symbolism of the elements of the story in his *The Samson-Saga and its Place in Comparative Religion* (London: Pitman, 1913).

14.   Oelman, *Marrano Poets*, 211.

15.   M. Menéndez y Pelayo, *Heterodoxos*, 2:263.

16.   Amador de los Ríos, *Estudios*, 549.

17. Amador de los Ríos, *Estudios,* 545. Pierce, on the other hand, is more lenient: The *Samson* . . . contains a vigorous story excellent for an epic" (*Poesía épica,* 315). Modern critics might be more comfortable with the term heroic to describe the *Samson.* Enríquez Gómez himself blurs any distinction between epic and heroic by employing only the latter term in his prologue, although it is clear that he regards his creation as an epic.

18. Menéndez y Pelayo, *Heterodoxos,* 2:263: "In Canto XIV, very close to the end there are half a dozen valiant, clear, terse and well-written verses that are like an oasis in the midst of all that frightful desert."

19. "The Religious Views of Antonio Enríquez Gómez: Profile of a Marrano," *Bulletin of Hispanic Studies* 56 (1983):206.

20. "Samson, whose birth is foretold and announced in this Haftorah, brought a temporary deliverance from the Philistine yoke. But he was utterly alone, and he wrought his intermittent feats of private revenge and daring alone, supported neither by enthusiasm for the national cause nor by active help from his people. He was a man, strong physically but weak morally, who suffered shipwreck through following 'the desire of the eyes,' and permitting himself to be ensnared by a heathen woman. His life came to nothing" (*Hertz Bible and Commentary,* 602).

21. The ancient tradition that made Samson a prototype of Christ and of a Christian Saint is discussed in depth in F. M. Krouse, *Milton's Samson and the Christian Tradition* (Princeton: Princeton University Press, 1949).

Chapter Eight

1. Maxim P. A. M. Kerkhof has called attention to another MS attributed to Enríquez Gómez that he found in the Municipal Archives of Amsterdam entitled "Inquisición de Lúcifer y visita de todos los diablos" (The inquisition of Lucifer and visit of all the Devils). Kerkhof has published a fragment of the work in *Sefarad* 38 (1978):319–31, but desisted in further study because C. Amiel announced that he was working on a complete edition of the composition.

2. For detail see Elliott, *The Count-Duke,* 547 ff.

3. See chapter 2, n. 16.

4. A reprinting of *The Lusitanian Triumph* from the Lisbon edition is found in João Franco Barreto's *Relação da embaixada a França em 1641* (Coimbra: University Press, 1918). The citations from the *Triumph* are noted by page numbers of Barreto's text.

5. Another encomium to Richelieu appears in Enríquez Gómez's introductory verses to Fernándes de Villareal's *Político cristianísimo* the year of the cardinal's death.

6. The dedication is to Margaret of Lorraine, duchess of Orléans. The Spanish connection that Enríquez Gómez always sought for these ded-

ications is announced as the part her family took in ridding Portugal of the Moors several hundred years previously.

7. The mirror device is also a feature of the *Samson,* book 10, where the Philistines use it to divine the hero's weakness.

8. The *Dialogues* of León Hebreo were originally composed in Italian by the exiled Portuguese author. Their fame was such that they were translated into Spanish in 1586 by another renowned literary figure, the Inca Garcilaso de la Vega. León Hebreo's difficulties with the Portuguese Inquisition would have made him a sympathetic figure for Enríquez Gómez.

9. The citations to the *First Pilgrim's Guilt* are to page numbers from the first edition of Maurry (Rouen, 1644).

10. Kirkconnell's investigations into the various representations of the creation myth failed to take into account this work of Enríquez Gómez. See his *Celestial Cycle.* The inclusion by Enríquez Gómez of the name du Bartas in his listing of French greats in the prologue to *Samson* points to some influence of this author, Guillaume de Saluste, Seigneur du Bartas. The works of du Bartas, *L'Uranie ou Muse Céleste* (Paris, 1573), and *La Septmaine, ou Création* (Paris, 1578), were famous in their time. See Kirkconnell, 569–70. Enríquez Gómez's title no doubt owes its inspiration to that of a Lope play, *La creación del mundo y primera culpa del hombre.*

11. Révah, for example, and also Amiel whose introduction to the *Pythagorean Century* announces a forthcoming work on Enríquez Gómez and *marrano* casuistry.

12. The power struggles of French politics during the years Enríquez Gómez spent there are incredibly complicated. It is difficult to determine exactly his sympathies, which at first seem to lie with the royal party and then with the opposition group led by Condé and Gaston d'Orléans. Michael McGaha, who is studying the matter, believes that Enríquez Gómez soon became disillusioned with Queen Anne's regency.

13. The page numbers after the citations from *Louis God-given* refer to the edition of René Baudry (Paris, 1645).

14. García Valdecasas draws attention to this identification in his *Las "Academias morales,"* 19–25. It now seems that the extent of criticism depends upon which version of the *Louis God-given* one reads. L. Reis Torgal has discovered that there is one version that includes a strong attack on the Spanish Inquisition and Spanish policies which is replaced in another version by a defense of the Portuguese restoration. Reis Torgal's article includes facsimiles of both. See his "A literatura 'marrânica' e as 'edições duplas' de António Henriques Gomes (1600–1663)," *Biblos* 55 (1979):197–228. C. H. Rose has also addressed this discovery in "Dos versiones de un texto de Antonio Enríquez Gómez un caso de autocensura," *Nueva Revista de Filología Hispánica* 30 (1981):534–45.

15. Gendreau-Massaloux and Rose, "Antonio Enríquez Gómez," (378), feel that the *Angelic Politics* was conceived as a reply to Quevedo's *Politics*. Likewise they see the *Louis God-given* as a response to Quevedo's *Carta al serenísimo Luis XIII rey de Francia* (Letter to the Most Serene Louis XIII, king of France, 1635) reproaching the king for favoring Richelieu over the Spanish Queen Anne's party.

16. Révah, "Un pamphlet"; the citations to the *Politics* are made from page numbers in Révah's article.

17. Massaloux-Gendreau and Rose, "Antonio Enríquez Gómez," suggest that Enríquez Gómez waited until Fernándes de Villareal left for Lisbon to print the second part and that the curious date mention' in *The Tower of Babylon* celebrates the publication of the clandestine section of the *Politics*.

18. Oelman's dissertation was the first to study the ballad, and his *Marrano Poets* also contains some English translations from it (see chapter 7, n. 1). Oelman has published the edited text twice more: "Antonio Enríquez Gómez's 'Romance al divín mártir Judá Creyente': Edited text with introduction," *Journal of Jewish Studies* 26 (1975):113–31, and a recent beautiful edition with introduction, edited texts, and reproductions of the manuscripts, *Romance al divín mártir, Judá Creyente [don Lope de Vera y Alarcón] martirizado en Valladolid por la Inquisición* (Rutherford, N.J.: Fairleigh Dickinson University Press, 1986). My citations are to the edition in the *Journal of Jewish Studies* and to portions of his English translation.

19. Amiel, for example, calls it "une des rares oeuvres sincères." See his introduction to the *Pythagorean Century*, xvii. Not everyone, however, is convinced that the "Ballad" is an Enríquez Gómez composition. Michael McGaha, in a paper given at the AATSP Conference in Los Angeles, 15 August 1987 (Sephardic Studies I) argues convincingly that the poem is in fact a combination of an actual work of Lope de Vera preceded and closed with sections written by Miguel de Barrios. McGaha is presently at work on a lengthy article on the matter. It should be noted that, for the sake of argument, Oelman raises the possible authorship of Barrios in his book but rejects it (95–96).

20. Oelman, "Antonio Enríquez Gómez," 114, n. 5.

21. Ibid., 119.

22. Ibid., 118.

Chapter Nine

1. For a study of this polemic see Glen Dille, "Antonio Enríquez Gómez alias Fernando de Zárate," *Papers on Language and Literature* 14 (1978):11–21.

2. C. H. Rose and T. Oelman have announced a forthcoming edition of this *loa*.

3. The MSS are of *The Noble is Ever Valiant, The Mountain Girl of Burgos,* and *The Masses of St. Vincent Ferrer.* The plays staged in Madrid were *The Valiant Campuzano* and *Danger at Each Step.* The printed plays were *The Valiant Campuzano, The Bishop of Crobia,* and the *Battle of Honor.* The two entr'actes were *The Shoemaker* and *The Mayor of Mayrenʳ*

4. Rose, "Las comedias políticas," 54–55.

5. Ibid.

6. They are *The Mountain Girl from Burgos, There is no Worse Evil Than Marriage,* and *The Virgin's Chaplain, St. Ildefonso.*

7. Two other plays at times attributed to Zárate are *St. ͡áeˑ* and *La culpa más provechosa y vida y muerte de Poncio Pilatos* (The most fortunate guilt and life and death of Pontius Pilate). The former is more often attributed to Francisco de Rojas Zorrilla and the later to Francisco de Villegas. Michael McGaha is presently editing *The Most Fortunate Guilt* and strongly suspects it as an Enríquez Gómez work. McGaha has also prepared for future publication critical editions of *La conversion de la Magdalena, Santa Táez, Las misas de S. Vicente Ferrer,* and a bilingual critical edition of *El rey más perfecto, S. Hermenegildo.*

8. *The Conquest of Mexico* (Seville: Vásquez, n.d.), 19. Carlos Romero Muñoz suspects that this play is closely based on a lost Lope de Vega play if not, in fact, the Lope play itself. See his "Lope de Vega y 'Fernando de Zárate': *El nuevo mundo* (y *Arauco domado*) en *La conquista de México,*" Studi di letteratura ispanoamericana 15–16 (1983):243–64.

9. *The Life and Death of the Cid Campeador and Noble Martín Peláez* (Salamanca: Santa Cruz, n.d.), 9. The inspiration for this play on the supposed or suspected cowardice of Martín Peláez, the Cid's nephew, may be from the strong Spanish ballad tradition. The *Romancero general,* BAE, vol. 10, p. 1, includes various ballads on this topic. See pages 535–37.

10. See David M. Gitlitz, "La angustia vital de ser negro: tema de un drama de Fernando de Zárate," *Segismundo* 2 (1975):65–85, and Glen Dille, "A Black Man's Dilemma in *Las misas de S. Vicente Ferrer,*" *Romance Notes* 20 (1979):87–93.

11. *To Change for the Better* in *Dramáticos posteriores a Lope de Vega* (BAE, vol. 47, p. 1), 537, column c.

12. See, for example, the comments of Romualdo Alvarez Espino, *Ensayo histórico-crítico del teatro español desde su origen hasta nuestros días* (Cádiz, 1876): "Zárate preferred the lives of the saints and the New Testament mysteries, developing his thoughts in harmony with the Catholic faith and impelled by a completely Christian religious enthusiasm" (223). See also Glen Dille, "The Christian Plays of Antonio Enríquez Gómez," *Bulletin of Hispanic Studies* 64 (1987):39–50.

13. *El vaso y la piedra*, in *Parte veinte y nueve de comedias nueva, escritas por los mejores ingenios de España* (Madrid, 1668), 85–86. This is only one of many passages to exalt the Trinity, Jesus, and Mary.

14. Rose suggests that Enríquez Gómez was influenced by the thought of Menasseh ben Israel and the Portuguese priest Antonio Vieira. For more on Ben Israel's teachings see A. J. Saraiva, "Antonio Vieira, Menasseh ben Israel et le Cinquième Empire," *Studia Rosenthaliana* 1 (1972):25–57.

15. *The Conquest of Mexico*, 2.

16. The citations from *The Presumptuous Lady and the Beauty* refer to page number and column from *Dramáticos posteriores a lope de Vega* (BAE, vol. 47, pt. 1). I am presently preparing an edition and translation of this play.

17. The citations from *The Chalice and the Rock* refer to page numbers in *Parte veinte y nueve*.

18. The reference to the siege of Vecelli of 1638 provides a *terminus a quo* for this drama.

19. H. Rennert wrote that *Diego de Camas* was staged by Manuel Vallejo on 22 May 1633. See his "Notes on the Chronology of the Spanish Drama," 338.

20. Coe, *Catálogo bibliográfico*, 90.

21. The citations from *The Valiant Campuzano* refer to page number column from the BAE, vol. 47, pt. 1.

22. See Glen Dille, "The Tragedy of Don Pedro: Old and New-Christian Conflict in *El valiente Campuzano*," *Bulletin of the Comediantes* 35 (1983):97–109.

Selected Bibliography

PRIMARY SOURCES

1. Printed Works

Academias morales de las musas. Bordeaux: Pedro de la Court, 1642; Valencia: Claudio Macé, 1647; Madrid: Fernández de Buendía, 1660; Madrid: Fernández de Buendía, 1668; Madrid: Juan García Infanzón, 1690; Barcelona: Rafael Figueró, 1704; Madrid: J. de Zúñiga, 1734.

La culpa del primer peregrino y el pasajero. Rouen: Laurent Maurry, 1644; Madrid: Juan García Infanzón, 1735.

Luis dado de Dios a Ana y Samuel dado de Dios a Elcana y Ana. Paris: René Baudry, 1645.

La política angélica. Part 1, Rouen: Laurent Maurry, 1647. Part 2, Rouen: Laurent Maurry, 1647.

El Sansón nazareno. Rouen: Laurent Maurry, 1656.

El siglo pitagórico y vida de don Gregorio Guadaña. Rouen: Laurent Maurry, 1644; Rouen: Laurent Maurry, 1682 (false place and date); Rouen: Laurent Maurry, 1726; Brussels: Francisco Foppens, 1727; Madrid: Antonio Espinosa, 1788.

La torre de Babilonia. Rouen: Laurent Maurry, 1649; Madrid: Bernardo de Villadiego, 1670; Amsterdam: Isaac de Córdoba, 1726.

Triunfo lusitano: recibimiento que mandó hacer Su Majestad el Cristianísimo Rey de Francia, Luis XIII, a los embajadores extraordinarios, que S. M. el Serenísimo Rey D. Juan el IV de Portugal le envió el año de 1641. Lisbon: Lourenço de Anveres, 1641; Paris, 1641.

La vida de don Gregorio Guadaña. In *Tesoro de los mejores autores españoles,* volume 38. Paris: Baudry, 1847. In *Novelistas posteriores a Cervantes,* BAE, volume 18. Madrid: Rivadeneyra, 1851–54. In *Obras en prosa festivas y satíricas.* Barcelona: La Maravilla, 1862. In *Biblioteca clásica española,* volume 38. *Novelistas del siglo XVII.* Barcelona: Daniel Cortizo, 1884. In *La novela picaresca.* Barcelona: Iberia, 1947; Madrid: Diana, 1951. In *La novela picaresca española.* Madrid: Aguilar, 1966.

2. Attributed Works (in MSS)

"La inquisición de Lúcifer y visita de todos los diablos," Municipal Archive of Amsterdam, MS.0 826. "Romance al divín mártir, Judá Creyente martirizado en Valladolid por la Inquisición," Oxford University, Bod-

leian Library, Oppenheimer Additional MS. 4°, 150, fols. 46ʳ–50ʳ.
Portugees Israelitisch Seminarium *Etz Haim*, Amsterdam, MS. 48 A
23.

3. Plays Listed in the Prologue to *Samson the Nazarene*
A lo que obliga el honor. In *Academias morales de las musas*.
A lo que obligan los celos. In *Parte 25* (1666) as of Zárate.
Amor con vista y cordura. In *Academias morales de las musas*.
El caballero de gracia.
"El capitán Chinchilla." Biblioteca Palatina de Parma, MS. CC° 28033.38.
Attributed to Francisco de Rojas Zorrilla.
La casa de Austria en España.
Celos no ofenden al sol. In *Flor de las mejores 12 comedias* (Madrid, 1652).
Contra el amor no hay engaños. In *Academias morales de las musas*.
Engañar para reinar. In *Doce comedias, 3ª parte* (Lisbon, 1649).
Fernán Méndez Pinto. Parts 1 and 2 in *La torre de Babilonia* (1670).
La fuerza del heredero.
El gran cardenal de España, don Gil de Albornoz. Part 2, Biblioteca Nacional
(Madrid) MS. 15, 152.
Lo que pasa en media noche.
La prudente Abigail. In *Academias morales de las musas*.
El rayo de Palestina.
La soberbia de Nembrot y primero rey del mundo. Suelta in British Library,
(Madrid? 1750?).
El sol parado.
El trono de Salomón.
"El valiente Diego de Camas." Biblioteca Nacional (Madrid) MS. 15,076.

4. Plays Attributed to Enríquez Gómez
Los bandos de Ravena y fundación de la camándula. Sevilla: Joseph Padrino,
n.d. Probably of Juan de Matos Fragoso.
La española de Florencia. Probably of Calderón de la Barca.
La hija del aire. Part 2. Probably of Calderón de la Barca.
Jerusalén libertada. Suelta, in British Library (Seville?, 1740?).
No hay contra el honor poder. In *Comedias escogidas, Iª parte* (1652). Has
been attributed to Jerónimo de Villanueva.

5. Plays Attributed to Fernando de Zárate y Castronovo
Antes que todo es mi amigo. In *Parte 22* (1665).
El capellán de la Virgen, San Ildefonso.
La conquista de México. In *Parte 30* (1668).
"La conversión de la Magdalena, o Santa María Magdalena." Biblioteca
Nacional (Madrid) MS. 16,955.

La defensora de la reina de Hungría. In *Parte 29* (1668).

Los dos filósofos de Grecia Heráclito y Demócrito. In *Parte 19* (1663).

Entremés del alcalde de Mayrena. In *Rasgos del ocio* (Madrid, 1661).

Entremés del zapatero. In *Rasgos del ocio.*

La escala de la gracia. In *Parte 35* (1671).

Los hermanos amantes y piedad por fuerza. In *Parte 40* (1675).

El maestro de Alejandro. In *Parte 24* (1666).

Mártir y rey de Sevilla, San Hermenegildo, o el rey más perfecto. Suelta
    (Valencia: Viuda de Joseph de Orga, 1763).

"Mayor mal hay en la vida." Biblioteca Nacional (Madrid) MS. 17,139.

El médico pintor, San Lucas. In *Parte 40* (1675).

Las misas de San Vicente Ferrer. In *Parte 23* (1665).

La montañesa de Burgos.

Mudarse por mejorarse. In *Parte 19* (1663).

No hay más mal que casarse.

El obispo de Crobia San Estanislao. In *Parte 15* (1661).

La palabra vengada. In *Parte 44* (1678).

La presumida y la hermosa. In *Parte 23* (1665).

El primer conde de Flandes. In *Parte 29* (1668).

Quererse sin declararse. In *Parte 21* (1663).

Quien habla más obra menos. In *Parte 44* (1678).

San Antonio Abad. In *Parte 30* (1668).

Santa Pelagia [or *La Margarita de los cielos y más firme penitencia*]. In *Parte
    44* (1678).

Las tres coronaciones del emperador Carlos V. In *Parte 40* (1675).

El valiente Campuzano. In *Parte 14* (1660).

El vaso y la piedra. In *Parte 29* (1668).

La vida y muerte del Cid campeador y noble Martín Paláez [or *El noble
    siempre es valiente o Martín Peláez*]. Suelta (Valencia: Joseph y Tomás
    de Orga, 1774).

6. Plays Attributed to Zárate and Others

A cada paso un peligro. Suelta (Valencia: Joseph y Tomás de Orga, 1776).
    Also attributed to Diego and José de Figueroa y Córdoba.

La batalla del honor. In *Parte 15* (1661). Also attributed to Lope de Vega.

La culpa más provechosa y vida y muerte de Poncio Pilatos. In *Parte 32*
    (1669). Also attributed to Francisco de Villegas.

La desgracia venturosa. In *Parte 37* (1671). Also attributed to Gaspar de
    Aguilar.

El gran sepulcro de Cristo [or *La Jerusalén restaurada ye el gran sepulcro de
    Cristo*]. Also attributed to Agustín Collado.

Matilde de Orleans. Possibly Confused with a drama of Lope de Vega or another by Antonio Marqués y Espejo.
"Santa Táez." Biblioteca Nacional (Madrid) MS. 17,047. Also attributed to Francisco de Rojas Zorrilla.

7. Modern Editions and Translations

A lo que obliga el honor. Edited by Silvia Wynter. M.A. thesis, University of London, 1953. A critical edition of Enríquez Gómez's important honor tragedy that includes an extensive introduction and bibliography.

Fernán Méndez Pinto: Comedia famosa en dos partes. Cambridge, Mass.: Harvard University Press, 1974. Edited by L. G. Cohen, F. M. Rogers, and C. H. Rose. Informative introductions and notes. One of the few Enríquez Gómez plays available in a modern edition.

El noble siempre es valiente: comedia de don Fernando de Zárate. Edited by Juan Porras Landeo. Ph.D. dissertation, Wayne State University, 1976. Valuable notes and bibliography, but Porras-Landeo does not accept Zárate as an alias for Enríquez Gómez.

Oelman, Timothy. "Antonio Enríquez Gómez's 'Romance al divín mártir Judá Creyente.' " *Journal of Jewish Studies* 26 (1975):113–31. Valuable comments on the ballad as well as a reprinting and English translation of the work.

———. *Marrano Poets of the Seventeenth Century: An Anthology of the Poetry of Joao Pinto Delgado, Antonio Enríquez Gómez, and Miguel de Barrios.* Edited and translated by T. Oelman. Rutherford, N.J.: Fairleigh Dickinson University Press, 1982. The selections for Enríquez Gómez are from *Samson Nazareno* and *Judá Creyente.*

———. *Romance al divín mártir, Judá Creyente don Lope de Vera y Alarcón martirizado en Valladolid por la Inquisición.* Edited by T. Oelman. Rutherford, N.J.: Fairleigh Dickinson University Press, 1986. A beautiful edition of the MSS of this ballad that includes reproductions of the MSS, transcriptions, and extensive notes. The lengthy introduction sets out Oelman's most recent thoughts on Enríquez Gómez's religious beliefs and is somewhat less sure of the poet's final Marranism.

El siglo pitagórico y vida de don Gregorio Guadaña. Paris: Ediciones Hispano-americanas, 1977. Edited by Charles Amiel. Exceptionally complete notes and appendixes. Indispensable for information on Enríquez Gómez.

"La Ynquisición de Luzifer y visita de todos los diablos." Edited by M. P. A. M. Kerkhof. *Sefarad* 38 (1978):319–31. A partial reprinting of a manuscript found in Amsterdam that has been ascribed to Enríquez Gómez.

SECONDARY SOURCES

Although most general critical histories of Spanish literature include brief assessments of some of the works of Antonio Enríquez Gómez, the following is a selection of materials offering specific information concerning the author.

Amador de Los Ríos, José. *Estudios históricos, políticos y literarios sobre los judíos de España.* Madrid: Díaz, 1848. One of the few nineteenth-century critical studies to find something good in Enríquez Gómez's works, although rather out of date today.

Atkinson, William. "Studies in Literary Decadence: The Picaresque World Novel." *Bulletin of Spanish Studies* 4 (1927):19–27. Considers, and criticizes, *The Pythagorean Century* in the last section of this article.

Barreto, João Franco. *Relação da embaixada a França em 1641.* Coimbra: Imprensa da Universidade, 1918. Not a readily obtainable book. Contains valuable information on the France of Enríquez Gómez's day. More important for the reprinting of *The Lusitanian Triumph* included in the appendix.

Besso, Henry V. *Dramatic Literature of the Sephardic Jews of Amsterdam in the XVIIth and XVIIIth Centuries.* New York: Hispanic Institute, 1947. Calls Enríquez Gómez one of the most outstanding writers of his time. Includes a brief analysis of *What Honor Obliges.*

Caro Baroja, Julio. *Inquisición, brujería y criptojudaísmo.* Barcelona: Ariel, 1947. Interesting work that contains general information on Enríquez Gómez and the Bartolomé Febos case. Suggests that Enríquez Gómez did finally decide for Catholicism.

———. *Los judíos en la España moderna y contemporánea.* 3 vols. Madrid: Arion, 1961. The most complete and modern work available on the subject. There is a huge and valuable bibliography.

Cid, Jesús Antonio. "Judaizantes y carreteros para un hombre de letras: A. Enríquez Gómez (1600–1663)." In *Homenaje a Julio Caro Baroja.* Madrid: Centro de Investigaciones Sociológicas, 1978, 271–300. Important for comments on Enríquez Gómez's life and work.

Cruickshank, Don. "The Second Part of *La hija del aire.*" *Bulletin of Hispanic Studies* 61 (1984):286–94. Reviews the polemic with regard to the authorship of this play which Rose has suggested may be Enríquez Gómez's. Cruickshank maintains that both parts of *La hija* are by Calderón.

Dille, Glen F. "Antonio Enríquez Gómez Alias Fernando de Zárate." *Papers on Language and Literature* 14, no. 1 (1978):11–21. Reviews the polemic as to whether Zárate was a pseudonym.

————. "Antonio Enríquez Gómez's Honor Tragedy *A lo que obliga el honor.*" *Bulletin of the Comediantes* 30, no. 2 (1978):97–111. Examines the play and compares it with Calderonian honor tragedy.

————. "A Black Man's Dilemma in *Las Misas de S. Vicente Ferrer.*" *Romance Notes* 20, no. 1 (1979):87–93. Brief study of characterizations in this play written under the Zárate alias.

————. The Christian Plays of Antonio Enríquez Gómez." *Bulletin of Hispanic Studies* 64 (1987):39–50. Discusses religious elements in the Zárate plays; suggests that the dramatist turned to Christianity in his later years.

————. "The Originality of Antonio Enríquez Gómez in *Engañar para reinar.*" In *Renaissance and Golden Age Essays in Honor of D. W. McPheeters,* edited by Bruno M. Damiani, 49–60. Potomac, Md.: Scripta Humanistica, 1986. A study of Enríquez Gómez's view of kingship in what is supposed to be his first play.

Fez, Carmen de. *La estructura barroca de "El siglo pitagórico."* Madrid: CUPSA Editorial, 1978. Confusing but still informative study of *The Pythagorean Century.*

García Gómez, Angel M. *The Legend of the Laughing Philosopher and Its Presence in Spanish Literature (1500–1700).* 2d ed. Córdoba: Universidad de Córdoba, Servicio de Publicaciones, 1984. Important for the chapter dealing with the topic in many of Enríquez Gómez's works.

García Valdecasas, José. *Las 'Academias morales' de Antonio Enríquez Gómez.* Seville: Anales de la Universidad, Serie Derecho, 1971. The most comprehensive work to date on the *Academies.* The author believes that Enríquez Gómez was a true Christian and that the work is primarily a veiled attack on the Inquisition.

Gendreau-Massaloux, Michèle, and Rose, Constance H. "Antonio Enríquez Gómez et Manuel Fernandes de Villareal: Deux destins parallèles, une vision politique commune." *Revue des etudes Juives* 136, nos. 3–4 (1977):368–88. Contains much valuable information concerning Enríquez Gómez's activities during the period of his French exile.

Gitlitz, David M. "La angustia de ser negro: tema de un drama de Fernando de Zárate." *Segismundo* 2 (1975):65–85. Lengthy character analysis that includes the source of this play and offers observations on Enríquez Gómez's dramaturgy.

Hanrahan, Thomas. *La mujer en la novela picaresca.* Madrid: José Porrua, 1967. Includes a complete section on the *Life of Don Gregorio Guadaña* especially as regards the female roles. Calls attention to the forceful and artful women characteristic of Enríquez's works.

Menéndez y Pelayo, M. *Historia de los heterodoxos españoles.* Madrid: Biblioteca de autores Cristianos, 1956. Although Menéndez finds Enríquez Gómez acceptable as a satirist, in the main he offers a negative assessment. Menéndez's remarks were very influential.

Oelman, Timothy. "Tres Poetas marranos." *Nueva revista de filología Hispánica* 30 (1981):184–206. More or less the same information included in the introductions in his *Marrano Poets.*

Pierce, Frank. *La poesía épica del siglo de oro.* Madrid: Gredos, 1968. Includes several references to Enríquez's *Samson* although, by and large, Pierce is not favorably disposed to any seventeenth-century epic. Especially useful for the chronological listings of Spanish epics in the appendix.

Porqueras Mayo, Alberto. *El prólogo en el manierismo y barroco españoles.* Madrid: CSIC, 1968. Finds interesting Enríquez Gómez's prologues. Reprints those from *Tower of Babylon* and *Samson.*

Profeti, Maria G. "Un esempio di critica 'militante': il prologo al 'Samsón nazareno' di Enríquez Gómez." *Quaderni di lingue e letteratura* 7 (1982):203–12. Includes a brief introductory study and a critical edition of this most important of the author's prologues.

Rauchwarger, Judith. "Antonio Enríquez Gómez's *Epístolas tres de Job:* A Matter of Racial Atavism?" *Revue des etudes Juives* 138 (1979):69–87. Part of a series by Rauchwarger concentrating on literary interpretations of Job. The most complete study to date of these poems that appear in *The Moral Academies.* Studies Enríquez Gómez's knowledge of Judaism.

Reis Torgal, L. "A literatura 'marrânica' e as 'edições dulpas' de António Henriques Gomes (1600–1663)." *Biblos* 55 (1979):197–228. Reis Torgal apparently was the first to notice the two editions of *Louis Godgiven.* In addition to his comments on their contents, this article includes facsimiles of both versions.

Révah, I. S. "Manuel Fernándes Vilareal: adversaire et victime de l'Inquisition portugaise." *Iberida revista de filologia* (Rio de Janeiro) 1 (April 1959):33–54; 3 (December 1959):181–207. The best source of information on an important figure in Enríquez Gómez's life.

———. "Un pamphlet contre l'Inquisition d'Antonio Enríquez Gómez: la seconde partie de la *Política angélica* (Rouen, 1647)." *Revue des etudes Juives* 131 (1962):81–168. Doubly important for the reprinting of the rare *Angelic Politics* and for the definitive biography of Enríquez Gómez which dispels the errors and myths of previous biographies.

Romero Múñoz, Carlos. "Lope de Vega y 'Fernando de Zárate': *El nuevo mundo* (y *Arauco domado*) en *La conquista de México.*" *Studi di letteratura ispano–americana* 15–16 (1983):243–64. Suggests that the Zárate play *La conquista de México* is either closely based on a lost Lope de Vega play on the conquest of Mexico, or is, in fact, the Lope play itself.

Rose, Constance H. "Antonio Enríquez Gómez and the Literature of Exile." *Romanische Forschungen* 85 (1974):63–77. An informative article concentrating on the play *Fernán Méndez Pinto* as a vehicle for Enríquez

Gómez's expressions concerning his exile.

———. "Las comedias políticas de Enríquez Gómez." *Nuevo Hispanismo* 2 (1982):45–56. A study of the figure of the king's minister in three of his "political" plays.

———. "Dos versiones de un texto de Antonio Enríquez Gómez: un caso de autocensura." *Nueva revista de filología hispánica* 30 (1981):534–45. Discusses in detail the two printings of the *Louis God-given*.

———. "Portuguese Diplomacy Plays a Role in the Printing of Some Peninsular Works in Rouen in the Seventeenth Century." *Arquivos do Centro Cultural Português* 10 (1976):523–41. Informative article on Portuguese efforts to propagandize the restoration of John IV through exiled Peninsular writers including Enríquez Gómez.

———. "Who Wrote the *Segunda Parte* of *La hija del aire.*" *Revue belge de philosophie et d'histoire* 54 (1976):797–822. In addition to the information it offers on several Enríquez Gómez plays, this article suggests that he, not Calderón, was the author of the second part of *La hija del aire*.

Roth, Cecil. "Romance sur l'execution de Don Lope de Vera." *Revue des etudes Juives* 97 (1934):105–11. Roth's work has lately been superseded by Oelman's. Roth believed that the ballad was actually a composition of Lope de Vera.

Serís, Homero. *Nuevo ensayo de una biblioteca española de libros raros y curiosos*. New York, 1969. Besides offering a valuable résumé of critical material on Enríquez Gómez, Serís comments on the holdings of the Hispanic Society and the Ticknor Collection.

Smieja, Florian. "Stanislaw Szczepanowski w Dramacie Fernanda de Zárate." *Kwartalnik Neofilologiczny* (Warsaw) 15 (1968):61–65. A general description of the Zárate play, *The Bishop of Crobia, St. Stanislaus*, which deals with an incident from Polish History.

Thacker, M. J. "Gregorio Guadaña: Pícaro-Francés o Pícaro-Galán." In *Hispanic Studies of Honor of Frank Pierce*, edited by John England, 149–68. University of Sheffield: Department of Hispanic Studies, 1980. The lengthiest and most complete study to date of the *Life of Don Gregorio Guadaña*, concentrating on its relationship to the Spanish *novelas cortesanas*.

Index